Beethoven

String Quartets
Op. 18, Nos. 1–6

Their Creation, Origins and Reception History
Incorporating
An Anthology of Selected Writings

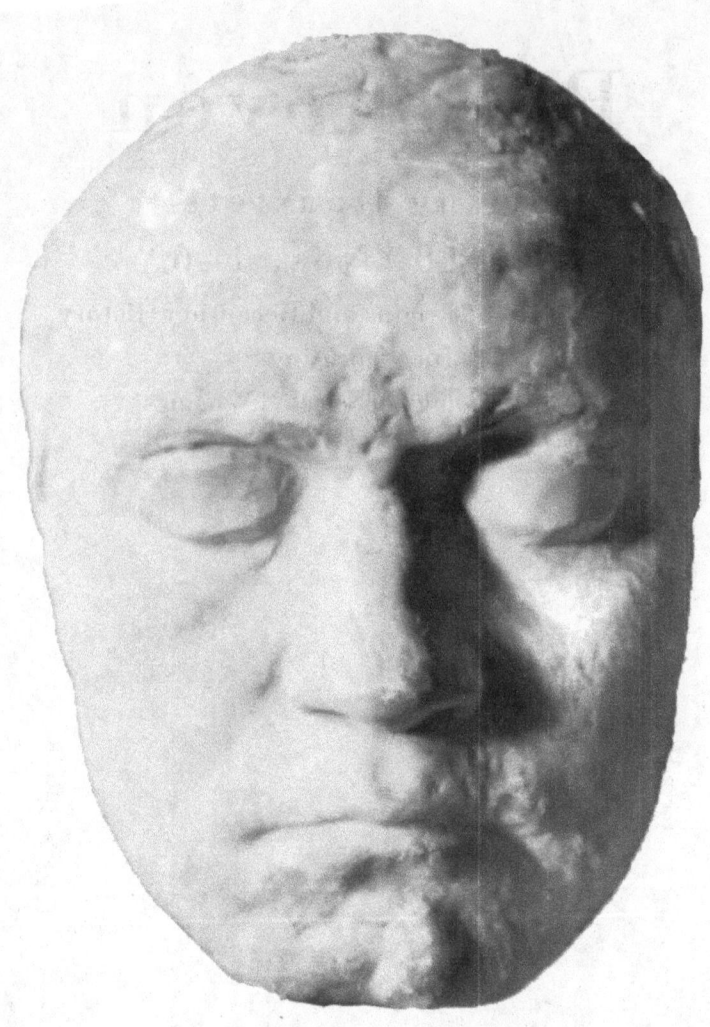

BEETHOVEN

As depicted by the life mask taken by Franz Klein in 1812
(derived from a copy in the author's possession)

BEETHOVEN
STRING QUARTETS OP. 18, NOS. 1–6

THEIR
CREATION, ORIGINS
AND
RECEPTION HISTORY

Incorporating an Anthology
of Selected Writings

Terence M. Russell

Jelly Bean Books

The right of Terence Russell to be identified as the
Author of the Work has been asserted by him in accordance
with the Copyright, Designs and Patents Act 1988.

Copyright © Terence M. Russell 2022

Published by
Jelly Bean Books
136 Newport Road
Cardiff
CF24 1DJ

ISBN: 978-1-915439-12-3

www.candyjarbooks.co.uk

All rights reserved.
No part of this publication may be reproduced, stored in a
retrieval system, or transmitted at any time or by any means,
electronic, mechanical, photocopying, recording or otherwise
without the prior permission of the copyright holder. This book is
sold subject to the condition that it shall not by way of trade or
otherwise be circulated without the publisher's prior consent in any
form of binding or cover other than that in which it is published.

CONTENTS

AUTHOR'S NOTE — I
INTRODUCTION — IX
EDITORIAL PRINCIPLES — XIII
BEETHOVEN'S FINANCIAL TRANSACTIONS — XV

BEETHOVEN'S STRING QUARTETS, OP. 18 NO. 1-6:
AN ANTHOLOGY OF SELECTED WRITINGS:
    Gerald Abraham — 1
    The Beethoven Quartet Society — 2
    Paul Bekker — 4
    Hector Berlioz — 4
    Leonard Bernstein — 7
    Leon Botstein — 8
    Fryderyk Chopin — 10
    Rebecca Clarke — 10
    Carl Dahlhaus — 12
    Claude Debussy — 14

Gabriel Fauré	15
Guarneri Quartet	17
William Henry Hadow	19
Fanny Hensel (Mendelssohn)	20
Gustav Holst	22
Hans Keller	22
Joseph Kerman	25
William Kinderman	26
Niccolò Paganini	27
Sergei Prokofiev	28
Philip Radcliffe	29
Alma Rosé	30
Arthur Shepherd	31
Robert Simpson	33
Igor Stravinsky	34
Bruno Walter	35

THEIR CREATION, ORIGINS AND RECEPTION HISTORY:

String Quartets Op. 18, Nos. 1–6	37
String Quartet in F major, Op. 18, No. 1	121
String Quartet in G major, Op. 18, No. 2	140
String Quartet in D major, Op. 18, No. 3	151
String Quartet in C minor, Op. 18, No. 4	162
String Quartet in A major, Op. 18, No. 5	180
String Quartet in B-flat major, Op. 18, No. 6	196
String Quartet arrangement: Piano Sonata in E major, Op. 14, No. 1	215

BIBLIOGRAPHY	222
INDEX	257
ABOUT THE AUTHOR	261

AUTHOR'S NOTE

I have cherished the idea of making a study of the life and work of Beethoven for many years. This statement requires a few words of personal reflection. I first encountered Beethoven in my early piano lessons — Minuet in G major, WoO 10, No. 2. At the same time I became acquainted with his piano pupil Carl Czerny — *Book One, Piano Studies*. My heart sank when I discovered the rear cover advertised a further *99* books in the same series — scales, arpeggios studies for the left hand, studies for the right hand — all the way to his Op. 824! By coincidence, my *Czerny Book One* was edited by Alec Rowley — who had the same surname as my music teacher. In my childish innocence, I often wondered why *he himself* never appeared to give me a lesson!

In my teenage years I found myself drawn ever closer to Beethoven's music in the manner that ferromagnetic materials are ineluctably held captive in the sway of a magnetic field. The impulse to which I yielded is well described in words the conductor Bruno Walter gave in one of his rare public addresses: 'It is my belief that young people at that age are more easily impressed by what is heroic and grandiose; that they more easily understand works of art in which passionate feelings are violently uttered in raised accents, and that the lighter sounds of cheerfulness are less impressive to them.' I do indeed recall the stirring effect made on me on first hearing the Overture *Egmont*, the unfolding drama of the Fifth Symphony and the declamatory opening chords of the *Emperor* Piano Concerto.

I resolved to read everything I could about Beethoven, starting with Marion Scott's pioneering English-language study of the composer in the *Master Musicians series*. My father took out a subscription for me for *The Gramophone* magazine, enabling me to read reviews of the new 'LP' recordings — none of which though I could afford! The LP was then — 1950s — beginning to supplant the 78 rpm shellac records, stacks of which could be purchased for as little as six pence each in 'old' money. At this same time I had the privilege of hearing Beethoven's music performed by the *Hallé Orchestra* under the baton of Sir John Barbirolli, and experienced the *Carl Rosa Opera Company* perform the composer's only opera *Fidelio*; I borrowed the piano-reduction score from the City Library to become better acquainted with this moving work — only to find the score's fists full of notes were well beyond my capabilities. Nonetheless, since then *Fidelio's* every note has been woven into my DNA. I also recall the period when the *London Promenade Concerts* were designated 'Friday night is Beethoven night'.

Through these influences I resolved to visit Vienna to see where Beethoven had lived and worked. But how? The support for such travel was beyond the means of my family. Fortunately in my final year at school (1959) an opportunity presented itself. I saw a poster that stated *WUS — World University Service* — required volunteers to work in the Austrian town of Linz to help relocate refugees who were living there in improvised wooden shacks — displaced and dispossessed victims of the Second World War. To those participating all expenses would be paid together with free accommodation — in one of the crumbling wooden shacks! From Linz, I planned to make my way to Vienna.

I applied to *WUS* and, despite being a mere school-leaver, I was accepted. The *WUS* authorities doubtless reasoned the building-trade skills I had acquired during my secondary education in the building department of a technical school would be useful. This proved to be the case. At the refugee camp I dug trenches and was allowed to assist as a bricklayer. All about me were wide-eyed children eager to help but mostly getting in the way. I recall one afternoon when a reporter from *The Observer* newspaper paid a visit to our construction site to gather material for an article he was writing on European post-war recovery — he generously admired my trenches and brickwork!

Of lasting significance was another visit, this time from a Belgian priest. He took a group of us to the nearby *Mauthausen* Concentration Camp, recently opened as a silent and solemn memorial to those who had perished there. It was a deeply moving experience. Years later I learned of the views of the ardent Beethovenian Sir Michael Tippet. After the horrors of the *Holocaust*, he posed the question for mankind: 'What price Beethoven now?' He posited: 'Could we any longer find solace in Beethoven's setting of Schiller's *Ode to Joy* and its utopian vision — "Be embraced you Millions"?'

My refugee contribution duly came to end and Vienna beckoned. On arrival there I found scenes reminiscent of *The Third Man* and *Harry Lime*. I recall, for example, encountering cobblestones piled high in the streets waiting to be replaced after having been disturbed by the heavy armoured vehicles that had so recently passed over them. But Vienna was welcoming. I visited the houses where Beethoven had lived and worked and paused outside others associated with him that were identified by a commemorative plaque and the Austrian flag. A particularly memorable occasion was attending a recital in the great salon within the palace of Beethoven's noble patron Prince Lobkowitz — the very one where the *Eroica* Symphony had been premiered. Ultimately, my steps led me to the composer's first resting place in the *Währinger Ortsfriedhof.* I paid silent homage to the great man and, as I did so, discovered nearby the resting place of Franz Schubert to whom Beethoven was an endless source of admiration and inspiration.

I felt a youthful impulse to discover yet more about Beethoven and his music. But absorption in musicology would have to take second place. My chosen career beckoned in the guise of architecture — 'the mother of the arts' and 'the handmaid of society'. There was room though for Beethoven's music and from that time on it has been my constant companion through attendance at recitals, in concerts and music-making in the home. And at home a reproduction of Franz Kline's 1812 study of the composer has greeted me each day for more than half a century.

On my retirement from a career in architectural practice, research and university teaching, the opportunity finally presented itself for me to devote time to researching Beethoven musicology. Having attained my eightieth year also emboldened me to make progress with my good intentions!

With these autobiographical remarks outlined I will say a few remarks about my working method — see also the comments made in *Editorial Principles.*

As a member of staff of The University of Edinburgh, I had the good fortune to have access to the *Reid Music Library*, formed from a nucleus of books bequeathed by General John Reid and augmented over the years by such custodians as Sir Donald Francis Tovey, sometime *Reid Professor of Music* and renowned Beethoven scholar. Over a period of three years, I made a survey of the many works in the Reid collection. I consulted each item in turn making records on paper slips — many hundreds — that I deemed to be relevant for my researches. I confined my searches to book-publications, as reflected in my accompanying bibliography. All of this was quite some years ago, the cut-off date for my researches being 2007. Beyond this date I have not surveyed any further works. I am mindful though that Beethoven musicology and related publication continue to be a major field of endeavour in the manner of the proverbial 'ever rolling stream'.

In the intervening years since completing my archival researches, personal tribulations associated with family illness and bereavement slowed my progress in giving expression to my projected intentions. Latterly, however, with renewed energy, and more time at my disposal, I have been able to make progress. My studies take the form of a set of monographs. These trace the creation origins and reception history of each of Beethoven's piano sonatas and string quartets. The resulting texts also incorporate contextual accounts of Beethoven and his contemporaries. Also included in my musicological surveys are two related Beethoven anthologies. The set of monographs in question, identified by short title, are:

Beethoven: An anthology of selected writings.
Beethoven: The piano sonatas: An anthology of selected writings.

The Piano Sonatas:
Op. 2—Op. 28
Op. 31—Op. 81A
Op. 90—Op. 111

The String Quartets:
Op. 18, Nos. 1—6
Op. 59, Nos. 1—3 (Razumovsky); Op. 74 (The Harp);
Op. 95 (Quartetto Serioso)
Op. 127, Op. 132 and Op. 130 (Galitzin)
Op. 131, Op. 135; Grosse Fuge, Op. 133 and Op. 134 (Fugue transcription)

I provide further information about these studies in the introduction to each individual monograph. Suffice it for me to state here the basic premise upon which my work is founded. I believe it is rewarding, concerning the life of a great artist, to find connections between who he *was* and what he *did*; in Martin Cooper's words 'between his personality, as expressed on the one hand in human relationships, and on the other in artistic creation'. (*Beethoven, The Last Decade*) That is not to say I consider it essential to the enjoyment of Beethoven's music to know this or that fact about it. His music can be enjoyed, as millions do, with — in Robert Simpson's apt phrase —'an innocent ear', for what it is and how it reaches out to us in purely musical terms without any prejudging of its merits based upon extra-musicological facts.

I must make a further point. I am mindful that a scholar who ventures into a field of study that is not rightly his may be regarded with some suspicion. In this regard I can but ask the reader to place his or her trust in me in the following way. I have attempted to bring to my work the care which publishers and their desk editors have required of me in my book writings relating to architecture — listed elsewhere.

As inferred, it is now more than sixty years since I paid homage to Beethoven in Vienna's *Währinger Ortsfriedhof* and my warmth of feeling towards the composer and his music have grown with the passing of the years. My studies are not intended to be propaedeutic — that would be pretentious. However, if in sharing with others what I have to say contributes to their knowledge and understanding of the composer, and thereby increases their own feelings towards him and his works, my own pleasure in bringing my work to completion will be all the more enhanced.

It is perhaps fitting that my studies should appear in Beethoven's 250th Anniversary Year — I must confess more by chance than design!

When Beethoven arrived in Vienna, he was unknown. He was armed though with a note of encouragement from his youthful friend and benefactor Count Ferdinand Waldstein. It contained the often-quoted words: 'Receive Mozart's spirit from Haydn's hands.' Some forty years later Beethoven passed away in the House of the black-robed Spaniards at 200 *Alservorstädter*, the *Glacis* where he had lived since the autumn of 1825. Soldiers had to be called to secure the doors to the inner courtyard of the house from the pressure of onlookers. His body was blessed in the *Alservorsttädt Parish Church*, schools were closed and perhaps as many as 10,000 people formed a funeral procession — an honour ordinarily reserved for monarchs. The *Marcia Funebre* from the composer's Op. 26 Piano Sonata was performed at the funeral ceremony. Franz Grillparzer read the funeral oration. Franz Schubert, who, as remarked in life so admired Beethoven, was one of the pallbearers. The composer's mortal remains were lowered into a simple vault. Beethoven now belonged to history.

Dr Terence M. Russell
Edinburgh 2020

INTRODUCTION

The subjects of this study are the creation origins and reception history of Beethoven's string quartets. It is one of three that broadly correspond with the generally accepted periods into which the composer's compositions are held to conform and which have been described as 'early', 'middle', and 'late' and their counterparts, 'imitative', 'heroic' and 'introspective'. In our first study the string quartets Op. 18, Nos. 1—6 are considered alongside the transcription for string quartet of the Piano Sonata in E major, Op. 14. In the second part are the string quartets Op. 59, Nos. 1—3 (Razumowsky), Op. 74 in E-flat major, (The Harp) and Op. 95 in F minor (Quartetto serioso). In the third part are the string quartets Op. 127, Op. 130, Op. 131, Op. 132, Op. 135 and the Great Fugue, Op. 133 together with Beethoven's four-hand keyboard transcription Op. 134.

We open this study with an anthology of writings bearing on Beethoven's achievements in the genre of the string quartet. Texts selected for inclusion are illustrative of views expressed about these compositions as conveyed through the sayings and writings of musicians, musicologists and performing artists. As such they provide insights into such considerations as the composer's aesthetic and creative impulse; his philosophical and intellectual outlook; the expressive nature of his writing; the challenges with which he confronts the performer — relating to questions of interpretation and performance — and, above all, the continuing legacy of his musical inheritance.

Following on from the anthology the collection of writings presented here derive from the string quartet compositions of Beethoven's so-called first period. They take the form of extended essays that may serve the reader as a source of reference — in the manner of programme notes to a recital. Accordingly, the remarks relating to each string quartet are 'free standing' and can be read independently. That said they are also interlinked by the events unfolding in the composer's life. An attempt has been made, therefore, to interrelate the individual essays so that they may be read as a continuous narrative — in typical book fashion. A summary outline of this narrative is provided in the Index for each individual string quartet. Thereby, the reader is provided not only with a guide to the contents discussed in each quartet-text but also has an over-arching time-line of the principal events bearing on Beethoven's life and work.

By way of an introduction to the individual essays in this part of our survey, we provide the following summary-outline bearing upon the compositions to which we make reference.

In the 1790s the string quartet held a place of special regard in social music-making. The Italian composer Giuseppe Cambini is credited with writing nearly 150 string quartets. He published an article in the music journal Allgemeine musikalische Zeitung of 1800 in which he states: '[If] music should not stir up or soothe the emotions, then it should at least draw our attention to itself and so divert us from the cares and griefs of our everyday life.' The contemporary mystical poet and musician Christian Schubart considered the string quartet expressed no less than 'the music-universe condensed into one work'. Haydn and Mozart had enriched this universe by enhancing the string quartet through their own powers of invention. In due course Beethoven progressively stamped his authority on the medium by enhancing its stature and transforming it almost beyond recognition, confronting both performers and listeners by challenging their expectations of easy music-making and straightforward comprehension.

Beethoven came late to the medium of the string quartet. Unlike Haydn and Mozart, he was not an accomplished string performer, although he had played the viola in his youthful days in Bonn. When Beethoven started work on his Op. 18 String Quartets he had been living in Vienna for six years and was already twenty-eight years old and was thirty before the set of six was completed. By way of comparison, we recall Mozart had written his String Quartet in G, K. 387 — his fourteenth and the first of the celebrated Haydn Quartets — when he was twenty-six, and Schubert had composed his String Quartet in A minor, D. 804 — his thirteenth, the so-called Rosamunde — when he was twenty seven.

It is understandable the youthful Beethoven should defer taking up the challenge of writing string quartets. Haydn, 'the father of the string quartet', was at the height of his powers and composing quartets at a steady rate, witness his Opp. 64, 71, 76 and 77 — a total of twenty works. In the 1790s, in the genre of chamber music, rather than writing quartets we find Beethoven composing such works as the Piano Trios, Op. 1; Sonatas for Piano and Cello, Op. 5; Serenade for String Trio, Op. 8; String Trios, Op. 9; Trio for Piano, Clarinet and Cello, Op. 11; Violin Sonatas, Op. 12; and the Septet, Op. 20 – revised later by Beethoven as his Trio Op. 38. These were categories of works for which Haydn had written very little or had ceased to compose some years previously. Thereby, Beethoven avoided direct comparison with his revered teacher.

When Beethoven completed his Op. 18, Nos. 1–6 the string quartet could still be performed by amateurs – albeit accomplished ones. Writing in the Centenary Issue of the Musical Times (Vol. VIII, No. 2, 1927), the English-born classical composer and accomplished violist Rebecca Clarke communicated the pleasure to be derived from playing the composer's quartets: 'Beethoven, with his ever new ideas, in which he never plagiarizes even himself, his amazingly individual polyphony and rhythm, and his all-embracing depth of feeling, will always be the ideal of those who really want to work at quartets. Into this form, the purest and most perfect that we know, he poured thoughts which could be expressed in no other way and which make his quartets unsurpassed to this day, and in working at them the player comes as near as is humanely possible to understanding the feelings with which they were written, and finds a delight which is lasting and can know no disenchantment.'

TMR

EDITORIAL PRINCIPLES

By its very nature a study of this kind draws extensively on the work of others. Every effort has been made to acknowledge this in the text by indicating words quoted or adapted with single quotation marks. Wherever possible, for the sake of consistency, I have retained the orthography of quoted texts making only occasional silent changes of spelling and capitalization. Deleted words are identified by means of three ellipsis points ... and interpolations are encompassed within square brackets [ ]. Quoted words, phrases and longer cited passages of text remain the intellectual property of their copyright holders.

I address the reader in the second person notwithstanding that the work is my own. It follows that I must bear the responsibility for any errors of misunderstanding or misinterpretation for which I ask the reader's forbearance. A collaboration I must acknowledge is the help I received from the librarians of the Reid Music Library at the University of Edinburgh. Over the three-year period it took me to compile my reference sources, they served me with unfailing courtesy, often supplying me with twenty or more books at a time. In converting my manuscript into book format, I wish to thank my editorial coordinator, William Rees, for his support and painstaking care. I would also like to thank Shaun Russell for his work designing the cover for each of the twelve volumes.

My admiration for Beethoven provided the initial impulse to commence this undertaking and has sustained me over the several years it has taken to bring my enterprise to completion. That said, I am no Beethoven idolater. I am mindful of the danger that awaits one who ventures to chronicle the work of a great artist. I believe it was Sigmund Freud who suggested that biographers may become so disposed to their subject, and their emotional involvement with their hero, that their work becomes an exercise in idealisation. In response to such a charge let me say. First, I am no biographer. I do however make occasional reference to Beethoven's personal life and his relationships with his contemporaries. Second, I acknowledge Beethoven has his detractors. Accordingly, I have not shrunk from allowing dissentient voices, critical of Beethoven and his work, to be heard. These, however, are few and are silenced amidst the adulation that awaits the reader in support of the endeavours of one of humanity's great creators and one who courageously showed the way in overcoming personal adversity.

TMR

BEETHOVEN'S FINANCIAL TRANSACTIONS

Beethoven's negotiations with his music publishers make many references to his compositions. Today they are recognised for what they are — enduring works of art — but referred to in his business correspondence they appear almost as though they were mere everyday commodities — for which he required an appropriate remuneration. Beethoven resented the time he had to devote to the business-side of his affairs. He believed an agency should exist, for fellow artists such as himself, from which a reasonable sum could be paid for the work (composition) submitted, leaving more time for creative enterprises. In the event Beethoven, like Mozart before him, had to deal with publishers largely on his own. Beethoven, though, did benefit in his business dealings from the help he received from his younger brother Kasper Karl (Caspar Carl). From

1800, Carl worked as a clerk in Vienna's Department of Finance in which capacity he found time to correspond with publishers to offer his brother's works for sale and — importantly — to secure the best prices he could. In April 1802 Beethoven wrote to the Leipzig publishers Breitkopf & Härtel: '[You] can rely entirely on my brother who, in general, attends to my affairs.' Whilst Carl promoted Beethoven's interests with determination, he appears to have lacked tact and made enemies. For example, Beethoven's piano pupil Ferdinand Ries — who for a while also helped the composer with his business negotiations — is on record as describing Carl as being 'the biggest skinflint in the world'. The currencies most referred to in Beethoven's correspondence are as follows:

- silver gulden and florin: these were interchangeable and had a value of about two English/British shillings
- ducat: 4 1/2 gulden/florins: valued at about nine shillings
- louis d'or: This gold coin was adopted during the Napoleonic wars and the French occupation of Vienna and Austria more widely. It had a value of about two ducats or approximately twenty shillings or one-pound sterling.

Beethoven was never poor — in the romantic sense of 'an artist starving in a garret'. On arriving in Vienna in 1792, he was fortunate to receive financial support from his patron Prince Karl Lichnowsky who conferred on him an annuity of 600 florins that he maintained for several years. Between the months of February and July of 1796, Beethoven undertook a concert tour taking in Prague, Dresden, Leipzig and Berlin. He was well received and wrote to his other younger brother Nikolaus Johann: 'My art is winning me friends and what more do I want? ... I shall make a good deal of money.' Later on, in 1809, Napoleon Bonaparte's youngest brother Jérôme Bonaparte offered Beethoven an appointment at his Court with the promise of an income of 4,000 florins. Alarmed at the prospect of losing Beethoven — now the most celebrated composer in Europe — three of Vienna's most notable citizens, namely, the Archduke Rudolph (Beethoven's only composition pupil), Prince Kinsky and Prince Lobkowitz settled on the composer the same sum of 4,000 florins. Inflation, however, brought about by the Napoleonic wars, soon eroded its value; personal misfortune to Lobkowitz and Kinsky also took its toll.

Beethoven undoubtedly had to work hard to secure a reasonable standard of living. Notwithstanding, despite his occasional straitened circumstances, he contributed generously to the needs of others. For example, he allowed his works to be performed free of charge at charitable concerts; in 1815 his philanthropy earned for him the honour of Bürgerrecht — 'freedom of the City'.

Beethoven earned a great deal of money when his music was performed, to considerable acclaim, at several concerts held in association with the Congress of Vienna (1814-15). He did not though benefit from it personally; he invested it on behalf of his nephew Karl. It is one of the misfortunes of Beethoven's life that in money-matters he was culpably improvident. This is poignantly evident in a letter he wrote on 18 March 1827 to the Philharmonic Society of London just one week before his death; the Society had made him a gift of £100. He sent the Society 'his most heartfelt thanks for their particular sympathy and support'.

TMR

*'No encomium, uttered or written, could add to the
splendour of so enduring an art-monument
as the sixteen string quartets of Beethoven.'*

Arthur Shepherd, *The string quartets
of Ludwig van Beethoven*, Cleveland: H. Carr, The Printing Press, 1935, pp. Vii–ix.

*'A cycle of Beethoven's quartets is of unique interest; his
spiritual development encompasses worlds. It's little
wonder that the complete Beethoven cycle is in such
demand; we're asked to play it at least once every season.
There's a bottomless well of fascination in these pieces.
New ideas seem to be coming up all the time. Much
remains enigmatic — even some of the markings. There's a
creative mystery that can never be entirely resolved.'*

Eric Blom, *Beethoven's pianoforte sonatas discussed*, 1938.

SELECTED WRITINGS

This part of our study consists of a compilation of writings bearing on Beethoven's achievements in the genre of the string quartet. They are illustrative of views expressed about these compositions, as conveyed through the sayings and writings of musicians, musicologists and performing artists. As such they provide insights into such considerations as the composer's aesthetic and creative impulse; his philosophical and intellectual outlook; the expressive nature of his writing; the challenges with which he confronts the performer relating to questions of interpretation and performance; and, above all, the continuing legacy of his musical inheritance

Where applicable, prefatory remarks are incorporated with the selected texts to provide the reader with the original context from which the various writings have been derived. The bibliography at the close of the work will also be of value to the reader wishing to discover more about the original sources and others publications not cited in the selected texts.

GERALD ABRAHAM

'In early Beethoven one is always very conscious of the beautifully clear-cut, more-or-less conventional form; in mature Beethoven one thinks less of the conventional because it is so beautifully matched with the organic content; in Beethoven's last period works the formal outline, though always present and always discoverable by those who take trouble to look for it frequently flouts convention and is generally concealed by the organic richness of the content.'

Gerald Abraham, *Beethoven's Second-Period Quartets*. London: Oxford University Press: Humphrey Milford, 1944, p. 71.

THE BEETHOVEN QUARTET SOCIETY

The Beethoven Quartet Society was a musical society established in 1845 in London with the professed aim of 'giving the most perfect performance possible of those beautiful compositions'. *The Society* was established by Thomas Alsager, a Beethoven enthusiast who was also a critic and manager of *The Times*. A measure of Alsager's eagerness to promote the better understanding of Beethoven's compositions is evident insofar as the first complete performance of the *Missa Solemnis* took place in Alsager's home on Christmas Eve in 1832. *The Society* had high ideals as can be inferred from its founding rules:

'(1): That the composition [selected for performance] should be of a highly refined and intellectual character;
'(2) That it should be played by the best artists, prepared by long practice and careful study of the author's design;
'(3) That the performance should be in the presence of an audience able to appreciate both the composition and its execution.'

As can be inferred from the above, prior study by the audience of the composer's scores of the string quartets was encouraged; thereby *The Society* expected 'all will listen with profound attention'!

The Society held its first concerts in *The Beethoven Rooms*, located in fashionable Harley Street. Later on these took place in *The New Beethoven Room* situated in Queen Anne Street. In its first season, *The Society* resolved to hold five recitals at each of which three Beethoven quartets were to be performed: one form the Op. 18 set, one from the middle period quartets Opp. 59, 74, 95, and one of the later quartets. A measure of the high standing of *The Society* was that its Membership was confined to fifty persons on payment of five guineas each. At the first recital, the String Quartets Op. 18, No.1, Op. 59, No.3 and Op. 127 were performed. Later on in the season, *The Society* achieved an English 'Beethoven first' by completing the entire cycle of his quartets with the exception of the *Grosse Fuge*.

Pamela J. Willetts, *Beethoven and England: An account of sources in the British Museum*, London: British Museum, 1970, pp. 55–8. See also entry for Hector Berlioz.

PAUL BEKKER
In his survey of Beethoven's writing for the string quartet,

the German music critic Paul Bekker writes:

> 'He began with trios and at last arrived, by way of the quintet, at the quartet. The first works of this group date from 1800 (the year which saw the last of the chamber works for wind instruments), and with them begins Beethoven's greatest path of achievement, the way which leads from the six quartets of op. 18 up to the five last which represent the coping-stone of his whole life's work. Everything he wrote, everything he experienced or achieved, is expressed in this series of works. Chamber music for strings alone is, indeed, the very heart and kernel of Beethoven's creative work, around which the rest is grouped, supplementing, explaining, confirming. His life is there faithfully mirrored, not in the "diary" form of both sonata improvisations, not in the monumental style of his symphonic works, but with absolute intellectual clarity, independent of the sensuous appeal of personal virtuosity or of the compelling force of great orchestral tone masses, and limited to the outwardly inornate form of "conversation" between four "individuals" of equal standing and privileges.'

Paul Bekker, *Beethoven*, London: J. M. Dent & Sons, 1925, p. 283.

HECTOR BERLIOZ

According to Berlioz's *Memoirs*, he appears to have become aware of the music of Beethoven at about the time of his death in 1827; Berlioz was then age 24. Despite being a relatively late-comer to the composer, he soon became one of his most ardent admirers. After attending one of the celebrated series of concerts by the newly founded *Société des Concerts du Conservatoire* in March 1828, he wrote to his sister Nanci:

> 'It is when you have heard the sublime instrumental compositions of the eagle Beethoven that you can see how right the poet is in exclaiming: "O divine music, speech is powerless and weak, and yields to your magic".' (*Correspondence générale)*

The impact of Beethoven on Berlioz is evident from the many references to him that occur in his letters and other writings; epithets abound such as 'immense', 'colossal', 'sublime', 'a giant' and 'a Titan'. In another letter to Nanci, written in 1829, he refers to attending Beethoven string quartet evenings in the home of the composer's former publisher Moritz Schlesinger. Apparently their newness was a challenge to the performers who 'played sometimes well, sometimes badly'.

Hugh Macdonald, editor, *Berlioz: Selected letters*, London: Faber and Faber, 1995, p. 62.

Berlioz was a friend of the German poet Heinrich Heine, who was given to referring to him as 'a colossal nightingale'. In 1843, Berlioz heard four brothers perform Beethoven string quartets under their family name *The Müller Quartet*. In a letter to Heine, Berlioz enthused:

> 'I regarded their performance of Beethoven quartets as one of the most extraordinary prodigies of modern art.'

For Berlioz, this group of players represented the ideal. He elaborates:

> 'Nowhere else in the world has perfection of ensemble, unity of sentiment, depth of expression,

purity of style, grandeur, force, spirit, and passion been carried to such a pitch. Such an interpretation of these sublime works give us, I think, the most exact idea of Beethoven's thoughts and feelings while writing them. It is the echo of creative inspiration, the rebound of genius!'

Ernest Newman, *Memoirs of Hector Berlioz from 1803 to 1865, Comprising his Travels in Germany, Italy, Russia, and England*, New York: Knopf, 1932, p. 296.

When on a visit to London in 1847, Berlioz made the acquaintance of *The Beethoven Quartet Society* (see above). Writing of his encounter, Berlioz remarks:

'The programme of each evening concert contains no less than three [string quartets], and nothing else. There is usually one in each of the three different styles of the composer; and it is always the last, from the third period (the period of Beethoven's allegedly incomprehensible works) that excites the most enthusiasm. There you can see English listeners following the unpredictable flight of the master's thought in miniature sores printed in London for this purpose.'

Berlioz was fortunate insofar as his apartment opened onto the staircase leading directly to the concert room. He relates:
'I had only to open the door to hear everything that was being performed.'

He describes how one evening the music so infiltrated his senses, it prompted him to exclaim:

'Wherever did Beethoven find those thousands of phrases, each one more poetic in nature than

> the last, and all different and original? ... And
> what skillful development! What unexpected
> flights! ... How swiftly that tireless eagle wings its
> way! How he soars and hovers in his harmonious
> sky!'

Hector Berlioz, *Evenings in the Orchestra*, Harmondsworth: Penguin Books, 1963, p. 216.

LEONARD BERNSTEIN

In his Introduction to *The Joy of Music*, the ardent Beethovenian Leonard Bernstein discusses the nature of our response to music and of the challenges posed by attempting to explain *meaning* in music. He illustrates the point by remarking:

> 'There have been more words written about the
> *Eroica Symphony* than there are notes in it ...
> And yet has anyone ever successfully "explained"
> the *Eroica*?'

He continues:

> 'Can anyone explain in mere prose the wonder
> of one note following or coinciding with another
> so that we feel that it's exactly how those notes
> *had* to be?'

Bernstein describes this challenge to our ordering of sensory perception as 'this magical block'. He cites the endeavours of the most rational minds in history, such as Plato and Socrates, to find a way through this 'mystic haze' that, notwithstanding, Bernstein asserts still confronts us. He writes:

> 'We are still, in our own day, faced with this magical block. We try to be scientific about it, in our bumbling way — to employ principles of physics, acoustics, mathematics, and formal logic. We employ philosophical devices like empiricism and teleological method. But what does it accomplish for us? The "magic" questions are still unanswered. For example, we can try to explain the "shape" of a theme from a Beethoven quartet by saying that it follows the formal principles of synthesis: that there is a short statement (thesis), followed by a "questioning answer" (antithesis), followed by a development arising out of the conflict of the two (synthesis). The Germans call this form "*Stollen.*" Others say "syllogistic." Words, words, words. Why is the theme beautiful? There's the rub. We can find a hundred themes shaped in this way, or based on variants of this principle; but only one or two will be *beautiful.*'

Leonard Bernstein, *The Joy of Music*, New York: Simon and Schuster, 1959, p. 12.

LEON BOTSTEIN

The Jewish-American conductor and scholar Leon Botstein reflects on the challenges posed by, and the rewards of, Beethoven's writing for the medium of the string quartet:

> 'At issue for both Beethoven and his listeners, even 200 years afterwards, is the struggle to conceive and transmit the sense of beauty and

goodness and the inner struggle with matters of existential meaning and truth in a way at once general and overarching and also individual and specific to the moment of hearing. In the cultural context of this century, in which ordinary language has become the object of distrust, music without words remains a refuge, a nearly logical but not mimetic mode of expression. In late Beethoven, the expression aspires to prophecy; to communicate across time and space, to connect the human community through a shared perception of art. Beethoven's musical and metaphysical achievements in the quartets is no less than the authentic attainment of aspirations that elude speech.'

Botstein concludes:

'Beethoven's discourse in the quartets cannot be corrupted or invalidated by repetition and familiarity. Their inexhaustibility and uncompromising vitality have confronted past auditors and modern listeners alike.'

Leon Botstein: *Music, Culture and Society in Beethoven's Vienna*, in Robert Winter and Robert Martin, editors, *The Beethoven Quartet Companion*, Berkeley: University of California Press, 1994, pp. 91–2.

FRYDERYK CHOPIN
Chopin appears to have admired Beethoven but only, in a manner of speaking, from a distance. It is known he had a particular respect for the composer's Piano Sonata Op. 26

— the one with the funeral march — and offered it to his pupils as a subject worthy of study. More generally, however, as Chopin's biographer Frederick Niechs remarks, he found certain passages in Beethoven 'too rudely fashioned', their structure 'too athletic' and their wraths 'too violent' (*Chopin*, Vol.2 p. 110). Notwithstanding these reservations, in April 1832, Chopin wrote to his friend and fellow composer Joseph Nowakowski in enthusiastic terms regarding Beethoven's music — Chopin was twenty-two at the time:

> 'I wish I could give you my ticket for the *Conservatoire Concert*. That's something that would exceed your expectations. The orchestra is unsurpassable. Today they are giving Beethoven's symphony with choir and one of his quartets played by the massed strings of the orchestra — violins, violas and 'cellos: fifty string players all told. This quartet is being repeated by special request. They did it at the previous concert. You could have imagined that no more than four instruments were playing, yet the tone of the violins could be compared to a Castle, the violas to a Bank, and the 'cellos to a Lutheran Church.'

Arthur Hedley, editor, *Selected Correspondence of Fryderyk Chopin: abridged from Fryderyk Chopin's Correspondence*, London: Heinemann, 1962, p. 111.

REBECCA CLARKE

Rebecca Clarke was an English born classical composer and accomplished violist — she was one of the first female professional orchestral players. A measure of her standing is that she was invited to contribute to the Beethoven

Centenary Issue of the *Musical Times*. In this she wrote — from her performer's viewpoint:

> 'The Beethoven quartets more than any others are pre-eminently for the player rather than for the listener. Brought into the world as they were by slow and laborious growth it is only by slow and laborious concentration that they reveal themselves fully. The listener who hears them casually cannot begin to understand them, as does the player who has lived with them for years and knows all their intricacies by heart. Most other chamber music — that by Mozart for instance — speaks more for itself; it is luminous, lighting its own way. In Beethoven, on the other hand, the player must himself illumine the hidden obscurities, and unless he well understands them he cannot hope to make others do so. Everything must be forgotten in this one aim, that is, provided technique can be more-or-less taken for granted, for we are dealing with something that needs far more than mere personal self-expression or attempted originality of interpretation. One feels that Beethoven himself never bothered much about whether he was original or not, he was too busy being so; and as to self-expression, it must have come so naturally to him and have been so unconscious that he very likely never thought about it at all. It even seems to me not quite right to stress unduly the importance of technique and ensemble; they are after all but the means to an end — a fact which is often lost sight of nowadays. How many times has one had to listen to a robot-like Beethoven, well oiled, drilled to the last degree, complete with every synthetic

emotion — and utterly lacking the vital spark that understanding alone can give.'

Clarke continues:

> 'Beethoven, with his ever new ideas, in which he never plagiarizes even himself, his amazingly individual polyphony and rhythm, and his all-embracing depth of feeling, will always be the ideal of those who really want to work at quartets. Into this form, the purest and most perfect that we know, he poured thoughts that could be expressed in no other way and which make his quartets unsurpassed to this day, and in working at them the player comes as near as is humanely possible to understanding the feelings with which they were written, and finds a delight which is lasting and can know no disenchantment.'

Rebecca Clarke: *The Beethoven Quartets as a Player sees them*, in: *Musical Times*, Special Issue: Vol. VIII, No. 2, 1927, pp. 178–90.

CARL DAHLHAUS

The German musicologist Carl Dahlhaus considers the challenge posed by the legacy of Beethoven's achievement. He first makes the generalization:

> 'However supreme Beethoven's symphonies and string quartets may have reigned in the concert repertoire, the later development of these eminently Beethovenian genres was, from

the standpoint of composition, checkered and disjoint.'

Turning to the efforts of other composer's who followed Beethoven, with regard to the medium of the string quartet, he elaborates:

'Mendelssohn's efforts to come to grips with Beethoven's late works shortly after their appearance left noticeable traces on his early String Quartets Op. 12 and Op. 13, but in this respect he seems to be exceptional. Revealingly, it was precisely the nineteenth century's most "genuine" composers of chamber music, Schumann and Brahms, who were obviously wary of the string quartet and tended to avoid it in favor of chamber music with piano rather than confronting the overpowering legacy of Beethoven. Not until the modern music of our century was the history of the string quartet, which virtually seeped away in the nineteenth century, resumed in representative bodies of works by Schönberg, Bartók, and Hindemith. And in spite of the radically new musical idiom, or perhaps under its protection, these works unmistakably took Beethoven as their starting point ... Thus, we have little cause to speak of a continuous history of the string quartet after Beethoven and under his influence.'

Carl Dahlhaus, *Nineteenth-Century Music*, translated by J. Bradford Robinson, Berkeley; London: University of California Press, 1989, p. 78.

CLAUDE DEBUSSY

Harold Bauer was an American pianist who lived in Paris for a number of years and became acquainted with Claude Debussy. Although there are passages in Debussy's writings where he acknowledges Beethoven's achievements, he, more generally, held the composer in low esteem. This is evident in Bauer's recollections:

> 'Debussy was the most violent of all the critics I ever met, in spite of his enthusiasms and the delicacy of feeling he seemed able to express, in words as in music. He satirized Wagner, he despised and detested Brahms, and he attacked Beethoven with such bitterness and sarcasm that it made one's blood boil. Once, in my hearing, he mentioned that he had "escaped" the previous evening from a concert where a Beethoven quartet was being played, just at the moment when "the old deaf one" (*le vieux sourd*) started to "develop a theme".

Bauer was incensed:

> 'There was something so hateful in the tone of his voice as he said this that I rose up indignantly and denounced him for his disrespect to the name of a great genius; and the result was, I regret to say, that our relations were broken on the spot and not renewed for a number of years.'

As originally recalled in Harold Bauer's *Autobiography*, *Harold Bauer*, New York: 1948, p. 82 and quoted in: Roger Nichols, *Debussy Remembered*, London: Faber and Faber, 1992, pp. 136-7.

GABRIEL FAURÉ

Beethoven's string-quartet writing exerted its intimidating influence on other composers through the nineteenth century and well into the twentieth (see entry under Carl Dahlhaus). We detect this in a letter that Gabriel Fauré wrote to his wife Marie in September 1923; at the time Fauré was residing in Annecy-le-Vieux. He informs her:

'I have undertaken a quartet for strings, without *piano*.'

This is a reference to his String Quartet in E minor, Op 121, his last work completed in 1924 shortly before his death. In his letter he continues:

> 'This is a genre which Beethoven in particular made famous, and causes all those who are not Beethoven to be *terrified* of it! Saint-Saëns was always afraid, and only attempted it towards the end of his life. He did not succeed there as he did in other kinds of composition. So you can well imagine I am frightened too. I have spoken of this to no one. I shall say nothing about it as long as I am nowhere near my objective: the end. When I am asked: "Are you working?" I reply shamelessly "No!" So keep this to yourself!'

J. Barrie Jones, editor, *Gabriel Fauré: A life in letters*, London: Batsford, 1989, p. 299.

In 1925, the Parisian publisher Libraire Félix Alcan posthumously published *Les Quatuors de Beethoven by the French musicologist* Joseph de Marliave. This work was widely read and is still available in reprint. In his study, de Marliave drew heavily on the work of the earlier, and pioneering, scholarship of the Austrian music critic and writer Theodor Otto Helm. His *Beethovens Streichquar-*

tette had been published in Leipzig in 1885 and some consider de Marliave's work to be essentially a translation and adaptation of Helm's study. The Preface to de Marliave's publication was contributed by his friend the composer Gabriel Fauré. He describes his late friend's work as 'a splendid memorial' to him and worthy of 'the honour of Beethoven'. We should add that de Marliave had perished in the Great War, thus delaying the publication of his work.

In 1925, an English translation of de Marliave was published as *Beethoven's Quartets*. In this, Fauré contributed his own views regarding these compositions:

> 'Each of these quartets is in itself an achievement of art and genius, and has a right to respect and consideration, demands the closest attention to detail, and, on the part of a conscientious critic, a proper understanding of the spirit that gave it birth, of its form, whether classical or re-created anew, or entirely novel, of its technique and of its style. He must realize the promise of the first quartets and how it materialized in those that followed, the musician's favourite methods, how they appear in the early movements and then later on in this long series of pieces, all different, but cast in a mould of almost unchanging form; then must be defined the slow but uninterrupted upward progress of the inner consciousness, of the inspiration, style, technique, from voluntary imitation to free creation. And finally the material provided in the Beethoven quartets demands a critical knowledge of the technique of string instruments.'

Gabriel Fauré, Preface to: Joseph de Marliave, *Beethoven's*

Quartets, New York: Dover Publications (reprint), 1961, pp. v–vi.

GUARNERI QUARTET

The Guarneri String Quartet was an American string quartet founded in 1964. It was admired for its rich, warm tone and had a particular affinity for the works of Beethoven and Bartók. The Quartet was notable for its longevity: the group performed for 45 years with only one personnel change when cellist David Soyer retired in 2001, to be replaced by Peter Wiley. The other members were Arnold Steinhardt, first violin, John Dalley, second violin and David Soyer, cello. Before the Quartet was disbanded in 2009, the group was interviewed by the American writer David Blum. The exchanges that followed shed light on the rapport that exists between such musicians and their response to the demands made upon them by the music. When the conversation turned to Beethoven and his first set of string quartets, the Op. 18, Steinhardt remarked on their need for 'a crystalline quality, a perfection ... an almost constant delicacy and precision'. He compared these works to those of Mozart that 'should always sound spontaneous, no matter how carefully they must be treated'. In contrast, he likened performing the late quartets to 'painting on a large canvas in broad strokes, splashing blobs of colour'. He singled out for particular mention the Finales of the Op. 131 and the *Grosse Fuge* and their 'wild frenzy'. Tree added:

> 'When coming to the *Grosse Fuge* [Beethoven] seems to sidestep the nineteenth century altogether and plant his feet squarely in the twentieth century in terms of dissonance, sonority, and sheer abandon.'

Commenting on the *Razumovsky* String Quartets, Op. 59, Dalley remarked on the extent to which Beethoven had changed the sonority of the quartet sound since his pioneering Op. 18:

> 'The four parts are more nearly equal in prominence; the lower voices have more resonance. The melodies have a more sustained cantilena quality. There is more concentrated sound ... fuller, richer than before.'

Of Beethoven's over-arching achievement in the genre of the string quartet, Soyer reflected:

> 'A cycle of Beethoven's quartets is of unique interest; his spiritual development encompasses worlds. It's little wonder that the complete Beethoven cycle is in such demand; we're asked to play it at least once every season. There's a bottomless well of fascination in these pieces. New ideas seem to be coming up all the time. Much remains enigmatic — even some of the markings. There's a creative mystery that can never be entirely resolved.'

When David Blum asked the Quartet if they always played the quartets in the same order, Dalley replied:

> 'Yes, whenever we play the cycle in six concerts. On occasion we've done it in five concerts, but that's very strenuous both for us and for the public. In deciding on the order in which we play the works we borrowed heavily from the Budapest Quartet version; their cycle was very well

conceived. Because of its full, declamatory beginning, we consider Opus 127 the ideal work to open the cycle. And we conclude with the last quartet, Opus 135. The six-concert cycle allows us to include the short movement Beethoven wrote as a substitute for the *Grosse Fuge*. We use it to conclude Opus 130 because we feel that the *Grosse Fuge* can, if necessary, stand on its own, as it often does.'

The following is the sequence of quartets when performed by the Guarneri String Quartet in their six-concert series: (1) Opus 127; Opus 18, No. 2; Opus 59, No. 3; (2) Opus 18, No. 3; Opus 95; Opus 132; (3) Opus 18, No. 4; Opus 18, No. 1; Opus 131; (4) Opus 74; Opus 18, No. 5; Opus 59, No. 2; (5) Opus 130; Opus 59, No. 1; (6) Opus 18, No. 6; Opus 133; Opus 135.

David Blum, *The Art of Quartet Playing: The Guarneri Quartet in conversation with David Blum*, London: Gollancz, 1986, pp. 157–8.

WILLIAM HENRY HADOW

Sir William Henry Hadow was a leading educational reformer in Great Britain, a composer and musicologist. He held high academic office at Durham and Sheffield Universities in the capacity of Vice Chancellor. Despite being in demand to serve on many national committees, he found time to write extensively on music. He made a particular study of Beethoven's Op. 18 String Quartets. At the close of his text he modestly states:

'Such a book as this can but open the door of the garden, and indicate the flower beds and the fountains, and the shady coverts where students of Beethoven may find enjoyment for a lifetime.'

In his final summation, he writes:

'It is important, it is even necessary for any progress, to learn, as matter of fact, the principles of musical architecture, and to note in what chief respects Beethoven adopted or modified them in his own practice. But it is when those facts have been ascertained that real understanding begins. Then it is the reader's privilege to study the music bar by bar, bringing to it a trained ear and a mind already furnished and equipped: his reward will be the continuous discovery of beauties which, when he first began, were beyond his imagination. Horace advises us to turn the Greek poets "with daily and with nightly hand": that is the advice that should be given to every student of Beethoven. Though we learn the notes until we are letter-perfect, we shall never master their secret: every time that we come back to it we shall meet it with fuller comprehension, like the face of a familiar friend which grows more beloved with every day of added experience and converse.'

William Henry Hadow, *Beethoven's Opus 18 Quartets*, London: Humphrey Milford at the Oxford University Press, 1926, p. 64.

FANNY HENSEL (MENDELSOHN)
After almost a century of neglect, it now recognized that

Fanny Mendelsohn should not be remembered for being merely the sister of her gifted brother Felix, but as a highly accomplished pianist and composer in her own right. Fanny had the misfortune to be constrained by attitudes prevailing at her time towards women. Notwithstanding her remarkable precocity, her father felt obliged to write to her in 1820 with the caution:

'Music will perhaps become his [Felix's] profession, while for *you* it can and must be only an ornament.'

Undeterred Fanny composed numerous works, including her String Quartet in E-flat major that has been described as being 'packed [with] a huge amount of emotion'.

Recalling her first attempts at serious composition, Fanny wrote to Felix in February 1835:

> 'I've reflected how I, actually not an eccentric or overly sentimental person, came to write pieces in a tender style. I believe it derives from the fact that we were young during Beethoven's last years and absorbed his style to a considerable degree. But that style is exceedingly moving and emotional. You've gone through it from start to finish and progressed beyond it in your composing, and I've remained stuck in it, not possessing the strength, however, that is necessary to sustain that tenderness. Therefore I also believe that you haven't hit upon or voiced the crucial issue. It's not so much a certain way of composing that is lacking as it is a certain approach to life, and as a result of this shortcoming, my lengthy things die in their youth of decrepitude; I lack the ability to sustain ideas properly and give them the needed consistency.'

Regarding the quality of so many of Fanny's compositions, many would today regard Fanny's self-disparagement as unjustified.

Marcia Citron, editor, *The Letters of Fanny Hensel to Felix Mendelssohn*, Stuyvesant, New York: Pendragon Press, 1987, p. 174.

GUSTAV HOLST

In 1903, Holst resolved to set upon a programme of study. He confided his intentions in a letter to his friend and fellow composer Ralph Vaughn Williams —a competent viola player. Beethoven was Holst's paradigm:

> 'As to how to study I feel rather floored again. But what I personally should like would be to have all of Beethoven's chamber music at my fingers' ends as Wagner apparently had: to be able to wallow in it — to soak it in and make it part of one's being. That is my idea.'

Jon C. A Mitchell, *A Comprehensive Biography of Composer Gustav Holst; With correspondence and diary excerpts: including his American years*, Lewiston, New York: Edwin Mellen Press, 2001, p. 38.

HANS KELLER

The Austrian-born British musician Hans (Heinrich) Keller made significant contributions to musicology and music criticism through the medium of his many writings and BBC broadcasts — some of which, as the present writer recalls, could be provocative. To his musical insights he brought the skills of being an active violinist and violist, deriving from the early part of his career. Keller had a deep admiration for the string quartets of Mozart. In his study of the composer her wrote:

> 'Not all of them may be absolutely flawless, but where they are, they represent a consummation of artistic perfection the like of which has, perhaps, never again been achieved in chamber music.'

Within the foregoing context, Keller remarked:

> 'With Haydn (from Op. 9 onwards) and Beethoven, a new quartet is a new quartet, revolutionarily unlike its predecessors, employing hitherto untried means of diversifying a basic idea. Mozart's originality does not similarly renew itself; it is always there, but often it has been there before. He tends to adhere to his own, highly original, conventions, whereas Haydn and Beethoven do not only break other people's conventions, but also their own. Consequently, any two great Mozart quartets are more alike in form than any two great Haydn or Beethoven quartets, and if we are honest, we do not always find it easy to say, on purely musical grounds, which Mozart quartet is the earlier and which the later.'

Hans Keller, *The Mozart Companion*, London: Faber & Faber, 1956, p. 102.

Writing of Beethoven's contribution to the genre of quartet writing he remarks:

> 'As for Beethoven, possibly humanity's greatest mind, his great quartets ... are, of course, far fewer than Haydn's, and therefore give a far less complete picture of his spiritual development. For another, while his evolution as a quartet composer eventually carried him into spheres of unheard-of — in fact unheard — expression where nobody, with the possible exception of Schoenberg, has been able to follow, let alone join him, it was inevitable that on the way, he had to sacrifice classical perfection to the extent of discovering the beauty of ugliness in general, and of an ugly quartet sound in particular ... In point of fact, a certain (very certain, acutely imagined) kind of imperfection, of both instrumental and sheer acoustic strain, became part and parcel of the creative act.'

Hans Keller, *The Great Haydn Quartets: Their interpretation*, London: J. M. Dent, 1986, p. 17.

Keller's characteristic acerbic style of music criticism is to be found in a review of a Beethoven recital given by the Blech String Quartet sometime in the 1940s. Founded by Harry Blech, the ensemble had by then established itself as one of Britain's finest. Notwithstanding, Keller wrote of their performance on the occasion in question in the following terms:

> 'I have the greatest respect for many of the Blech Quartet's achievements, and even for some inspired moments in the present interpretation, but moments are not enough for this work [late Beethoven]. The early and middle Beethoven always manages to fight his way through even a

bad performance, but even the greatest possible representation does not do justice to the late Beethoven, and anything worse is worse than nothing. This is not perfectionism, but a reminder that the performer's responsibility towards the public should depend on his responsibility towards the composer: If you cannot give the composer his due, soil his linen in private. Of course each of us must play late Beethoven from the cradle to the grave, but most of us should only let the listener in when we can already see our grave, and maybe our way out of it.'

Donald Mitchell and Hans Keller, editors, *Music Survey: New Series 1949–1952*, London: Faber Music in association with Faber & Faber, 198, p. 98.

JOSEPH KERMAN

The American critic and musicologist Joseph Wilfred Kerman briefly considers the position of Beethoven in relation to the evolution of the string quartet:

'[To] consider the history of the string quartet is to assess how Beethoven with his three periods was caught up in that history, as much as how he contributed to it. If we are to see three phases in the history of the quartet during Beethoven's lifetime – the amateur, and the private – we must also see how Beethoven's relation to each was different. In the first his role was that of participant. To the second he served as a sort of prophet. The third was his own unique, private vision ... The final privatization of the string quartet was Beethoven's special contribution, one that — except for the overriding historical impact of his works — stands outside of history ... The first audience of the string quartet was an actual audience; the second can only be thought of in terms of potential and the third was an ideal audience that consisted, paradoxically, of no audience at all ... And because in his last period Beethoven often gives the impression of shutting out an audience, listeners ever since had to get used to a situation in which they are suddenly made privy to a singular colloquy, now hushed, now strident, but always self-absorbed. The conversation of the classical string quartet is obviously designed to be heard and, within a discreet circle, overheard. Listening to certain movements of late Beethoven quartets, one feels sure that neither of these situations holds. The music is sounding only for the composer and for one auditor, an awestruck eavesdropper: you.'

Joseph Kerman: *Beethoven Quartet Audiences: Actual, potential, ideal* in: Robert Winter and Robert Martin, editors, *The Beethoven Quartet Companion*, Berkeley: University of California Press, 1994, p. 25 and pp. 26–7.

WILLIAM KINDERMAN
The American scholar, pianist and musicologist William Kinderman gives his estimation of Beethoven's string quartets:

'No group of compositions occupies a more central position in chamber music than Beethoven's string quartets, yet the meaning of these works continues to stimulate debate. The achievements of Haydn in his Op. 33 collection and Mozart in his famous "Haydn" set had already brought the string quartet to peaks of stylistic development by the 1780s. The refined cultural position of the genre was reflected in the old adage, echoed by Goethe in 1829, that in a quartet "one hears four reasonable people conversing with one another".' [Goethe was writing to the German composer and conductor Carl Friedrich Zelter]

Kinderman continues:

'Building on the conversational aura and integrated textures of these models, Beethoven used the quartet as the medium for some of his boldest and most advanced ideas. These works convey wit and humour, pathos and drama, and the last quartets in particular seem to push beyond established traditions to discover whole new seas of thought and feeling.'

William Kinderman, editor, *The String Quartets of Beethoven*, Urbana, Ilinois: University of Illinois Press, 2005, p. 1.

NICCOLÒ PAGANINI

We customarily associate the name of Niccolò Paganini with the art of violin playing at its most virtuosic, as, for example, enshrined in his 24 Caprices for solo violin, Op. 1. References to his performance in chamber works are hard to come by. One such has been left by Paganini's contemporary, the violinist Karl Guhr. He was leader and conductor of theatre orchestras in both Frankfurt-am-Main and Paris. Guhr made a close study of Paganini's style of playing that was subsequently published in the December 1829 issue of the *Revue Musicale*. Guhr recognized Paganini's playing had 'opened boundless horizons to fantasy, imagination and technique', but considered his virtuosity disposed him to get carried away and, when performing the work of another composer, to depart from his intentions. Guhr writes:

'This terrible originality ... has its peculiar weakness. It is impossible for him to ever escape from his own creative self. That is why Paganini falls so far from his best when he plays the compositions of other masters.'

Guhr was privileged to here Paganini perform as a member of a string quartet. This, however, disposed him to level further criticisms against the virtuoso:

'Although, when he plays the quartets of Beethoven and Mozart, he is entranced by their mighty genius, he cannot escape from himself. Ideas of his own break athwart the conceptions of the great masters, and, carried away by his amazing facility, he has to be on his guard against introducing *tours de force* of his own.'

Of particular interest to string players is Guhr's summing up of the chief differences between the playing of Paganini and that of other violinists. He cites:

> 'His method of tuning his instrument; his method of bowing; his practice of combining the sound produced by the bow with a left-hand *pizzicato* accompaniment; his use of harmonics natural and artificial; his performances on the G string only; and his incredible *tours de force*.'

As derived from: Renée de Saussine, *Paganini*, Westport,

Connecticut: Greenwood Press, 1976, p. 174.

SERGEI PROKOFIEV

At the start of 1930, Sergei Prokofiev toured America where he gave twelve symphony concerts and eleven chamber recitals. In these, he performed works of his own composition that, according to his own account, were generally well received — unlike some years previously when his music was considered too modern for many ears. On his return home from America, later that year, he relates how he started work on his String Quartet op.50. This had been commissioned by the Library of Congress in Washington and may be taken as an indirect tribute to Prokofiev's acceptance as a modern composer. He relates:

> 'Before starting work on the quartet I studied Beethoven's quartets, chiefly in railways carriages on my way from one concert to another. In this way I came to understand and greatly admire his quartet technique. Perhaps this explains the somewhat "classical" idiom of the first movement of my quartet.'

Christopher Palmer, editor, *Sergei Prokofiev: Soviet Diary 1927 and other writings*, London: Faber and Faber, 1991, pp. 290–1.

PHILIP RADCLIFFE

The English scholar, musicologist and composer Philip Radcliffe outlines his views on Beethoven's string quartets:

> 'The quartets give as full and varied a picture of

[Beethoven's] personality as do the symphonies and the sonatas; their whole character is, however, inevitably affected by the medium for which they were written. In his earlier years it was the piano that stimulated Beethoven to his boldest flights of imagination, and in the early quartets there is nothing as passionate as the slow movements of some of the sonatas of the period, such as Op. 10, No. 3 in D major. The Op. 59 and Op. 74 Quartets are rich and massive in texture, but do not show the stormy explosiveness of the *Appassionata Sonata,* or the first movement of the Fifth Symphony. It is not surprising that, in his last years, his increasing interest in polyphony found particularly full expression in the writing of string quartets.'

Radcliffe continues:

'One of the most impressive indications of the colossal range of Beethoven's genius is the fact that he, greatest and most widely loved of symphonists, should, notwithstanding, have written more quartets than symphonies and shown an increasing interest in this branch of composition in his last years. Nothing can be gained by exalting either portion of his work at the expense of the other; Wagner expressed his views in words with which many will agree:

"Give me Beethoven's symphonies and overtures for public performance; his quartets and sonatas for intimate communion".'

Philip Radcliffe, *Beethoven's String Quartets*, Cambridge:

Cambridge University Press, 1978, derived in part from Radcliffe's Introduction and p. 188.

ALMA ROSÉ

Alma Rosé was the violinist daughter of Arnold Rosé who formed the Arnold Rosé String Quartet in 1882. The Quartet's repertoire was based around the works of Haydn, Mozart and Beethoven but was also recognized for its championing of the works of modern composers; for example, it premiered Schoenberg's First and Second String Quartets. A review from one of the Quartet's all-Beethoven recitals conveys the power of the composer's music to work on our emotions. The recital in question was the last to be given by the Quartet and inevitably feelings amongst the audience, possessed of this awareness, were running high. The works performed included the Quartets in E-flat, Op. 74; C-sharp minor, Op. 131; and A major, Op. 18, No. 5. The reviewer Stefan Zweig reported:

'When the last measures of the Beethoven, played more beautifully than ever by the Rosé Quartet, had died away, no one left his seat. We called and applauded, several women sobbed with emotion, no one wished to believe this was farewell. The lights were put out to make us leave. Not one of the four or five hundred enthusiasts left his seat. A half hour, a full hour, we remained as if our presence could save the old hallowed place.'

Richard Newman, *Alma Rosé: Vienna to Auschwitz*, Portland, Oregon: Amadeus Press, 2000, p. 42.

Alma had a successful career of her own but which was to end tragedy. With the onset of the Second World War, and being of Jewish origin, she was interred in Birkenau Concentration Camp where she subsequently perished. For a time she was allowed to create a small chamber orchestra.

Her friend and fellow inmate Anita Lasker-Wallfisch survived to recall a performance of the Sonata *Pathétique* arranged by Alma for three violins and cello. Her account is deeply moving. She recalls:

> 'How can I describe that evening ... It was a link with the outside, with beauty, with culture – a complete escape into an imaginary and unattainable world ... We lifted ourselves above the inferno of Birkenau into a sphere where we could not be touched by the degradation of concentration camp existence.'

Richard Newman, *Ibid*, pp. 261-2.

ARTHUR SHEPHERD

Arthur Shepherd was an American composer and conductor but is known in Beethoven musicology primarily for his survey of the composer's string quartets. This had its origins in a series of Beethoven recitals that Shepherd attended in Cleveland during May and June 1935. Of these, he enthused:

> 'Those who were fortunate enough to attend will recall an artistic experience that will not easily slip from remembrance.'

Shepherd appears to have resolved to retain a measure of his own experience by writing up the programme notes he had prepared for the recital series. From his published study, we quote the following prefatory extracts.

> 'No encomium, uttered or written, could add to the splendor of so enduring an art-monument as

the sixteen string quartets of Beethoven.'

'Had the composer of the *Eroica*, the Ninth Symphony, and the *Missa Solemnis* eschewed the chamber-music forms entirely, his place among the immortals would still be incontestable, but it remained for the quartets and the last five piano sonatas to add final confirmation to the supremacy of his genius. For listener, student and performer, the Quartets constitute a majestic highway that traverses that province of the tone-realm which is at once most hazardous and most rewarding; they require no pious novitiate for their enjoyment, but it cannot be denied that they demand both intellectual and spiritual cooperation.'

'It becomes greatly advantageous to hear and study these works consecutively, for they provide, as no other series could, a clear and complete record of the composer's creative progress through the several stages so ardently characterized by Franz Liszt as *the Youth, the Man,* and *the God.*'

Arthur Shepherd, *The String Quartets of Ludwig van Beethoven*, Cleveland: H. Carr, The Printing Press, 1935, pp. Vii–ix.

ROBERT SIMPSON

Robert Wilfred Simpson was an English composer and a long-time serving producer for the BBC. Members of an older generation will recall his scholarly and informative broadcasts for the *Third Programme* in several of which he explored the music of Beethoven. Writing of the composer's string quartets he remarks:

> 'Beethoven's quartets may not be summed up. They represent most of the main stages in his development, though not all; the piano sonatas show a more continuous process, but the quartets reach further into his last period. Falling conveniently into three groups (or four if you regard Op. 74 and Op. 95 as a separate pair), they reveal Beethoven at crucial stages in his incomparable career. There is nothing else like them in the whole of music except in Beethoven's own work, and they reveal, like the sonatas and the symphonies, that of all composers he possessed the widest, deepest, most active and most realistically hopeful genius. It is a platitude to say that his range of expression is Shakespearean; so it is, but he has a commitment to humanity that Shakespeare does not reveal. There has been no greater artist; and it is to be doubted whether any can match him.'

Robert Simpson, *The Chamber Music for Strings* in: Denis Arnold and Nigel Fortune, editors, *The Beethoven Companion*, London: Faber and Faber, 1973, pp. 277–8.

IGOR STRAVINSKY

Stravinsky alludes to what he refers to as the string quartets 'inborn powers':

> 'The string quartet was the most lucid conveyor of musical ideas ever fashioned, and the most singing — i.e., *human* — of instrumental means; or rather, if it was not that, natively and necessarily,

Beethoven made it so. As for inborn powers, it could register a faster rate of harmonic change than the not yet fully chromatic orchestra of Beethoven's time, which was further impeded by a weight problem and balance problem. It is a more intense medium, furthermore, partly by the same tokens; and a more pleasing one, long-term, as colour: to me at any rate, and in my case partly because I am least conscious of the colour element in it. Its sustaining powers are greater than those of wind-instrumental ensembles, and its ranges of speeds, and of degrees of soft volumes, are wider. Compared with the piano, its advantages are in polyphonic delineation and in the greater variety of dynamic articulation and nuance.'

Igor Stravinsky, *Themes and Conclusions*, London: Faber and Faber, 1972, p. 256.

BRUNO WALTER

On 19 October 1966 Bruno Walter appeared before the public in an unfamiliar guise. He delivered a lecture at the University of London Institute for Education. His subject was *A Musical Education*. He opened with remarks that would have had such prescience for Beethoven, shortly after his arrival in Vienna, when he wrote to his old friend, the physician Franz Gerhard Wegeler, informing him of the progressive loss of his hearing — a circumstance that would eventually determine no less than the future direction of his life and art. Walter posed the question:

'And what of sound itself, the supreme element in communication, the uninterrupted and continuous apprehending of our environment which the aural gift ensures?'

He elaborated:

> 'Sound is indeed the supreme medium of communication, and how much more significance do words hold when they are restored to sound, in the voice of a loved one ...'.

Turning to sound as music, Walter argued:

> 'Sometimes it is important to forget words altogether and let music take over, as we do when we listen to a Beethoven quartet.'

This prompted Walter to tell his audience about a circumstance concerning a remarkable woman and how, amidst her harrowing circumstances, she found solace in Beethoven's music that gave her the strength to endure her adversity. The woman in question was the mother of the conductor Antal Dorati. Being wartime, and having Jewish connections, she was taken into custody — a euphemism. Walter relates:

> '[She] found herself herded into a small room with dozens of others, where they were kept for many days with no food and no facilities of any kind. Most of the others went out of their minds, but she kept sane by methodically going through the four parts of each of the Beethoven quartets, which she knew individually by heart.'

Bruno Walter, *Theme and Variations: An autobiography*, London: H. Hamilton, 1948, p. 103.

BEETHOVEN AND VIENNA STRING QUARTETS OP. 18, NOS. 1–6

'It was as the incarnate spirit of Mozart, moulded by Haydn's virile talent, that Beethoven was to appear to the musical world when the six quartets of Op. 18, following close upon the First Symphony, were published in two uniform series nine years later. In these works of Beethoven's youth the clarity and freshness of Haydn are found linked with the grace of Mozart, but so far from slavish imitation of these two masters, they form, as it were, the crowning achievement of their art.'

Joseph de Marliave, *Beethoven's Quartets*, 1961 (reprint — originally published in 1917), pp.1–2.

'[In] Beethoven's Op. 18 the balance is perfect, the interest is distributed with an entirely even hand. He has, indeed, less virtuosity than Haydn, though he demands more concentrated intelligence; the steady light which illumines his work is diffused over the whole canvas.'

William Henry Hadow, *Beethoven's Op. 18 Quartets*, 1926, pp. 7—8.

'The composition of string quartets was important in several ways to Beethoven in 1798. It meant, first of all ... entry upon a major musical genre which he had not yet tried. This entry itself may be seen as a step in his steady apprenticeship in all braches of composition. There can be little doubt that at this period in his life Beethoven had embarked on a more or less planned assault on the entire territory of music.'

Joseph Kerman, *The Beethoven Quartets*, 1967, p. 10.

'To underestimate Beethoven's earlier works in the light of his later achievements is one of the commonest blunders of criticism, and one of the most natural. It is all too easy to take for granted that the Op. 18 Quartets are works of genius and then to treat them as advanced student essays; more than one writer has been guilty of this, and with the best of intentions ... Despite some inequalities ... these six works, sometimes to the point of recklessness, express a wider range of colour and feeling than any group of six by Haydn and Mozart.'

Robert Simpson, *The Chamber Music for Strings* in: Denis Arnold and Nigel Fortune, editors, *The Beethoven Companion*, 1973, p. 241 and p. 246.

> 'Compared to Beethoven's late quartets, [Op. 18] have been thought of as "early works" and wanting in some aspects. This is to do grave disservice to these extraordinary first fruits of Beethoven's genre, and also to remove them from their highly important position in the history of music ...'.

H. C. Robbins Landon, *Haydn: the Years of 'The creation', 1796–800*, 1977, p. 504.

> 'Beethoven's [early] chamber music for strings, which includes three string trios, six string quartets and two string quintets, marks a stage in [Beethoven's] gradual liberation from reliance upon the piano as the anchor of his compositional style.'

Maynard Solomon, *Vienna: early years*, in: *Beethoven*, 1977, p. 100.

> 'The fact that emerges most obviously from a survey of these six works is that Beethoven was already a master of the problems of writing a string quartet ... The six works all have their own individual character, those in F major and C minor giving on the whole the most complete picture of the composer.'

Philip Radcliffe, *Beethoven's String Quartets*, 1978, pp. 44.

> Notwithstanding their evident roots in *galanterie* ... the six quartets [Op. 18] ... already embody a taste for experiment in directions clearly seditious of the old polite order.'

Bernhard Jacobson, Liner notes to: *Ludwig van Beethoven; The early string quartets*, Op. 18, Alban Berg Quartet, EMI, 1981.

> '[Beethoven] was the first quartet composer to enter the medium in the full knowledge of his inheritance, and of what was expected of a quartet in the 1790s — something very different from what was expected in the 1770s when Mozart began ... Certainly Beethoven felt pressed to produce only his best ... With this first collection, Beethoven had changed the nature of the quartet ... and he had also changed the sound.'

Paul Griffiths, *The String Quartet*, 1983, p. 84.

> 'When the string quartet originated as a genre, in Haydn's period, six compositions were required as a work — an opus. This unwritten law of European music's golden age bears witness to true richness ... The opuses of Haydn, Mozart and Beethoven, consisting of groups of six string quartets, are the greatest masterpieces of the literature or within the genre.'

János Kárpáti, Introduction to: *Bartók's Chamber Music*, 1994.

> 'All six quartets demonstrate that Beethoven had fully absorbed the idiom as used by Mozart and Haydn. No other composer had matched their sophistication, and Beethoven probably saw himself as their true heir in this genre, as in the symphony.'

Barry Cooper, *Beethoven: The Master Musicians Series*, 2000, p. 93.

> 'Unlike Mozart in his "Haydn" Quartets, Beethoven's Op. 18 cannot ... be viewed as a response to Haydn's latest works. Instead, the stance is a broader one. Beethoven's understanding of the genre had taken several years to develop and reflected a general understanding of the quartet repertoire from the 1780s and early 1790s rather than an exclusive knowledge of one striking set.'

David Wyn Jones in: Robin Stowell, editor, *The Cambridge Companion to the String Quartet*, 2003, p. 211.

> 'What unifies the early quartets [Op. 18] is simply their classicism, though it is a classicism already placed under threat by the force of Beethoven's powerful musical personality. The writing is lithe and aphoristic, with abrupt switches of between soft and loud, violent changes of key, unexpectedly volatile scale passages, [and] dramatic use of all four instruments.'

Conrad Wilson, *Notes on Beethoven: 20 Crucial Works*, 2003, pp. 15–16.

> 'The six quartets of Op. 18 are the magnum opus of Beethoven's first decade at Vienna, and they stand somewhat apart from his later contributions to the quartet medium. Although less admired in writings about the composer than the *Razumovsky* Quartets or the late quartets, the Op. 18 quartets are probably the most frequently performed and they occupy a key historical position at the threshold to the nineteenth century.'

William Kinderman, editor, *The String Quartets of Beethoven*, 2005, p. 13.

Beethoven took up residence in Vienna in November 1792 in order to continue his studies in Europe's musical capital with Joseph Haydn, having been granted leave of absence from his duties in his hometown of Bonn by the Elector Maximilian Franz. His first musical appointment was at the Bonn Court of the Elector who, in time, recognised his employee's talent and sponsored Beethoven's visit to Vienna so that he could study with Haydn and thereby perfect his skills. For his part, Beethoven was conscious of his lack of formal training and readily agreed to participate in the venture, even though it entailed departing from his hometown and circle of friends. Haydn, in his capacity as Kapellmeister to Prince Nicholas Esterhazy, had commended Beethoven warmly to the Elector. He had been introduced to the little known, but brilliantly gifted young composer, when coming home from his first London tour. He had planned to take Beethoven with him to London on his return there for the summer season but the political situation in Europe conspired against this. Instead, Haydn agreed to give Beethoven lessons in Vienna where he was acknowledged as the leading composer of the day.

Beethoven arrived in Vienna to find the city still sorrowing from the death of Mozart who had died there in straitened circumstances in December 1791. This is recalled in the following incident. Before leaving for Vienna, on 29 October 1792, Beethoven invited several close friends to a farewell meal at which they each inscribed his *Stammbuch* (family album) with a dedicatory message. Amongst the contributors was Count Ferdinand von Waldstein whose name today we associate with the Piano Sonata in C major, Op. 53 – *The Waldstein* – of which he was the dedicatee. He sent Beethoven on his way with the often-quoted words: 'You are now going to Vienna in fulfilment of your long-frustrated wishes. Mozart's genius still mourns and is weeping over the death of its pupil ... Through uninterrupted diligence, you shall receive *Mozart's spirit from Haydn's hands.*'[ii][iii] It later transpired the arrangement suited neither of them; Beethoven became dissatisfied with Haydn's instruction and his own unorthodox ways were uncongenial to the more prosaic Haydn. We consider their relationship more closely in due course.[iv]

Waldstein was eight years older than Beethoven and was about forty-two when the Piano Sonata Op. 53 was dedicated to him. The two men became acquaintances from about 1788 when Waldstein had been summoned to Bonn to perform official diplomatic duties by Maximilian Franz – the Grand Master of the *Teutonic Order* of which Waldstein was himself a knight. Beethoven's early biographer Franz Gerhard Wegeler describes Waldstein as being 'the first person to recognize Beethoven's great talent' and it is probable he may have rendered discrete financial support, and related assistance, to the young composer. Waldstein had a genuine love of music and for the *Carnival Sunday* of 6 March 1791, the two young men collaborated in writing the music required for the spring aristocratic festivities – a masked ball known as the *Ritterballet* or 'Knight's Ballet' for which the participants dressed in old-style German costume.[v]

Another claimant to be one of the first to recognize Beethoven's abilities was the composer Christian Gottlob Neefe. He gave his youthful protégée keyboard instruction, based on Bach's *Das wohltemperirte Clavier*, together with a grounding in thoroughbass and the principles of composition. As early as 1783 (when Beethoven was a mere thirteen years old) he is on record as declaring: 'He will assuredly become another Wolfgang Amadeus Mozart, if he continues as he has begun.'[vi] When he was settled in Vienna, Beethoven did not forget the debt he owed to his former teacher and on 26 October 1793 he found time to write to him: 'I thank you for the advice you have very often given me about making progress in my divine art. Should I ever become a great man, you too will have a share in my success.'[vii]

When the Elector Maximilian granted Beethoven leave of absence from his duties in Bonn, he conferred on him an allowance of 100 Viennese thalers (about 150 florins) to cover his basic living expenses. This was about the sum he had been paid in his capacity as assistant organist to Neefe.[viii] In Vienna, the cost of living was high. For example, a bachelor living in central Vienna needed an income of at least 960 florins to cover his basic needs and 1200 florins to allow for luxuries and entertainment.[ix] Anxious to secure further financial support, on 23 November 1793 Beethoven wrote a supplicatory letter to Maximilian Franz in which he stated: 'My sole endeavour is to render myself absolutely worthy of your Electoral Excellency's highest favour. With this in view I have employed this year all the powers of my soul for the benefit of music in order to be able during the coming year to send to your Electoral Excellency something that will reflect your magnanimous treatment of me.' Beethoven is referring here to works that his teacher Haydn was about to send to Maximilian Franz as testimonies to the progress he had been making in the art of composition.[x]

On the same day, 23 November, Haydn did indeed write a long letter to the Elector on behalf of his pupil. He listed several compositions recently composed by Beethoven and offered them as proof of his diligence and application to his studies. He says, prophetically: 'On the basis of these pieces, expert and amateur alike cannot but admit that Beethoven will in time become one of the greatest musical artists in Europe, and I shall be proud to call myself his teacher.' Haydn stressed the need for his pupil to receive financial support, asking the Elector if he would allocate him an allowance of 1000 florins to provide for his subsistence and to enable him to continue with his music studies.[xi] A month later the Elector responded curtly and dismissively. He rejected Haydn's testimony that the compositions he had received were adequate evidence of Beethoven's progress on the grounds he considered (wrongly) that most of the compositions had been undertaken when Beethoven was still resident in Bonn. He concluded: 'I wonder, therefore, whether he should not begin his return journey here ... for I doubt he will have made any important progress in composition and taste during his present stay.'[xii] Beethoven's response to the Elector was characteristically defiant. He resolved to make his own way in the world by the fruits of his labours. Moreover, he remained in Vienna and never again set eyes on his native hometown.

We have remarked that Beethoven became dissatisfied with Haydn's instruction. He admired the older composer, who was then at the height of his powers and was in demand both in Vienna and London; over the years Beethoven acquired many of Haydn's works including the autograph of *The London Symphony* that came into his possession after Haydn's death in 1809.[xiii] It appears though that Haydn was too pre-occupied with his own compositions to give Beethoven's studies the time and attention Beethoven expected; his exercises were returned, supposedly corrected, but with numerous errors overlooked.[xiv] These circumstances came to the attention of the composer and music teacher Johann Baptist Schenk. He made Beethoven's acquaintance in 1792 and in his *Autobiography* he writes: 'I saw the composer, now so famous, for the first time and heard him play ... He offered to improvise on the pianoforte. Having struck a few chords and tossed off a few figures as if they were of no significance, the creative genius gradually unveiled his profound psychological pictures. My ear was continually charmed by the beauty of the many varied motives which he wove with wonderful clarity and loveliness into each other.' Schenk became aware Beethoven had been studying counterpoint with Haydn for some six months and that he was dissatisfied with his studies. He agreed to give Beethoven additional instruction on the grounds that his collaboration should not be made known to Haydn. He states: 'I gave him the familiar textbook of Joseph Fux, *Gradus ad Parnassum*, and asked him to look at the exercises that followed.' Schenk relates his instruction commenced in August 1792 and lasted until May 1793. He generously exonerated Haydn's lax supervision on the grounds that when he returned to Vienna, from London, 'he was intent on utilizing his muse in the composition of large masterworks, and thus laudably occupied could not well devote himself to the rules of grammar'.[xv]

Further testimony to Beethoven's need for formal instruction is his relationship at this period with Antonio Salieri. He was no less celebrated than Haydn as a composer and teacher and was a dominant figure in Vienna's musical scene. Beethoven turned to Salieri for instruction in vocal composition and the setting of Italian texts. His debt to Salieri is reflected in his later dedication to him of his Violin Sonatas Op. 12 and the set of Variations *La stessa, la stessima* (WoO 73) derived from Salieri's opera *Falstaff*.[xvi]

When Haydn departed Vienna for his second visit to London in mid-January 1794, Beethoven turned to the greatly admired theorist and master of counterpoint Johann Georg Albrechtsberger. He was organist and *Kapellmeister* at Saint Stephan's Cathedral and was much sought after by young composers.[xvii] Although Albrechtsberger was something of a dry, painstaking theorist many of Beethoven's studies with him of the old-fashioned contrapuntal curriculum still survive — evidence of both his diligence and respect for the learned pedagogue.[xviii]

The recollections of the pianist and composer Ferdinand Ries are relevant to this part of our narrative. Sometime in late 1801, or early 1802, Ries commenced piano lessons with Beethoven and soon became a trusted companion to the composer. Beethoven relied upon Ries to copy out his scores and to perform various secretarial duties. Reflecting on his master's relationships with his teachers, Ries writes: 'I knew them all well; all three [Haydn, Albrechtsberger and Salieri] valued Beethoven highly, but were of one mind touching his habits of study. All of them said Beethoven was so headstrong and self-sufficient that he had much to learn through harsh experience which he had refused to accept when it was presented to him as a subject of study.' He adds: 'Beethoven found Albrechtsberger's "dry rules" irksome and was not readily disposed to Salieri's, Italianate school of dramatic composition that was then in vogue — although he did value Antonio Salieri's advice regarding the setting of Italian words.'[xix] Beethoven's eminent biographer Alexander Thayer, with his wider perspective of the composer's life and work, observes: 'It is now known that the "dry rules" of Albrechtsberger could make a strong appeal to Beethoven as appertaining to theoretical study, and that the old method of composition, to which he remained true all his life, always had a singular charm for him as a subject of study and investigation.'[xx xxi]

Vienna's claim to be Europe's musical capital of the world at the close of the eighteenth century, and the first decades of the nineteenth, was in no small part associated with the status held at this period by the symphony and the string quartet — in the words of Barry Cooper 'the two noblest and most elevated forms of instrumental music'.[xxii] The symphony afforded the composer an opportunity for the public display of his compositional craft, whilst the string quartet held sway in the more intimate environment of the salon — where the interplay between the four instruments had the authority and interest of informed conversation. Thereby the first quartets of Haydn, published in 1764, were described as *quators dialogues*. He would elevate this aspect of his art in 1781 with his set of six Quartets, Op. 33.

Igor Stravinsky's views are relevant here: 'The string quartet was the most lucid conveyor of musical ideas ever fashioned, and the most singing — *i.e.* human — of instruments ... As for inborn powers, it could register a faster rate of harmonic change than the not yet fully chromatic orchestra of Beethoven's time ... It is a more intimate medium, furthermore, partly by the same tokens, ... a more pleasing one ... Its sustaining powers are greater than those of wind-instrument ensembles, and its ranges of speeds, and of degrees of soft volumes, are wider.'[xxiii]

Beethoven's contemporary, the mystical poet and musician Christian Schubart, considered the string quartet expressed no less than 'the music-universe condensed into one work'.[xxiv xxv] Haydn and Mozart had enriched this universe 'by enhancing the quartet with ever more elaborate and novel strategies of musical realization'. In due course Beethoven would enrich and elaborate the genre with his own particular blend of wit, humour and challenges to both listeners and performers, 'deflating [their] expectations of easy comprehension with respect to the parallels between music and the assignment of meaning in the imagination'.[xxvi] Through these, and other devices, Beethoven would progressively stamp his authority on the medium of the string quartet by enhancing its stature and transforming it almost beyond recognition. But such developments were still some years in the future.

In the 1790s the string quartet held a place of special regard in social music-making. The Italian composer Giuseppe Cambini is credited with writing no fewer than 149 string quartets. He published an article in the music journal *Allgemeine musikalische Zeitung* of 1804 (we discuss the influential *AmZ* later) in which he states: '[If] music should not stir up or soothe the emotions, then it should at least draw our attention to itself and so divert us from the cares and griefs of our everyday life.' He cites Haydn's symphonies for possessing such virtues and suggests 'chamber music is even more likely to do so, since it is heard in smaller halls and played by smaller ensembles'. Cambini recognised the challenges of performing well 'for to perform a "true" quartet ... requires exhaustive rehearsal by each player alone and by the quartet as a whole'.[xxvii] Such views would doubtless have appealed to Viennese musicians, professional and serious amateur alike, who regarded the members of the quartet family 'as the most subtle of the crafted instruments, capable of challenging the human voice'. The string quartet was seen as 'perfect both expressively and texturally, intimate yet complete' in which the four performers 'exemplified the Viennese ideal of civilized discourse'.[xxviii]

The Vienna into which Beethoven entered in 1792 had been witness to the interplay of the two great masters of the genre of string quartet writing, Haydn and Mozart. They had not only shared their works with each other but had also performed together in occasional quartet sessions.[xxix] Haydn's six string quartets Op. 20 are considered to be a milestone in the history of the genre in which he invested the medium with the profoundly expressive connotations of 'seriousness, learning and lofty connoisseurship', characteristic of the philosophical and political ideas sweeping Europe under the impulse of the Age of Enlightenment.[xxx] Haydn's Op. 20, No. 1, in particular, seized Beethoven's imagination since he made a fair copy of it — quite a studious undertaking — sometime between 1794–96.[xxxi]

By his own admission Haydn composed his six quartets Op. 33, of 1781, 'in an entirely new and special way', endowing them with further levels of musical wit and invention. Moreover, during the years 1793–99, Haydn composed a further fourteen of his sixty-eight quartets, justly earning him the soubriquet 'The father of the string quartet'. For his part, Mozart paid homage to Haydn by dedicating to him six of his 23 string quartets — the so-called 'Haydn' Quartets (K. 387–K. 465) composed between the years 1782 to 1785. After hearing these, Haydn made his now-famous remark to Mozart's father Leopold: 'Before God, and as an honest man, I tell you that your son is the greatest composer known to me either in person or by name. He has taste, and, what is more, the most profound knowledge of composition.' Not surprisingly, in light of these illustrious precursors, it was not only natural, indeed imperative, that Beethoven should direct his compositional skills to the string quartet if he were to fulfil his destiny — we recall his words to his old teacher Neefe: 'Should I ever become a great man, you too will have a share in my success.'

Beethoven came late to the medium of the string quartet. Unlike Haydn and Mozart, he was not an accomplished string performer, although he had played the viola in his youthful days in Bonn. When Beethoven started work on his Op. 18 string quartets he had been living in Vienna for six years and was already twenty-eight years old and was thirty before the set of six was completed. By way of comparison, we recall Mozart had written his String Quartet in G, K. 387 — his fourteenth and the first of the 'Haydn' Quartets — when he was twenty-six, and Schubert had composed his celebrated String Quartet in A minor, D. 804 — his thirteenth, the so-called *Rosamunde* — when he was twenty seven. It has often been remarked that Beethoven developed more slowly than other great composers, or, as Joseph Kerman more appositely states 'he came to produce works of real consistency and authenticity only later in life'.[xxxii]

As a virtuoso pianist, Beethoven had already been lionised in Vienna's musical salons, captivating audiences with the powers of his improvisations and later embodying in his compositions for the keyboard the new textures and melodic constructions that had come to him via his ten fingers. By not being a natural string player such resourcefulness was not available to him in writing for the string quartet in the manner he desired — that is as 'high art expressed in concentrated musical logic'.[xxxiii] He had to discover what Philip Downs describes as 'the integrity of voice' by slow and patient discovery.[xxxiv] Basil Lam remarks in similar fashion: 'Whatever the cause, the marvellous certainty of technique and invention of the early works from Op. 1 [three Piano Trios] to Op. 9 [three String Trios] was slow to develop in the string quartet.'[xxxv xxxvi]

Beethoven had other reasons for deferring writing for the string quartet, as H. C. Robbins Landon eloquently states: 'Beethoven, in the very first Viennese years, was very careful to avoid writing music in genres wherein his muse would be in direct confrontation with that of the older man [Haydn].'[xxvii] In the 1790s Haydn was still publishing string quartets at a steady rate, witness his Opp. 64, 71, 76 and 77 — a total of twenty works. When only fifteen, Beethoven had composed three quartets for piano and strings (WoO 36) that he modelled on sonatas by Mozart. Perhaps for this reason he held them back from publication but later drew on melodic ideas from them for the Piano Sonatas Op. 2, Nos. 2 and 3. Ideas from these discarded works were also later used in the Sonata *Pathétique*. These quartets were not published until 1828, the year after the composer's death. In the 1790s, in the genre of chamber music, rather than writing quartets we find Beethoven composing such works as the Piano Trios, Op. 1; Sonatas for Piano and Cello, Op. 5; Serenade for String Trio, Op. 8; String Trios, Op. 9; Trio for Piano, Clarinet and Cello, Op. 11; Violin Sonatas, Op. 12; and the Septet, Op. 20 (revised later by Beethoven as his Trio Op. 38).[xxviii] These were categories of works for which Haydn had written very little or had ceased to compose some years previously. As evidence of Beethoven's creativity at this period, mention may also be made of his Piano Sonatas Opp. 2, 7, 10, 13 and 14 (ten in number); Piano Concerto No. 1, Op. 15; Symphony No.1 in C, Op. 21 and Romance for Violin & Orchestra, Op. 50.

Musicologists agree that the origins of the Op. 18 String Quartets owe much to the experience Beethoven gained in writing his early string trios.[xxix] It is a medium in which, in a manner of speaking, 'every note counts'. As Robert Simpson explains: 'The essence of classical music is momentum generated by vigorous reactions between tonal, harmonic, rhythmic and thematic elements in equally functioning proportions ... [It] is more difficult to create a sonority productive of momentum with three than with four parts.' The players, for one thing, have to revert to such practices as double-stopping to give added weight and richness of sound to the medium. Writing of his personal experience of hearing Beethoven's String Trio in C minor, Op. 9, No. 3, Simpson enthuses: 'I suddenly and for the first time heard it as perhaps it seemed to its first hearers; the furious perfection of its first movement must have struck them with great force, and the more perceptive of them must have been overwhelmed by its unprecedented concentration and structural tension, to say nothing of the unheard-of richness and power of Beethoven's writing for three instruments.'[xl]

Beethoven's String Trio in E flat Op. 3 was modelled on Mozart's Divertimento in E flat K. 563 and is of extra-musicological interest. A copy of the trio, probably in the form of a set of manuscript parts, was taken to England by the chaplain to the Archbishop of Cologne the Abbé Dobbeler. These eventually came to the attention of the composer William Gardiner of Leicester who heard the work performed sometime between 1793 and 1796 (1794 has been suggested as the most probable), thereby laying claim to be one of the very first performances of Beethoven's music in England. Of the work in question, Gardiner enthused in his *Music and Friends* (1838): 'This composition, so different from anything I had ever heard, awakened in me a new sense, a new delight in the science of sounds ... It was a language that so powerfully excited my imagination, that all other music appeared tame and spiritless.'[xli]

The String Trios Op. 1 have been described as: '[The] first which lift [Beethoven] above mediocrity and which astonished contemporaries as not merely talented, but assured and mature expressions of his capacity.' Of these works, Ferdinand Ries remarks 'Beethoven's three trios were first heard by the musical world at one of Prince

Lichnowsky soirées' (to which we make further reference shortly). He relates that nearly all the foremost artists and amateurs were invited, among them Haydn whose opinion was awaited with intense interest. Ries continues: 'The trios were played and caused an immediate sensation. Haydn said many pleasant things about them but advised Beethoven not to publish the third in C minor.' This offended Beethoven who thought it to be the best of the three. According to Ries: 'He took Haydn's remark very ill and got it into his head that Haydn was envious and jealous of him.' He adds: 'I must say that when Beethoven spoke to me of all this, I believed little of it.' Ries subsequently raised the matter with Haydn himself who conceded that he had cautioned Beethoven not to publish but for the sincere reason 'he thought this particular trio would not be so quickly and easily understood or be favourably received by the public'.[xlii] Paul Bekker, reflecting on this incident, comments: 'Haydn's known and straightforwardness and integrity make it highly unlikely that he was envious or jealous of Beethoven, but it is very probable that the C minor Trio shocked him and that he felt its publication imprudent.'[xliii]

The String Trios in question were subsequently published in 1795 by the firm of Artaria & Co. as the composer's official Opus 1. Haydn's biographer Giuseppe Carpani records in his study of the composer (*La Haydine*, 1823): 'Haydn was asked once by one of my friends what he thought of "that young composer". The old man replied with all sincerity: "His first works pleased me considerably, but I must admit that I don't understand the later ones. It seems to me that he [now] continually improvises".' Landon remarks, this quotation may not belong precisely to the period of composition of Beethoven's Op. 18 String Quartets but it serves to illustrate a degree of estrangement between master and pupil.[xliv] As Paul Bekker observes, Haydn was now in his sixties and perhaps found it difficult to become reconciled to the reality that a new generation of composers had grown up, pre-eminently represented by Beethoven, who were drawn to the 'wild expression of naked emotions' and all too ready to rebel against 'traditional bounds and limitations'.[xlv]

Further testimony to the tension that existed between Beethoven and Haydn, in their master-pupil relationship, became apparent with the publication of Beethoven's Piano Sonatas Op. 2. These were announced on 9 March 1796 in the *Wiener Zeitung* ('Vienna Journal') bearing the dedication to Haydn — the only professional composer to receive such a dedication from Beethoven with the exception of Antonio Salieri. Haydn, however, had wished to have the Title Page inscribed 'Pupil of Haydn' but Beethoven resisted. He acknowledged he had received instruction from Haydn but asserted 'he had never learned anything from him'.[xlvi] In later years Beethoven renounced these headstrong views and even spoke of his mentor with respect and affection. There was the occasion, for example, when the composer and publisher Anton Diabelli called on Beethoven to present him with a lithograph of Haydn's rather modest birthplace — in the village of Rohrau in Lower Austria. It gave Beethoven much pleasure prompting him to remark: 'Just see the little house, and such a great man was born in it.'[xlvii]

Before continuing with our discussion of the creation origins of the Op. 18 String Quartets, we consider for a moment the role of the music patron in Viennese society at the period under consideration. This will lead us to in due course to the salon of Prince Lichnowsky where the Op. 18 quartets received their first performances.

In the eighteenth century the support of the artist had

been the preserve of princes and noblemen to whose service the artist was committed. Haydn comes to mind in his role as Kapellmeister to Prince Esterhazy from whom he received a regular salary. It is also well documented how Mozart had to strive in order to achieve his independence from being regarded as a mere liveried servant to the Archbishop of Salzburg.[xlviii] The social historian Leon Botstein observes: '[The] support of music by noble families in the late eighteenth century was in part a competitive social display, exemplified by the large presentation rooms of Vienna's baroque and neoclassical palaces.'[xlix] The interplay of music, architecture and culture came to the fore amidst such surroundings particularly when banquets were held at which hired musicians would perform *Tafelmusik* ('table-music') — what today we would call 'background music'.

In her study of the politics of music in Vienna, Tia de Nora remarks how musical patronage and social hierarchy were mutually interlocked. It was in the salons of the aristocracy that Beethoven first gave expression to his more radical departures from musical orthodoxy through the medium of his pianoforte improvisations. These departures progressively found their way into his published works and, thereby, could be appreciated by the wider musically inclined members of the public. The awareness, and growing appreciation, of Beethoven's originality was also disseminated to wider audiences through the medium of such journals as the *Allgemeine musikalische Zeitung*.[l]

At the beginning of the nineteenth century, the more open-minded and musically educated members of the nobility began to show greater respect for the performing artist as an individual. Beethoven was to benefit from this change of attitude and, indeed, to help bring it about. We have identified several of the compositions Beethoven composed shortly after his arrival in Vienna. Reflecting on these Cooper comments: 'The seemingly random succession of Beethoven's genres in the late 1790s was dictated largely by the preference of various patrons. Sometimes the commissioner received the dedication when the work was finally published.' Beethoven's chamber works also reflected the general popularity of the various musical genres during this period but which were also genres that he found congenial to his evolving style of musical expression. As Cooper concludes: 'Beethoven was free to decide if [a commissioned] work were to be technically easy to play [and] Beethoven was free to dictate the content and style of the music and to explore musical problems and innovations of his own choice'.'[li]

One of Beethoven's most generous patrons was Prince Karl Lichnowsky. He had been a pupil and friend of Mozart and was a pianist of some ability. The composer's Piano Trios, Op. 1 were first performed at one of Lichnowsky's soirées in late 1793 or early 1794 and Beethoven later dedicated them to him. The Prince had in his service a quartet of young string players headed by Ignaz Schuppanzigh. A professional musician, he established a close relationship with Beethoven and remained devoted to him throughout his life.[lii] By way of illustration, Schuppanzigh's Quartet gave the first performances of the string quartets, Op. 95 (*Quartetto Serioso*), Op. 127, Op. 130 and Op. 132.

In addition to his soirées, Lichnowsky also made his salon available for regular Friday morning concerts. We gain a glimpse into these musical and social events from one of Beethoven's piano pupils at this period. She was a gifted young maiden by the name of Fräulein Elisabeth von Kissow. At an early age she showed pronounced musical talent, prompting her father to send her to Vienna to receive instruction. Such was her ability she was invited to perform at Count Lichnowsky's musical entertainments. Later in life

Elisabeth, as Frau von Bernhard, recalled her musical impressions of the time when she received her instruction from the composer: 'I still remember clearly both Haydn and Salieri sitting on a sofa on one side of the small music-room, both carefully dressed in the old-fashioned way with perruque [periwig], shoes and silk hose, whereas even here Beethoven would come dressed in the informal fashion of the other side of the Rhine, almost ill-dressed.'[liii] During his early years in Vienna there is evidence though that Beethoven made attempts to overcome his social and sartorial deficiencies. Entries from an account book, recording his personal income, reveal he acquired black silk stockings, boots, and incurred expenses for a wig maker (!) and a dancing master (!) — although, with regard to the latter, his piano pupil Ferdinand Ries recalls: 'He could never learn to dance in time, and his clumsy movements lacked all charm.'[liv]

Beethoven's star was rising and publishers would soon be eager to accept his works – largely on his own financial terms. Doubtless, in recognition of the composer's rising accomplishments and his growing admiration of him, Lichnowsky conferred on his protégée an annuity, in effect a stipend, of 600 florins – about sixty pounds sterling. The Prince's intention was to provide Beethoven with some financial security. The payments continued for several years until he received a more secure annuity in 1809 from three of Vienna's most notable citizens, namely, the Archduke Rudolph (Beethoven's only composition pupil), Prince Kinsky and Prince Lobkowitz.[lv] This annuity was set at 4000 florins, the equivalent of an upper-middle class income. However, personal misfortunes to Kinsky and Lobkowitz, combined with inflation, soon undermined its purchasing power. Of Lobkowitz's support, Schindler remarks: 'The great love this princely family felt for Beethoven was constant and unwavering.' He adds: 'In fact, for ten to twelve years, nearly all Beethoven's works were first tried out in the music circle of Count Lobkowitz.'[lvi]

An article published in a contemporary issue of the *Allgemeine musikalische Zeitung* places Beethoven's annuity in its contemporary context — and also reveals how little the average musician received for his labours. A player in an orchestra could expect to earn from 200 to 300 gulden (about 20—30 pounds sterling). In the Austro-Hungarian Empire at this time the gulden was a standard unit of currency and was the equivalent of the Austrian silver florin (about two English shillings or a half-crown depending on currency values). Violinists were in the worst position because, the article states, 'they are expected to play for nothing since ten dilettante can readily be found who will do so with great pleasure'. A teacher of pianoforte could earn a decent living but 'must possess enough self-denial to serve willingly the houses that support him' and, furthermore, 'to give lessons 'morning, noon and night'. On a more positive note, the article concludes: 'But as there are exceptions ... amongst musicians, so there are worthy houses to which the above complaints do not apply.'[lvii] Clearly, the household of Prince Lobkowitz was one of these and Beethoven was fortunate to secure a patron who valued his gifts so highly.[lviii] [lix]

Beethoven was pleased with his newfound security as can be inferred from a letter he wrote to his friend from his days in Bonn — and the composer's later biographer, Franz Gerhard Wegeler. Beethoven informed him that Prince Lichnowsky had granted him an allowance of 600 florins on which he could draw until he had obtained a secure appointment. He added: 'My compositions bring me in a good deal: and I may say that I am offered more commissions than it is possible for me to carry out. Moreover, for every composition I can count on six or seven publishers, and even more, If I want them; people no longer come to an arrangement with me, I state the price and they pay.'[lx] He wrote to his younger brother Nikolaus Johann in similar terms: 'I am well, very well. My art is winning me friends and renown.'[lxi] This was no idle boast. In due course Beethoven's patrons Prince Lichnowsky and Prince Lobkowitz would cease to be the only intermediaries between the composer and his public. Beethoven soon commenced dealings with the long-established firm of Breitkopf & Härtel of Leipzig and other publishing houses of this time including: Schott of Mainz (1773), Artaria (1780) and Cappi (1796) of Vienna, Simrock (1790) of Bonn, Hofmeister & Kühnel (1800) of Leipzig — taken over by Peters in 1814, Mollo (1800) of Vienna, and Schlesinger (1800) of Berlin.

Evidence of the extent to which Beethoven was beginning to secure the attention of publishing houses is apparent from a letter he received from the music publisher Gottfried Christoph Härtel. He wrote to Beethoven in encouraging terms. He states how pleased his publishing house would be 'to do everything that circumstances allow' to further his compositions, especially 'piano sonatas without accompaniment, or with accompaniment of violin, or of violin and violincello'. Härtel adds a touch of flattery: 'The fame of your talents is established firmly enough.' Härtel concludes by requesting where Beethoven's portrait may be seen so that a likeness could be taken for its publication alongside his series of 'the most prominent composers'. An engraving of Beethoven duly appeared in the October issue of Volume 6 of the *Allgemeine musikalische Zeitung* (1803–804). Johann Neidl created this from a drawing by the artist Gandolph Stainhauser — made sometime in 1800.[lxii]

With Beethoven's growing fame as a composer came the additional obligations for him to assume responsibility for transacting the business side of his affairs. Many letters between the composer and his publishers survive and bear testimony to Beethoven being astute in business matters and aware of the commercial value of his compositions. We cite the following as illustrative. At about the same time as the String Quartets Op. 18 were being prepared for publication, Beethoven had occasion to write to the Vienna publisher Anton Hoffmeister (not be confused with Friedrich Hofmeister of Leipzig). He brought out first editions of the *Sonata Pathétique*, the Second Piano Concerto and the First Symphony. Beethoven suggested twenty ducats (about ten pounds sterling) for the Septet, which was already becoming popular, and the same for the First Symphony. The Piano Concerto Op. 19 was offered at half price (ten ducats), Beethoven giving the reason: 'I do not consider it to be one of my best concertos.' He also asks for twenty ducats for the Piano Sonata Op. 22 describing it as 'a first-rate composition'. Beethoven tells Hoffmeister how much he dislikes the business-side of a composer's life and laments: 'There ought to be in the world *a market for art* [Beethoven's italics] where the artist would only have to bring his works and take as much money as he needed.' He laments how he has to be both an artist and, to a certain extent, to be a businessman as well. He then takes a swipe at the Leipzig music critics who had remarked unfavourably on certain of his compositions: 'Just let them talk ... they will certainly never make anyone immortal, nor will they ever take immortality away from anyone upon whom Apollo has bestowed it'. Beethoven clearly considered himself to be one so favoured by the gods.[lxiii]

We have remarked how Johann Baptist Schenk had been 'charmed by the beauty of the many varied motives' which Beethoven could weave into his playing when improvising at the keyboard. We pause for a moment in our discussion of the Op. 18 String Quartets and consider Beethoven the pianist.

When Count Ferdinand Waldstein sent Beethoven on his way to Vienna with his parting words of farewell, he made him a gift of a small, portable pianoforte by the German builder Tufenbruch. Although this would soon be rendered inadequate for the composer's ever-demanding needs, he retained the instrument all his life — probably as a gesture of appreciation to his friend. Beethoven's diary entries show that for some time following his arrival in Vienna, he hired various instruments that cost him about half his monthly house rent.[lxiv] As a child Beethoven had been required to practice for hours at the keyboard by his demanding father who sought to portray him to the world as a second Mozart — even resorting to falsifying his son's age. Later in life, Beethoven recalled how he had practised 'until the blood had burned beneath his fingernails'. Not surprising, in the 1790s he was well equipped to present himself in the salons of Vienna as a performer possessed of formidable keyboard skills. This is just as well since 'Romantic pianists were viewed as conquering titans whose individual feats expressed the heroic dimensions of human nature'.[lxv] A gifted performer could make a living by progressing from one salon to another to display his talents. Moreover, patrons not infrequently invited their own protégées to vie with each other in pianistic contests — first one performing then the other, each attempting to outshine his rival in pianistic display.

Not long after his arrival in Vienna, Beethoven found himself obliged to match his musical skills against those of the Czech pianist Joseph Gelineck — whose playing had impressed Mozart. On being invited to take part in a pianistic contest with Beethoven, Gelinek rashly boasted: 'We are going to thrash him soundly! I'll work him over!'

In the event he found himself outclassed both as a pianist and improviser. A few days later, quite dejected, he bemoaned: 'That young man is possessed of the devil. Never have I heard such playing! He will play me and all of us to death! And how he improvised!' Beethoven had apparently improvised on a theme of Gelinek's choosing and then performed compositions of his own (unspecified) that Gelinek regarded as 'wonderful and grandiose to the highest degree'. He adds how Beethoven achieved effects 'such as we have never even dreamed of'.[lxvi] Gelinek does not appear to have borne any ill will to Beethoven. He went on to make a piano arrangement of the composer's First Symphony and wrote a set of variations for piano on the *Allegretto* of the Seventh Symphony.

At this period Beethoven composed several sets of piano variations including WoO, 67 (1794); WoO 69 (1795); WoO 71 (1796); and WoO 73 (1799). His pre-occupation with this genre of compositions is, in part, explained in a letter he wrote in June 1794 to Eleonore von Breuning, a close friend who has been described as the composer's 'first serious love'.[lxvii] He had sent her a set of his variations with the remark: 'I should never have written down this kind of piece, had I not already noticed fairly often how some people in Vienna [his pianistic rivals] after hearing me extemporize of an evening would note down on the following day several peculiarities of my style.' Beethoven resolved to forestall his rivals, whom he describes as 'his sworn enemies' and 'to take revenge on them in this way'.[lxviii] In the context of Beethoven's writing for the keyboard, and his relationship with women, mention may be made here of Count Lichnowsky's first wife, Princess Marie Lichnowsky. She was one of Beethoven's most ardent admirers and had a close friendship with Beethoven. In recognition of her untiring efforts on his behalf he inscribed to her the piano score of his ballet *The Creatures of Prometheus*.

We have so far discussed Beethoven's arrival in Vienna and his having become established in the capital's salons. We now direct our attention to his turning to the to the medium of the string quartet, how this came about and its subsequent fulfilment in the form of the String Quartets, Op. 18.

Beethoven's biographer Franz Wegeler records that sometime in 1795 the music lover and patron of the arts, Count Anton Apponyi asked Beethoven to compose a quartet for him for which he would receive payment. Apponyi had encountered Beethoven at one of Lichnowsky's morning concerts and was aware he had not yet written a work in this genre. He was eager to secure his services in this manner as he had similarly commissioned Haydn to compose his sets of string quartets Op. 71 and 74. The Count generously proposed, contrary to the prevailing custom, that he did not want to claim exclusive possession of the proposed quartet before its publication. It was the convention of the period for the person who had commissioned, and paid for, a particular work to receive exclusive rights to a copy of the manuscript text for a stipulated period — typically a year. Only after the expiry of this period was the composer free to publish and derive further income from his composition. Despite repeated urgings by Wegeler, on Beethoven's behalf, he did not respond to Apponyi's request. In his account, Wegeler claims Beethoven twice set about the task and that the first effort resulted in the Violin Trio, Op. 3 and the second in the Violin Quintet, Op. 4. Modern-day authorities consider this may not be strictly accurate on the grounds it is now believed Beethoven had worked on these two compositions sometime previously. Thayer adds there is evidence though that Beethoven did not entirely reject Apponyi's proposition. He cites the contrapuntal studies undertaken for Albrechtsberger in 1795 that include a minuet in A flat for string quartet — found amongst sketches for the B-flat Piano Concerto. In addition, sketches exist from this period for the Piano Sonata in E, Op. 14, No. 1 that Beethoven was eventually (1802) prevailed upon to transcribe for string quartet.[lxix] Kerman conjectures: 'Was the [transcription of the Piano Sonata in E, Op. 14, No. 1] made in memory of an original intention to cast this music for strings?'[lxx] Of related interest is an exercise Beethoven composed for Johann Albrechtsberger that authorities consider shows 'real contrapuntal mastery'. In this study, Beethoven explored fugal treatment that he subsequently arranged for string quartet (Hess 30).[lxxi]

A formative influence on Beethoven's writing for the medium of the string quartet appears to derive from the Silesian-born composer and theorist Emanuel Aloys Förster.[lxxii] He was highly respected as a musician and could count Mozart and Haydn amongst his acquiantances. Beethoven met Förster at Prince Lichnowsky's music sessions where he also heard performances of his string quartets. Förster's own home was also a regular venue for music making, especially for the performance of string quartets; the regular periods of these quartet meetings were Sunday at noon and Thursday evening. Beethoven also spent other evenings with Förster 'when the conversation would usually turn to musical theory and composition'. Thayer describes Förster as a musician who was highly esteemed by Beethoven and who, on one occasion at least, referred to him as his 'alter meister' — 'old master'. He was twenty-two years older than Beethoven and Thayer adds: 'The elder not only appreciated the genius of the younger, but honoured him as a man; and spoke of him as being not only a great musical composer, but ... of a most honourable and noble nature.'[lxxiii]

Writing of the period of gestation of the String Quartets Op. 18, the distinguished musicologist and educationalist Sir William Henry Hadow states: 'Förster, a competent teacher and an adventurous quartet-writer, held twice a week at his house musical parties which were attended by some of the most famous virtuosi of the time: Schuppanzigh who became Beethoven's favourite first violin, Linke the 'cellist, Weiss the greatest viola player in the city, and many others.' Beethoven had free access to Förster's house and was a constant visitor, disposing Hadow to surmise: 'It may be taken as positive that the six quartets [Op. 18] were tried here in manuscript and discussed between the composer and the performers.'[lxxiv] [lxxv] Hadow is referring here in particular to Joseph Linke and Franz Weiss. Beethoven had a particular regard for Linke's musicianship and it is for him he probably composed his two Cello Sonatas, Op. 102. Linke also had the distinction of being acquainted with Schubert and took part in the performance of several of his chamber works.[lxxvi] Of the other members of Schuppanzigh's string quartet, Thayer writes: 'They were during these years but laying the foundations for future excellence and celebrity as performers of Mozart's, Haydn's, Förster's and Beethoven's quartets.'[lxxvii]

Ignaz Schuppanzigh's String Quartet is worthy of additional remark. In the winter of 1804–05, Schuppanzigh formed his Quartet with the express intention of giving public concerts — thereby laying claim to being one of the very earliest professional string quartets. Its members varied from time to time and if a particular player was absent, another would take his place. These included Beethoven's close friend Nikolaus Zmeskall von Domanovez. A civil servant by profession, he was an excellent cellist and held regular string quartet sessions in his own apartment — Haydn dedicated his String Quartets, Op. 20 to him.[lxxviii] A regular second violinist in Schuppanzigh's string quartet was Karl Holz. Like Zmeskall, he was a civil servant but was much admired by Beethoven for his performing skills. The two became friends and for a period Holz helped Beethoven as his unpaid assistant. He is remembered today in Beethoven musicology for the two humorous canons WoO 197 and WoO 198 that were dedicated to him in 1826. Beethoven's death the following year is said to have affected Holz deeply.[lxxix] Another of Schuppanzigh's second violinists was Joseph Mayseder. He joined the Quartet around 1800 and later performed in several of Beethoven's orchestral concerts.[lxxx]

At Lichnowsky's Friday morning recitals the Prince would occasionally perform himself. Ignaz von Seyfried, a musical contemporary of Beethoven who is remembered, amongst other things, for his recollections of the composer (1832) said, of Schuppanzigh's Quartet: 'If one wished to understand and appreciate to the full any chamber music of Beethoven's one should hear it played by these fine artists.'[lxxxi] Friedrich Reichardt, a writer on music, heard Schuppanzigh perform at the close of 1810 and remarked: 'Herr Schuppanzigh himself has an original, piquant style most appropriate to the humorous quartets of Haydn, Mozart and Beethoven – or, perhaps more accurately, a product of the capricious manner of performance suited to these masterpieces.'[lxxxii] In similar laudatory fashion, Thayer enthuses, in a remark that goes to the heart of quartet playing: 'Each of [Schuppanzigh's] performers ... knowing precisely the intentions of the composer, acquired the difficult art of being independent and at the same time of being subordinate to the general effect. When Beethoven began to compose quartets he had therefore, a set of performers schooled to perfection by his great predecessors, and who already had experience in his own music through his trios and sonatas.'[lxxxiii]

Prince Lichnowsky's admiration for Beethoven was such that he presented the composer with a fine quartet of Italian instruments; this may have been at the suggestion of Schuppanzigh. As Joseph Kerman remarks, the gesture was more symbolic than practical; Beethoven, unlike either Haydn or Mozart, could not make use of them himself.[lxxxiv] The set consists of: a violin made by Giuseppe [Joseph] Guarnerius of Cremona from the year 1718; a second violin made by Niccolo [Nicholas] Amati in the year 1667; a viola made by Vincenzo Ruger in 1690; and a cello of Andrea [Andreas] Guarnerius of the year 1712. Beethoven's seal — an ornate 'B' — was inscribed on the neck of each instrument. These details were conveyed to Thayer by the cellist and collector of musical memorabilia, Aloys Fuchs who owned more than 1400 musical autographs.[lxxxv] The instruments are now on display at the Beethoven Museum in Bonn. The Catalogue of this collection dates the Amati violin 1690 and the Guarnerius violincello 1675. It should be noted that some modern-day commentators believe that the attributions given by Fuchs to Thayer may be 'overly generous' but no one has yet undermined them.[lxxxvi]

In considering Beethoven's resolve to embark on writing for the medium of the string quartet, it will be useful to make a brief summary here of the considerations to which we have so far made reference. Beethoven had arrived in Vienna armed with Waldstein's letter of encouragement, and with it implied access to the salons of the princely nobility; he had been lionised in these same salons as one of the foremost virtuosi pianists of the day — unrivalled in his powers of improvisation; moreover, he had gained experience in writing string trios and other instrumental combinations featuring string instruments; his growing reputation had been acknowledged in the *Allgemeine musikalische Zeitung*

— Europe's premier music journal; he had before him the inspirational string-quartet models of Haydn and Mozart; he had benefitted in writing for the string quartet under the pedagogical influence of Emanuel Aloys Förster and his more general studies in composition with Antonio Salieri; he had heard elevating chamber music performed at Prince Lichnowsky musical events; and finally, in this context, he had the stimulus of direct contact with the Schuppanzigh Quartet — the most accomplished in Vienna.[lxxxvii] All that was now required to encourage Beethoven to embark on his career as a composer of string quartets was a commission from a patron.

This duly came from Prince Joseph Franz Lobkowitz who promoted music in Vienna in many ways. His mansion house was known as 'the true residence and academy of music' and Lobkowitz himself as 'a true and insatiable music enthusiast'.[lxxxviii] For example, one of the earliest performances of the *Eroica* Symphony took place in the great salon of Lobkowitz's house that served as a concert hall. It was also here in 1795 that Lobkowitz first heard Beethoven play and later that year he was one of the subscribers to the composer's Piano Trios, Op. 1. This was the start of a long and fruitful relationship with Beethoven who, in recognition of the Prince's support, subsequently conferred upon him the dedications to the *Eroica* Symphony and the Fifth and Sixth Symphonies (jointly with Count Razumowsky); the Triple Concerto, Op. 56; and the String Quartet, Op. 74 (*The Harp*).

Prince Lobkowitz commissioned Beethoven to compose the String Quartets, Op. 18 in the autumn or winter of 1798—99 for which he received a fee of 400 florins. At the same time he also commissioned a similar set of quartets from Haydn — his Op. 79. In Landon's words 'thus Lobkowitz was host to the latest quartets by both composers at the same time'.[lxxxix] The sequence of Beethoven's quartets, in their numbering and order of creation, was different to that by which they are known today. He placed what is considered to be 'the most vigorously adventurous' of the six quartets first, thereby seeking to secure the attention of the musically discerning public that valued novelty and innovation.[xc] We discuss this in more detail in our later remarks bearing on the individual compositions. The following is a brief summary – expressed in terms of the quartets' present-day terminology. Beethoven began work on the third quartet in D major in late autumn 1798, completing it at the beginning of 1799. Between January and March of that year he wrote the first quartet in F major followed by the second one in G major that was probably completed later in May. Thus, he was able to deliver copies of these first three quartets to Prince Lobkowitz by the beginning of October 1799.[xci] Evidence derived from the composer's sketches (see following) indicates that work was started on the fifth quartet in A major following completion of the first three quartets, with its own completion in the autumn of 1799. Subsequently, he wrote the fourth quartet in C minor and finally the sixth quartet in B-flat major that was composed in the spring or summer of 1800. At this time he also made a thorough revision of the first three quartets and presented all six Quartets Op. 18, in their final form, to Prince Lobkowitz later that autumn.[xcii]

Mention has been made of Beethoven's sketches that are now recognised as forming an integral part of his compositional method. The earliest of these derive from the composer's days in Bonn. It was then he developed what he used to refer to as 'his bad habit' of outlining his preliminary thoughts in sketch-draft form. They have different functions within the creative process and range from cryptic first ideas to longer passage and score-like elaborations. He used small pocket sketchbooks for composing outdoors — typically in the countryside. These fitted into his coat pocket and were always on hand to record ideas as they occurred in his imagination. About two hundred individual sheets of sketches date back to Beethoven's days in Bonn. These have been assembled into two large gatherings, the larger of which is now preserved in the British Library and is known as the 'Kafka Sketchbook' (more correctly 'miscellany') — taking its name from its one-time owner Johann Nepomuk Kafaka. Beethoven later systematised his sketching procedure by binding together bundles of pocket-sized sheets that he could take with him on his much-loved strolls in the country; later still he made use of ready-bound sketchbooks.[xiii] These provided him with the means of not only sketching more systematically but also more extensively, particularly as his compositions grew in scale and complexity posing related challenges in solving large-scale problems of musical continuity and construction. Today the sketchbooks that have survived have, like the Kafka Sketchbook, acquired the names of their various owners — to which we make occasional reference in our subsequent narratives.[xciv]

Beethoven set down ideas for a new piece starting on a fresh page, frequently noting ideas for different movements alongside each other. As his powers of invention took hold he inserted further thoughts cramming them into any available space or even going back to make use of pages previously left blank. As a consequence sketches for different compositions co-exist side-by-side, many to be discarded but others to be fully worked into the compositions we know and cherish today. In his lecture 'Questions about music' Roger Sessions, in his role as Charles Eliot Norton Professor, remarked: 'Beethoven could have made a great deal out of any one of the earlier versions [of his sketches] ...

Obviously it would have been a different piece, and since that piece is not in existence, we can never know what it would have been like.'[xcv] Gustav Nottebohm, a pioneer in the study and decipherment of Beethoven's sketchbooks, has this to say: '[In] spite of this unsystematic procedure, it is evident that as a rule Beethoven was clear about his objectives from the start; he remained true to his original conceptions, and once an idea was grasped, he carried it through to the end ... We may seek [in the sketchbooks] the artist himself, in the unity of his whole character and spirit, and in the harmony of his inner powers.'[xcvi] In his scholarly commentary to Beethoven's sketchbooks, Alan Tyson suggests they may have 'performed a special function for him in maintaining his morale as well as in facilitating his creative processes'. They did indeed become indispensible to him and at times, when his working method came up in conversation, he was given to quoting from Schiller's *Joan of Arc*: 'Without my banner I dare not come.'[xcvii] In his reflections on Beethoven's creative process, the Hungarian-American musicologist Paul Henry Lang invokes the following evocative lines from Wordsworth's *The Prelude*: 'Dust as we are, the immortal spirit grows/ Like harmony in music; there is a dark/ Inscrutable workmanship that reconciles/ Discordant elements, makes them cling together'.[xcviii]

During Beethoven's early years in Vienna his sketching had became so elaborate that by 1798 he found it more convenient to work with a ready-made manuscript sketchbook in preference to loose single sheets. The first such book is known as Grasnick 1 and dates from about late summer 1798 to early 1799. This coincides with the period, as remarked, when he started work on the String Quartets, Op. 18. Cooper comments: 'Thus the change to sketchbooks may have been a conscious policy to help him cope with the peculiar compositional problems of the genre; this supposition is supported by the fact that the first pages of the sketchbook as it now stands are devoted largely to work on the first quartet to be written (No. 3 in D major).'[xcix] Grasnick 1 is today preserved in the *Staatsbibliothek zu Berlin Preussischer Kulturbesitz* with the reference number 'Mus. Ms autograph Beethoven Grasnick'. The sketchbook originally had 48 leaves − a standard size in Beethoven's time. However, its first nine leaves were removed probably before the collector of autograph scores, Friedrich August Grasnick, acquired it in the middle of the nineteenth century.[c]

A further source for the origins of the String Quartets Op. 18 is the companion sketchbook Grasnick 2. Along with its namesake, it originally formed part of a large number of manuscripts and documents that Grasnick obtained from the widow of the Viennese collector Alloys Fuchs. He purchased these at the auction of Beethoven's estate on 5 November 1827 that took place following the composer's death. The chief contents of Grasnick 2 are the following: Op. 18, No. 1 − all four movements; Op. 18, No. 2 − all four movements; Op. 18, No. 4 − early sketches for the first movement; and Op. 18, No. 5 − all four movements.[ci]

Two other sketch sources require mention. The first of these is the so-called Autograph 19E. This consists of a collection of loose leaves on which Beethoven worked in the late spring and summer of 1800. The string quartets represented therein include: Op. 18, No. 1 − final revisions that were also worked on a year earlier; Op. 18, No. 2 − finale revisions; and Op. 18, No. 6 − finale revisions.[cii] In the summer and autumn of 1800 until March 1801, Beethoven made use of a sketchbook known as Landsberg 7. This is a substantial compilation of some 93 leaves. It was one of eight such sketchbooks acquired in 1862 by the former Berlin Royal Library from the estate of the collector

Ludwig Landsberg. He had obtained the sketchbook from the music publisher Artaria & Co. This sketchbook includes ideas for the first movement of Op. 18, No.1.[ciii]

The American musicologist Stephanie Schroeder comments: 'The gestation period of two and a half years for the Six Quartets Op. 18, as can be documented in his sketches and part copies, was an unusually long one for Beethoven. He not only revised the individual works of the set during this period, but he also revised their order within the whole, finally choosing an overall structure wherein the more unusual quartets — No. 1 and No. 6 — serve as a frame for the others.'[civ][cv]

No autographs of the String Quartets, Op. 18 have survived but the copies Beethoven presented to Prince Lobkowitz are today preserved in the Music Department of the National Museum in Prague where they are catalogued in the Lobkowitz Archive as Collection X, He. 44.[cvi] Beethoven duly received payment of 200 florins from Prince Lobkowitz for the last thee quartets Op. 18 on 18 October 1800, having presented the manuscript to him some time previously.[cvii]

It is at this period he probably also gave him the manuscript of the revised version of the first three quartets. Publication did not take place immediately however. As remarked, it was the custom of the day for Lobkowitz to have prior rights to the compositions. Consequently, Nos. 1–3 were not published until June 1801 with Nos. 4–6 following in October.[cviii] Evidence Beethoven had completed the Op. 18 Quartets at this period comes indirectly from a letter Countess Josephine von Deym wrote to her sister in December 1800 in which she enthused: 'Yesterday we had music ... Beethoven, that real angel, let us hear his new Quartets [Op. 18], which have not been engraved yet, and are the greatest of their kind ... You can imagine what a treat it was for us!' H. C. Robbins Landon, the source for this quotation remarks: 'No doubt the younger generation much preferred Beethoven's language and considered Op. 18 the greatest achievement [to date] in the field of the quartet.' He further reflects: 'Haydn's Op. 77 may even have seemed something of an anti-climax after the great spiritual heights of [his] Op. 76.'[cix]

In passing we may add Beethoven had a great affection for Countess Josephine von Deym and several love letters survive bearing testimony to his feelings for her. The origins of their relationship began when Josephine commenced piano lessons with the composer soon after her arrival in Vienna. It has been conjectured Josephine was the subject of Beethoven's impassioned *Immortal Beloved* letter dating from 1812. It was never sent and was only discovered amongst his possessions following his death. In music, Beethoven gave declaration to his feelings for Josephine in his *Andante favori* (WoO 57), thought by some to have been intended as the middle movement of the tempestuous *Waldstein* Piano Sonata, Op. 53. Josephine died in 1821 at the time Beethoven was at work on his last two piano sonatas Op. 110 and Op. 111. Some musicologist maintain these works may be regarded as requiems for Josephine in which they detect reminiscences of the *Andante favori* theme in the sonatas' repeated melodic theme that suggests her name recast as *Jo-seph-ine*.

On 22 April 1801 Beethoven once more corresponded with Franz Hoffmeister regarding the publication of his Opp. 19—22. He apologised for his tardiness concerning business matters on the grounds 'perhaps the only touch of genius which I possess is that my things are not always in good order'. Regarding the String Quartets Op. 18 he reassured Hoffmeister: 'The quartets could certainly be published in a few weeks.'[cx] This was something of an exaggeration. Beethoven commenced work on preparing the Op. 18 Quartets for publication in the spring or early summer of 1801. Confirmation of this comes from a further letter he wrote to his friend Count Nikolaus Zmeskall von Domanovez who, as previously remarked, was then working in his capacity as a civil servant — at the Hungarian Court Chancellery in Vienna. Zmeskall had to endure much leg pulling from Beethoven. Some one hundred letters and notes to him survive in which he is often greeted with the salutation 'little count' and 'little baron' — and worse. In his letter Beethoven informs his friend: 'I have to deal with that important proof-reading of the quartets [Op. 18], a task that cannot be postponed, since they are to be engraved on the following day.'[cxi] Zmeskall rendered many services to the composer and duly received his reward in 1816 by being the dedicatee of Beethoven's F minor String Quartet, Op. 95.

The String Quartets Op. 18, were eventually published at the Vienna printing house of Tranquillo Mollo. He had already brought out the composer's Trio for piano, clarinet and cello, Op. 11 (1798) and the Piano Sonatas Op. 14 (1799) — the first one of which, as we have remarked, Beethoven transcribed for string quartet. The Title Page bears the designation: 'Six quatuors pour deux Violons, Alto et Violoncello, composé et dédiés à Son. Altesse. Monseigneur. le Prince Regnant de Lobkowitz, par Louis van Beethoven. Oeuvre. 18; Ire (2e) Livraison. à Vienne, chez T. Mollo [Edition No 159].'[cxii] The work was not, however, undertaken to Beethoven's satisfaction. In a letter to Hoffmeister he had cause to complain: 'Herr Mollo recently published my quartets again [presumably a reference to the second set Nos. 4, 5 and 6], but full of mistakes and errata — on a large scale and on a small scale.'[cxiii]

The creative process of publishing six collected works

as a single opus was a legacy from the late eighteenth century. We have remarked that both Haydn and Mozart had composed string quartets in groups of six. Beethoven's similar procedure is open to interpretation as carrying 'overtones of both emulation and competition'.[civ] Moreover, at this period publication practice decreed that a single quartet or sonata did not carry sufficient 'weight' to be regarded as a single work worthy of its own opus number. In Beethoven's lifetime however — and not least through his own efforts — the publication of several works under a single opus number became more rare. By the end of his life such was the standing of Beethoven's string quartets (and other of his chamber works) that they acquired the status of a symphony or other orchestral works and were assigned their own opus numbers.[cv]

It has been suggested the originality of much of Beethoven's Op. 18 may have been the cause for Haydn not completing his projected Op. 77 Quartets. After finishing the first two in the set he began work on the third of which the two inner movements only were completed — later published separately as his Op. 103. Paul Griffiths observes this cannot be attributed to the great master's failing creative powers since he still had before him *The Creation* and the *Harmoniemesse*.[cvi] More plausibly, Landon conjectures: 'We believe that Haydn's refusal to go on with the [Op. 77] series stems from ... his first direct confrontation with Beethoven as a composer.'[cvii]

From our earlier remarks it will be evident Beethoven did not compose his Op. 18 in a vacuum. In the words of Bernhard Jacobson: 'Beethoven from the start nourished himself from the copious musical resources of his environment with a vivid sense of what was valuable in it.' He cites such lesser musical figures of the day as Johann Stamitz, Johann Nepomuk Hummel and Beethoven's counterpoint teacher, already mentioned, the Silsean-born Aloys Förster. To these we may add the names of such other contemporise as Haydn's pupil Ignaz Pleyel, Luigi Boccherini — whose contribution was to make the cello more prominent in the string quartet — and Carl Dittersdorf who had the distinction of playing quartets with both Haydn and Mozart. Although Beethoven benefited from their innovations Jacobson adds: 'Most of these men count for comparatively little in our time, partly because they were too much of their own.' But, he adds the important qualification: '[Their] music represented a living tradition.'[cxviii] The works of these composers served not only as models for such young composers as Beethoven but also served as a challenge to their artistic ingenuity.

Beethoven's particular debt to Haydn and Mozart in the genre of string quartet writing has been mentioned. In his pioneering study of the Beethoven string quartets, Henry Hadow suggests Haydn and Mozart advanced nearer to what he characterises as the ideal of a 'quatour dialogue'. Of the quartets of the older master he writes: 'For melody, for purity of transparent style, Haydn's are in their kind unsurpassed: in balance of instruments they seem to belong to an earlier generation than Beethoven.' He singles out for special praise the first violin parts that in his estimation 'are always brilliant and characteristic'.[cxix] In his discussion of Haydn's later tonal experiments, Landon cites how his slow movements not only possess 'profundity' but are also 'bathed in a curiously impersonal and remote melancholy' that he considers is best captured in the German word *Wehmut* (melancholy/wistfulness/nostalgia). He refers to the manner in which Haydn, in these late works, constructed movements featuring 'long and sustained lines' adding: 'It is one of the aspects of Haydn's style which he transmitted directly to Beethoven, whose Op. 18 Quartets have slow movements of this same density and sustained thought.[cxx]

Paying tribute to Haydn's originality, musicologist David Wyn Jones argues: '[In] many ways Haydn's Op. 76, in particular, is more free-thinking than Beethoven's Op. 18, with two quartets, Op. 76 Nos. 5 and 6 beginning with a movement not in sonata form [as was the convention of the period] and two finales (Op. 76, Nos. 1 and 3) setting off unexpectedly in the minor key before returning to the home major tonic; more generally, there is a variety, sometimes an idiosyncratic variety of scoring and textural density, in Haydn's quartets not apparent in Beethoven's first essays in the medium.'[cxxi] With regard to Haydn's final quartets it is assumed Beethoven would have seen these in manuscript form at one of Prince Lobkowitz's musical gatherings, before completing his own Op. 18. With the eventual publication of Haydn's Op.76 Beethoven would have been able to study his master's work more closely, possibly prompting him to make the revisions to his own set.

With regard to Beethoven's debt to Mozart, writing in the fifth edition of Grove's *Dictionary of Music and Musician* (1954) William McNaught could not resist being provocative: 'Among superlative things it is idle to make comparisons; but it may help to characterise some aspects of classical style to put it that Beethoven wrote the best music for string quartet and that Mozart's was the best string-quartet writing.' Phillip Radcliffe is more restrained, content to remark that in early Beethoven 'there are innumerable turns of phrase that can be found not only in Mozart but in the work of any composer of the period'. He concludes: 'Beethoven could frequently achieve a polished and unobtrusive profundity of the kind generally associated with Mozart, but this could not be fully realised until his idiom had become thoroughly individual, in the gentler and more lyrical works of his second period, which are fully as characteristic and significant as those of stormier vein.'[cxxii]

Evidence of Beethoven's estimation of Mozart's string quartet writing is that between the years 1798 and 1800 he copied out Mozart's String Quartet in G major K. 387 – some 26 pages of manuscript that bear testimony to his industry and wish to better understand his illustrious predecessor's compositional technique.[cxxiii][cxxiv]

In his estimation of Beethoven's debt to Mozart and Haydn, Joseph de Marliave invokes the prophetic words of encouragement with which Ferdinand Waldstein sent Beethoven on his way to Vienna (see our opening remarks): 'It was as the incarnate spirit of Mozart, moulded by Haydn's virile talent, that Beethoven was to appear to the musical world when the six quartets of Op 18, following close upon the First Symphony, were published in two uniform series nine years later. In these works of Beethoven's youth the clarity and freshness of Haydn are found linked with the grace of Mozart, but so far from slavish imitation of these two masters, they form, as it were, the crowning achievement of their art.' Douglas Johnson has considered what he describes as 'the new procedures' that set Mozart and Haydn apart from their contemporaries and which formed part of Beethoven's inheritance. He cites the following: 'The distribution of thematic material through the texture and the natural and easy use of polyphony ... Control in the handling of key relationships ... Concern with organic relationships among the parts of a movement ... [and] The creation of instability within thematic statements.'[cxxv]

Perhaps the most self-evident influence of Haydn and Mozart on Beethoven's Op. 18 is the very fact that he composed a set of six quartets in emulation of their legacy, notably Haydn's 'Russian Quartets', Op. 33 and Mozart's 'Haydn Quartets'. Kinderman comments: 'It is in the context of [Beethoven's] ambitious struggle with the legacy of Haydn and Mozart that we may view Beethoven's single compositional project of [his] first decade in Vienna: the set of six Quartets, Op. 18, written during 1798—1800.' He adds: 'Beethoven knew these works intimately, and reminiscences of both of his distinguished predecessors can be detected in his Op. 18.'[cxxvi]

We have seen that string quartet writing was a new departure for Beethoven and solving the balance between the various instruments was one of the challenges he had to confront. Writing of this Hadow enthuses: '[In] Beethoven's Op. 18 the balance is perfect, the interest is distributed with an entirely even hand. He has, indeed, less virtuosity than Haydn, though he demands more concentrated intelligence; the steady light which illumines his work is diffused over the whole canvas.'[cxxvii] Maynard Solomon finds Beethoven's adherence to tradition more evident in the first three quartets, whereas in the later ones he considers 'Beethoven began to alter the weight and textures of the movements within the usual structure'. In support he quotes Joseph Kerman: 'Beethoven suddenly seems to have thrown the classic framework in doubt.' He elaborates: 'The opening movements are lightened, and since the finales are composed in sonata form rather than in the characteristic rondo form, the climax of each cycle tends to be transferred to the close of each work.'[cxxviii] In the Op. 18 set William Kinderman finds Beethoven both looking back at tradition and simultaneously forwards to his own manner of expression: 'Not infrequently, a tension can be felt in these early quartets between a refined, courtly rhetoric and a powerful directness of expression that is typical of Beethoven.'[cxxix]

For Beethoven — the virtuoso of the keyboard *par excellence* — the writing of string quartets required the mastery of new technical skills. This entailed new challenges in managing the musical texture as shared between the various instruments. In Kerman's words: '[A] musical conception for four string instruments demands more contrapuntal control than one for piano or for piano and instruments ... The four instruments of the quartet ... are always individuals, always sensitive, always exposed.'[cxxx] Notwithstanding that Beethoven was making these new musical departures he revealed a mastery of the medium. In the words of Bernhard Jacobson: 'Among the most striking symptoms of [Beethoven's] individuality even at this early date is his egalitarian texture of the quartets ... in this chamber music, Beethoven carries the independence of the four instrumental parts a large step further than his precursors ... Beethoven was the first great composer to move with complete naturalness to a level of independence in the part-writing [of] quartets ...'.[cxxxi]

Despite this level of self-assuredness, the sketches reveal Beethoven had to strive to achieve what Kinderman characterises as 'a tight unity of organization in crafting these pieces' whilst at the same time 'pursuing heightened dramatic oppositions within and between individual movements'. On the basis of his study of the composer's creative process he adds: 'The surviving musical sketches and other sources cast a revealing and suggestive light on his compositional struggles and aesthetic goals.'[cxxxii] Landon pays tribute to Beethoven's grasp of the string quartet medium as a whole but finds him wanting in the full understanding of setting music for string instruments: 'The form of the Op. 18 music is of supreme technical mastery, but the string technique is not yet completely assured: many vexing passages, which do not lie well in the string player's hands, make Beethoven's difficult task [all the more] complicated.'[cxxxiii]

Beethoven's adherence to tradition is evident in his adoption of sonata form. He makes use of this for the first movements of all six quartets, for the slow movement of the first, the *scherzando* of the fourth, and the finales of the second, third and fifth.[xxxiv] However, whilst content to work within the confines of the sonata principle, he explores its implications 'by diversifying its operation, by annexing new tonal areas and incorporating much complex, even ostentatious, contrapuntal work'.[xxxv] In a further nod to tradition, in the first four quartets Beethoven follows Haydn's characteristic procedure of placing the slow movement second. Of these movements Landon remarks: 'The confrontation with the dense, dynamically much more "loaded" slow movements of Beethoven's Op. 18 must have particularly struck contemporary listener's. Here was Haydn's transparent, rhythmically "open", intensely lyrical music set against a much more technical task.'[xxxvi] Perhaps Beethoven's audiences at Prince Lichnowsky's morning recitals would also have been struck by his codas. As Hadow comments: 'The coda ... which before [Beethoven's] time was often no more than an "Amen" ['so be it'], was sometimes extended by him until it was as long or nearly as long as the rest of the movement altogether.'[xxxvii]

With the composition of the Op. 18 String Quartets Beethoven set performers new challenges. As Tully Potter comments: One only [has to hear] a student or young professional quartet struggling with Beethoven's music to realise that, even in Op. 18, he was asking a great deal. The notes do not always lie easily under the fingers and Beethoven is always demanding a higher degree of expression than any other quartet composer.'[xxxviii] Outlining his views regarding the interpretation of the Op. 18 set, Robert Martin, the cellist member of the Los Angeles based Sequoia String Quartet, suggests players should consider the following when shaping a performance 'overall character; tempo; tone colour; rhythmic contours; dynamics and balance; phrasing; and intonation.' Reflecting on the views of fellow string quartet players he observes: 'One hears over and over again: "He [Beethoven] added the metronome marks long after he wrote the pieces." "He was deaf." "How accurate was the metronome he was using?" "He seemed prone to extremes".' Martin concludes that when all things are taken into consideration: 'The piece still has to "work" ' and this 'springs from the players' roles as performers and their consideration of the effectiveness of the performance.'[cxxxix] Michael Tree, the viola member of the Guarneri String Quartet endorses the spirit of these remarks in his own observations: 'Even if we were to subscribe wholly to Beethoven's metronome markings, the tempo would change from night to night, whatever our intentions. Tempo is something organic.'[cxl] When in conversation with musicologist David Blum, Arnold Steinhardt, first violin member of the Guarneri String Quartet, remarked on the need to perform the Op. 18 Quartets with 'a crystalline quality, a perfection ... an almost constant delicacy and precision'. He compared these works to those of Mozart that 'should always sound spontaneous, no matter how carefully they must be treated'.[cxli]

It is fortunate for Beethoven musicology that the journal *Allgemeine musikalische Zeitung — AmZ — (General music newspaper)* had its inception in 1798. It was founded by the firm of Breitkopf and Härtell and combined reviews of recent music with reports from its correspondents on the musical life of Europe's major cites. During its first twenty years it was edited by Friedrich Rochlitz, a prolific writer and amateur composer. It provides contemporary accounts of the reception of many of Beethoven's compositions. These vary in their nature from adulation to scepticism; his last works were largely ignored for being considered beyond comprehension. During the period under consideration, however, performances of Beethoven works were regularly reported in Vienna, Leipzig, Berlin, Mannheim and Prague

— a measure of the composer's emerging standing as the foremost composer of the day.[cdii]

A review of the first three String Quartets Op. 18 appeared in the *AmZ* issue of 26 August 1801; we recall that Mollo issued the six quartets in two sets in the summer and autumn of 1801. The reviewer writes: 'Distinguished among the recent works appearing here are splendid pieces by Beethoven (Mollo and Co.). Three quartets offer valid proof of his art, but they must be played frequently and well since they are very difficult to perform and are by no means popular.' These sentiments found similar expression in another contemporary review: 'The quartets demanded repeated playings and rehearsings and study to permit a deeper appreciation of their coherence and shape.' However, with the passing of time the reviewer for the *AmZ* came to regard Beethoven's first six quartets as being no less than classical models. An entry in issue *AmZ* 13 of 1811 praises the works for their 'unity, utmost simplicity, and adherence to a specific character in each work ... which raise them to the rank of masterworks and validate Beethoven's place alongside the honoured names of our Haydn and Mozart'.[cdiii]

Beethoven's piano pupil Ferdinand Ries made an arrangement of the String Quartets, Op. 18 for piano trio. This was published by Nikolaus Simrock in Bonn in 1806 with Ries's opus number 60. Simrock wrote to Beethoven on 21 May informing him of this in the following terms: As an experiment Ferdinand Ries had arranged one of your String Quartets, Op. 18, for [piano] ... which made me decide to publish all six as Op. 60. In order to give you a pleasant surprise, I already instructed J. Traeg [Viennese music publisher] to deliver you a copy of the first two numbers ... The rest have been sent off to you already; I hope that they will receive your complete approbation.'[cdiv]

The arrangement on the Title Page reads: 'Six grandes

Sonates pour le piano Forte, Violin oblige et Violincelle ad lib.' In its July issue for 1806 the *AmZ* published a review of Ries's arrangement that is described as referring to '[Beethoven's] famously known violin quartets' — suggesting the extent to which they had by then become established in the string-quartet repertoire. The review is concerned only with Nos. 1 and 2 in the set. Of the arrangement the reviewer remarks: '[Because] the arrangement is made so reasonably ... one willingly desires to hear these ingenious products again, notwithstanding that they cannot possibly be performed and be as exceptional as in the original version and on the original instruments.' The reviewer adds — with a sting in the tail: '[In] spite of their austere and unmanageable nature, one can hardly get enough of listening to them, assuming of course that one manages to understand them.'[cxlv] Beethoven's own response to the Ries-Simrock enterprise in not recorded.

We consider next the early reception of Beethoven's string quartets with particular reference to the Op 18 set. We commence first with some general recollections concerning string-quartet music from the contemporary writings of Johann Friedrich Reichardt — to whom we have made previous reference. On Thursday 15 December 1808, Reichardt heard performances of string quartets by Haydn, Mozart and Beethoven — the works are not specified. He considered all three composers to be 'real humourists [who] had widened the genre, each according to his individual nature'. Haydn is esteemed for his 'charming and original nature ... and cheerful humour'. Mozart is praised for his 'stronger nature and richer imagination' and the manner in which '[he] expressed the highest and deepest of his nature'. Reichardt then reflects on the work of Beethoven whose originality somewhat disturbed him: 'Beethoven had at an early age made himself at home in this place [Vienna] and it only remained for him, if he were to express his own nature also in his own forms, to erect his daring, stubborn tower, on the top of which no one could easily build anything without breaking his neck.'[cxlvi]

A passage in the autobiography of Louis Spohr provides additional testimony that Beethoven's Op. 18 String Quartets were considered to be too in advance of convention for the taste of many. Spohr himself was an accomplished violinist, the composer of eighteen violin concerti and an innovator in the art of string playing; Spohr also suggested improvements in the shape of the violin chinrest. Moreover, he was on familiar terms with Beethoven. Sometime in 1808 he rehearsed the composer's so-called *Ghost* Trio, Op. 70, Beethoven taking the piano part. Spohr considered the master's playing to be somewhat harsh and careless — probably occasioned by the onset of his deafness. When on concert tour in Leipzig, Spohr was anxious to display his abilities as a string player. His wish was gratified when he received an invitation to perform at an evening party arranged by a devotee of music. Spohr narrates: 'I selected for the occasion one of the finest of Beethoven's six new quartets.' He does not identify which of the quartets was selected, but his reference to the six compositions as being 'new' suggests the period in question must have been shortly after their publication. He describes how his fellow string players 'could not enter into the spirit of the performance' and, moreover, how the audience lost interest and began to chatter 'so loud that it almost overpowered the music'. At this, to the dismay of his host, Spohr stopped playing and put his violin back in its case. His host apologised and, in a friendly tone suggested: 'If you could perhaps play something more adapted to the taste of my friends, I feel sure you would have a very attentive and grateful audience.'[cxlvii]

Sometime later, when on tour in Berlin, Spohr did not

fare much better. On this occasion he was invited to perform at a party given by Prince Antoni Radziwill, a patron of the arts and himself an accomplished cellist. Once more Spohr selected a quartet from Beethoven's Op. 18 in the hope it would please the assembled guests who included several distinguished, musically inclined participants — the distinguished cellist Bernhard Romberg being one of them. Spohr was mistaken. He states: 'The musicians of Berlin knew as little of Beethoven's quartets as the musicians of Leipzig and could neither play nor appreciate them.' At the close of the performance, although Romberg was on friendly terms with Beethoven, he found the composer's compositions hard to understand and said bluntly: 'My dear Spohr, how can you play such stuff!'[cxlviii]

Some twenty years after the composition of the Op. 18 set, contemporary accounts indicate Beethoven's first essays in quartet writing had not only found acceptance but were held in high regard. By then, of course, they had long been superseded by the composer's much greater attainments in the genre. An assessment of the Op. 18 appeared in 1830 in the May issue of the Berlin journal *Iris im Gebiete der Tonkunst*. The article in question was devoted to the first printing in score of the quartets. The reviewer remarked how they are 'known to the world as six glittering jewels'. He explains he is concerned only with the new edition that had just been published in full score for the first time. He describes their merits as 'unsurpassable'. The edition was in octavo format and, the reviewer adds, 'joins the similar editions of Haydn's and Mozart's quartets and even excels them perhaps in external elegance'. He described the enterprise as 'a highly meritorious undertaking' and looked forward 'to the similar publication of the composer's other quartets, quintets and the Septet' — the latter being still very popular with the public.[cxlix]

An early pioneer of Beethoven's string quartets outside of Vienna was the violinist-composer Karl Möser. In 1812 he became concertmaster of the Court Opera in Berlin where the following year he established a regular series of quartet recitals — to rival those of their kind organised in Vienna by Schuppanzigh. His chamber series lasted until 1843. Under Möser's sponsorship Beethoven's quartets became familiar repertory pieces; furthermore, in his programming he was adventurous — if not audacious. For example in 1828 he realised a performance of the composer's challenging String Quartet in A minor, Op. 132 and in subsequent concerts performed, Op. 59, Nos. 2 and 3 (from the *Razumovsky* set), Op. 74 (*The Harp*) and Op. 95 (*Quartetto Serioso*). From a recital given in 1833, which featured quartets from Op. 18, one reviewer was disposed to comment: 'Beethoven's first and fourth Quartets make no less an impression than before, [especially] in a superbly bowed and precise performance.'[d]

In England *The Beethoven Quartet Society* did much to promote the awareness of the composer's string quartets. Established in 1845, its avowed intention was 'to honour Beethoven' and 'to study his works from score'. The Society was the first in England to present performances of the complete cycle of Beethoven string quartets, running from April – June 1845.

In France Beethoven's string quartets took time to find audiences appreciative of their worth. In his pioneering study *The Beethoven Quartets* (1925), the French musicologist Joseph de Marliave records the Op. 18 were performed soon after their publication 'but were little understood'. Ferdinand Ries was in France in 1809 and wrote to Beethoven from Paris saying his works were little known or played, least of all the quartets. It appears at this period French musical circles were generally less willing to listen to chamber music than the German public and for a long time declined to take up the composer's quartets. Over time this state of affairs changed. De Marliave remarks that the celebrated violinist and composer Pierre Baillot 'appreciated the beauty of the works' and became 'the self-constituted champion both of the first and later quartets'. Apparently, though, even he was forced by public indifference and a general lack of comprehension to abandon their performance for a time. During the winter of 1826–27, The Baillot Quartet did play most of the Op. 18 Quartets and received a favourable notice in the *Revue musicale* of 1827. The quartets disappeared from the repertoire for the concert seasons 1830 – 34 but after then de Marliave relates 'they were at last included in the regular repertoire of various chamber-music societies, and regularly played'.[cli]

Beethoven's pioneering biographer Anton Schindler, writing in the 1860s, found the composer's level of originality in the Op. 18 Quartets to be on a level comparable to that of his early piano sonatas: 'A pronounced personal style in melody and phrase structure is apparent as early as the Op. 2 Sonata in F minor, or the E major Adagio in the third Sonata of the same group or in the Sonata in E-flat major Op. 7 ... not to mention ... the six Quartets Op. 18 which, entirely free from any stylistic influence, already bear the mark of the truly individual Beethoven style, as if they were the products of later years.'[clii] It must be conceded that Schindler was something of a Beethoven idolater and his views here, regarding the Op. 18 String Quartets, do not take adequate account of Beethoven's debt to Haydn and Mozart.

De Marliave's estimation of the Op. 18 is more measured: 'They have all the grace and brilliant charm of a painting by Raphael, yet, hidden beneath the sweet untroubled smile a shade of sadness lingers, where one thought to see nothing but the tender emotion of another Mozart. But joyous or sad, this music breathed so living a vitality, and a melodic power so abundant, that already it was obvious that Beethoven must soon find the traditional form a constraint.' He continues: 'In this respect the Op. 18 Quartets are inferior to the six great quartets of Mozart, which witness the subordination of technique to musical idea in a manner inspired by true genius ... these works [of Mozart] reveal freedom and flexibility, a harmonic freshness, that perfectly reflects the play of a supple imagination. They give the impression of smooth and adequate perfection that one misses in the Op. 18. One feels that Beethoven must create a new musical form in which to express the world of new ideas surging in his troubled soul [a reference to the composer's onset of deafness], and this end is not to be reached without some conflict between form and inspiration.'[cliii]

Modern-day authorities are broadly united in their acknowledgement of the merits of Beethoven's achievement — as reflected in our selection of opening quotations. His Op. 18, although perhaps not as self-assured as his early piano sonatas or the String Trios, Op. 9, are recognised for the manner in which they speak a new language, were a part of the composer's 'artistic emancipation', and are amongst the most intellectually challenging and appealing of his compositions to date. We close our account of the creation origins and reception history of these pioneering works through the words of a selection of contemporary authorities.

Arthur Shepherd writes: '[One] is impressed more than ever with Beethoven's clear intention to assimilate with the utmost thoroughness the principles, style and technique of his two great predecessors. It may be observed, too, that no creative artist less sure of himself would have dared to proceed so far in direct emulation of his models; but it is well to recognize the difference between fidelity to a pre-established design and slavish imitation of conventions.'[cliv]

Joseph Kerman is of the view: '[The] Op. 18 Quartets will be granted to be erratic works. There are bad spots within many of the movements; and within total compositions, some movements succeed as wholes better than others ... Characteristically, Beethoven was beginning to question the very nature of the undertaking he was engaged in ... When his interest did flare in [the] later quartets, it flared more imaginatively than ever, in ways that shed light ahead ... All in all, the best-realized movements are probably the dance and dancelike numbers.' Kerman acknowledges the Op. 18 set is also about ambition: 'Ambition bristles especially in the numerous passages of formal counterpoint, which seem on the one hand to be looking for some tougher, more individual means of expression, and on the other hand to be chasing the shadow of Albrechtsberger and Haydn ... In both technique and expression, Beethoven was more interested in following up dazzling new ideas than in polishing classic medallions.'[clv]

Philip Radcliffe believes what emerges most obviously, from a consideration of the six works that constitute Beethoven's Op. 18, is that he already possessed mastery of the challenges of writing for the string quartet. In particular: 'The fugal passages, in whatever mood, are always successful and he has fully realised that a contrapuntal texture need not necessarily be fugal, or even imitative.' Whilst Radcliffe does not consider Beethoven's slow movements reach the supremely high level of those in Mozart's Quartet in C major, K. 465, or Haydn's Quartet in F major, Op. 77, No. 2, he regards passages in Beethoven's Op. 18 'show the same feeling for logical, non-fugal counterpoint'. He cites the *Andante* of the Quartet in D major and the *Adagio* of the Quartet in B-flat major. He also draws attention to Beethoven's frequent use of *sforzandi* in his quartet writing that is also characteristic of the early piano sonatas: 'Sometimes it gives an unexpected jolt to an otherwise placid tune, such as that of the Trio of the Minuet of the Quartet in A major, or the Finale of the Quartet in B-flat major; more often it leads to a rhetoric more emphatic and vehement than that of Haydn or Mozart.' Radcliffe concludes: 'At this stage, Beethoven is not in the mood for the heroics of the *Pathétique* Sonata ... but in Op. 22 and Op. 18 he is able to use some of the idiom that is in no way revolutionary, but has far more independence and imagination than several more externally ambitious works of the same period, such as the Septet and the First Symphony.'[clvi]

In his commentary to the recordings of the Op. 18 Quartets by the Alban Berg Quartet, musicologist Bernhard Jacobson reminds us that the set is not monolithic and that the individual works manifest their own distinctive qualities. He finds Beethoven, at first, enjoying the Haydn-Mozart tradition but then gradually focusing on the aspects of quartet writing more adequate to his own creative needs. At his best, Jacobson maintains, Beethoven confronts his two greatest forebears 'as if to exorcise their oppressive presence'. This is a direct reference to Haydn, first in the G major Quartet, Op. 18, No. 2 and then more emphatically still, Mozart, in the Quartet in A major, Op. 18, No. 5. These quartets, Jacobsen asserts 'are invested with exactly the weight they ought to bear for a composer now experienced enough to know how much he owes them and confident enough to ... know how much he can and must achieve himself ... Altogether, the G major and A major quartets represent an extraordinary stylistic achievement'.[clvii]

H. C. Robbins Landon also regarded Beethoven's Op. 18 as 'a formidable achievement', in parts 'theatrical' — notably the D minor *Adagio affettuoso ed appassionato* from No. 1 — and richly adorned in a 'marvellously professional language'.[clviii]

Joseph Kerman, recognising Beethoven's even greater future achievements in the genre of string-quartet writing, concludes:

> '[Our] taste for them [Op.18] can never be quite the same as partaking of "masterpieces of art". They will doubtless always remain a merely mortal, not "celestial", nourishment.'[clix]

String Quartet in F major, Op. 18, No. 1

> 'As the work stands it is gratifying to the performer and offers pleasant not over-difficult problems to the listener, and shows the skill of the composer in handling the quartet instruments, among which the violin is still given the most prominent place.'

Paul Bekker, *Beethoven*, 1925, p. 311.

> 'The Quartet in F is the biggest and in obvious ways the most impressive [of the Op. 18]. Its first and last movements, besides lasting appreciably longer than corresponding movements in the other quartets, make a more brilliant effect — the first by means of thematic manipulation, the last by proliferating form. The second movement, if not quite the longest slow movement, is the only one in the minor mode and by far the most emotional. The *Scherzo* ... runs the fastest and

> runs the farthest in harmonic range.'

Joseph Kerman, *The Beethoven Quartets*, 1967, p. 30.

> 'Ultimately, individual works of art are all that
> exist, and that is how they are to be experienced
> ... We cannot get out of Op. 18, No.1 what
> Beethoven put into it if we listen to it with the ears
> we use for the *Grosse Fuge* or even the *Razu-
> mowsky* Quartets. And it is what the composer
> put into each work that is what we should try to
> find, rather than damaging the concentration of
> our perception by telling ourselves what it was
> that he was not yet ready to say.'

Robert Simpson, *The Chamber Music for Strings* in: Denis Arnold and Nigel Fortune, *The Beethoven Companion*, 1973, p. 242.

> 'The young master who could command such
> resources [as here evident] had no need to imitate
> even Haydn or Mozart, and to adopt an attitude
> of patronage to this quartet is mere impertinence
> ... Perhaps because it was completely composed
> twice over, this quartet is the most varied in
> expression, and the most masterly in overall
> design, of the six works comprising Op. 18.'

Basil Lam, *Beethoven String Quartets*, 1975, pp. 14—18.

In our overview of the String Quartets Op. 18, Nos. 1—6 we remarked that Beethoven placed the F major Quartet, No. 1 at the head of the series since it is 'the grandest and most immediately impressive'.[clx] We recall the influence of Beethoven's friend, the violinist Ignaz Schuppanzigh, regarding his suggested ordering of the compositions. In the case of the F major Quartet he encouraged Beethoven to give it first place for being 'the most brilliant' and, on the surface, 'the most impressive piece'. Furthermore, its first movement and finale are the longest movements in this position in the entire opus. In his survey of the composer's musical evolution, Michael Broyles discusses what he describes as the 'stylistic dualism' that is to be found in early Beethoven. This disposes him to find 'pairing' within contemporaneous compositions. He thereby pairs the first of the String Quartets of Op. 18 with the First Symphony, Op. 21.[clxi] Philip Radcliffe also draws attention to the parallels to be found within Beethoven's early compositions, citing from this period the Piano Sonata in B-flat major, Op. 22 that he considers has the most in common with Op. 18, No. 1: 'Its Adagio is less poignant than that of the Quartet in F, but the two movements, both in 9/8 time, have the same mixture of flowing Italianate melody with rich and nostalgic harmony of the Teutonic kind.'[clxii] In his estimation, Robert Simpson was unequivocal that Op. 18, No. 1 was the strongest and most concentrated of all six works, remarking: 'The F major shows the most perfect mastery of all the early quartets, both in equality of part-writing and succinctness (as well as breadth) of form.'[clxiii] Basil Lam was so moved by the composition as to enthuse: 'Beethoven's polyphonic treatment is great Beethoven of any period, and reveals the full power of the quartet medium in a way without precedent in any of the masterpieces previously given to it.'[clxiv]

The creation origins of the String Quartet in F major are intimately associated with the clergyman-violinist Karl Amenda. Beethoven became acquainted with him in 1799 at the chamber-music sessions held in the household of Prince Lobkowitz where Amenda was employed. He soon became Beethoven's closest friend; it is a measure of the closeness of the composer's feelings towards Amenda that he was one of the first to whom Beethoven confided the onset of his deafness. When Amenda had to return to his native Courland, Beethoven made him a gift of the first version of the F major quartet. On 25 June 1799, Beethoven wrote to Amenda inscribing on the first violin part: 'Take this quartet as ... memories of our friendship, and whenever you play it recall the days we spent together and the sincere affection felt for you then and which will always be felt by ... your warm and true friend Beethoven.'[clxv] The Quartet remained in the possession of the Amada family to the end of the nineteenth century. In 1904 the possessor of the Quartet, Frau Pastor Anna Kawall née Amenda, allowed the work to be published.[clxvi] Today the Amenda version of the F major String Quartet survives in the Beethoven House Archives in the form of a set of parts in the hand of a professional copyist.[clxvii] In this copy the piece is described in Beethoven's hand as 'Quartetto No. II', implying that, at that stage in the Op. 18 compositional sequence, the F-major Quartet was not planned to commence the series.

Reflecting more generally on these circumstances, Joseph Kerman comments: 'The very existence of this music in two forms tells us something about the ambience of the string quartet at that period. It tells us that pieces circulated in what might be called "trial versions", works in progress that would evidently be touched up or recast after being played and discussed by friends and patrons. The "finalization" represented by publication could be left for later.'[clxviii]

On 1 July 1801, Beethoven wrote to Amenda primarily to confide in him the realization he was losing his hearing. Towards the end of this moving letter he refers to the F major quartet with the plea: 'Be sure not to hand on to anybody your quartet, in which I have made some drastic alterations. For only now have I learnt how to write quartets.'[clxix] A comparison of the two versions of the music is illuminating insofar as it reveals Beethoven's capacity for self-criticism and self-improvement. Authorities who have studied the composer's surviving sketches, bear testimony to the rigour with which he revised both the smallest motifs and the largest compositional units, and how to make the music sound in terms of the voicing and scoring for the individual instruments so as to bring the four parts into more equal prominence. Simpson likens Beethoven's revisions to 'an absorbing study in clarification and in the closer articulation of counterpoint and form'.[clxx] In his comparison of the details of the two versions of Beethoven's quartet writing, Paul Bekker considers the revisions display 'a freer, more soloistic treatment of the accompanying parts, a clearer individualisation of the violoncello cello part and greater tonal delicacy in the ensemble effects'.[clxxi] Based on his study of Beethoven's sketches, Barry Cooper draws attention to the changes in texture that he finds 'becomes smoother and more linear' and in which 'motifs are made to stand out more clearly, while fussy accompaniment figures such as oscillating patterns are eliminated'.[clxxii] One illustration of this aspect of Beethoven's newfound self-control is that a particular gruppetto figure (a turn motif) that occurs in the first version no fewer than 130 times is reduced to a leaner 104 repetitions in the published version.[clxxiii]

Beethoven's piano pupil Ferdinand Ries made an arrangement of the Op. 18 String Quartets for piano trio, prompting a review of them in the 16 July 1806 issue of the *Allgemeine musikalische Zeitung:* 'Whoever is concerned with hearing an ingenious composition and making it available for others to hear, let him acquire them, particularly No. 1 (F major), which in the original is also one of the reviewer's favourites of these quartets and which can also be played on the pianoforte much better than No. 2 (G major).'

The reviewer commended the quality of the publisher's engraving for being free from errors, adding 'that is not a trifle in such music!'[clxxiv] Twenty years later, the Op. 18 String Quartets had long been assimilated into the concert repertoire. We infer this from a review of the compositions that appeared in the *AmZ's* sister music journal the *Berliner Allgemeine musikalische Zeitung*. In the issue for 22 November 1826 the writer expressed caution concerning the composer's most recent ventures into the genre of quartet writing but found favour in his early works: 'Beethoven showed himself worthy of his forerunners in the first quartet in F major with that genius that we admire in astonishment from the oldest up to his most recent artistic creations, even if we cannot always grasp them and discover the context for the ideas. These older quartets [Op. 18] are nevertheless quite clear, grand, and new in invention, as in the combination of harmonies.' The concertmaster for the quartet series that had prompted this review was Karl Möser, then a leading figure in Berlin's music scene. The reviewer praised him for 'comprehending the spirit of Haydn's humour, Mozart's soul, and Beethoven's sublime genius'.[clxxv]

Concerning the early reception of Beethoven's chamber music in France, something of this may be discerned from the following circumstances. In the winter of 1847—8, the violinist Théophile Tilmant founded the *Société de musique classique*. This society played several Beethoven quartets at regular intervals, especially those of Op. 18. In the programme of its opening concert in 1849, the Quartet in F Op. 18 was performed. The critic of the *Revue et Gazette musicale de Paris* recorded: 'The originality of the great symphonic writer already breaks through the influence and manner of Mozart in brilliant flashes; the work was performed with fine ensemble and subtlety of feeling.'[clxxvi]

In our Preface we have noted that in England *The*

Beethoven Quartet Society pioneered the performance of the composer's string quartets. In their very first recital, held in 1845, the players gave a rendering of Op. 18, No.1. Later in the season the entire Beethoven quartet cycle was performed with the exception of the *Grosse Fuge*.[clxxvii]

Beethoven designates the first movement of the F-major Quartet *Allegro con brio*, a directive to perform the music at 'a fast tempo with spirit'. The opening motif has the power to seize the listener's immediate attention. Perhaps a parallel may be found in the strident opening notes of the String Quartet Op. 95 (*Quartetto Serioso*). Beethoven's manner in the F major has been described variously as; 'beautifully incisive'[clxxviii]; 'crisp ... unforgettable'[clxxix]; 'the very touchstone of motivic integration in the High Classical style'[clxxx]; and 'full of fits and starts based on heady, thematic, rhythmic and harmonic contrast'[clxxxi]. In his commentary to the recording of the work by *The Alban Berg Quartet*, Bernhard Jacobson draws attention to Beethoven's originality: '[In] idiom and mood, the riveting unison principle theme of the *Allegro con brio* immediately raises Beethoven-ness to a new power.' He invokes the composer's later dramatic quartet opening to which we have just alluded: '[Here] is the same man as we find in the pithier unison opening of the F minor Quartet, Op. 95 of 1810.'[clxxxii] The manner in which Beethoven's invests such vigour and animation in the first movement, derived from the pervasive rhythm of the opening theme, disposed Lam to dismiss as 'absurd' the notion that in early Beethoven he was 'cautiously following Haydn and Mozart'. Although Beethoven may not have been following his former teacher 'cautiously', Lam does concede the composer's debt to Haydn is evident; he cites an early version of the opening theme being reminiscent of the older master's Quartet in B flat, Op. 50 No. 1.[clxxxiii] Likewise, David Wyn Jones finds Beethoven's F major

Quartet to be 'the most obviously Haydnesque work in the Op. 18'. He draws attention to the opening movement of Haydn's quartet in D major, Op. 76, No. 2, which, as he observes, 'was a very recent example of this kind of concentrated writing for the medium'. He also suggests the first movement of Haydn's Quartet Op. 50, No. 3 in E flat may also have been a stimulus to Beethoven.[clxxxiv]

A comparison between the published edition of the F major Quartet and that of the Amenda version reveals the extent to which Beethoven modified his thoughts so as to refine the overall proportions of the movement. In this context Cooper draws attention to the frequent deletions Beethoven made in order to achieve the balance he required; we have previously cited, by way of illustration, the curtailment of the number of occurrences of the opening figuration. Other transformations were more Draconian: 'In the first movement of the Quartet Op. 18, No. 1, Beethoven originally planned both halves to be repeated, as is clear from the early version he sent to Karl Amenda; but when he undertook a thorough revision of the quartet the second repeat was cancelled.'[clxxxv]

The opening of the first movement that springs forth seemingly so spontaneously caused Beethoven a great deal of trouble as he reshaped his first thoughts to the finished 'sharply defined profile'.[clxxxvi] Reflecting on its compositional origins — as revealed in the composer's surviving sketches — Arthur Shepherd draws attention to Beethoven's characteristic, and painstaking, striving for simplicity: 'It is difficult to believe that so blithe and naïve a theme, as that which launches this first quartet, is one of those laboriously wrought ideas that found its definite form only after much contemplation.'[clxxxvii] No fewer than sixteen pages exist in the composer's sketchbooks for the period 1798–9 and 1800 (see our remarks to String Quartets Op. 18, Nos. 1–6).

These reveal, in Marion Scott's words, 'Beethoven chiselling his first subject' and then, not satisfied, submitting it to more 'refining and retouching'.[clxxxviii]

Joseph de Marliave offered a somewhat mixed estimation of the F major Quartet's first movement. He regarded it as 'an interesting example of Beethoven's technical brilliance' and of his skill 'in working a theme', a device he considered 'had been carried to perfection by his predecessors'. But in his judgment the music has 'too many passages of unison and harmonic padding ... the young musician [shows] mastery over form [but] at the same time a certain failure of inspiration'. He more generously acknowledged the extent to which Beethoven's creation, regarded as a whole, had moved many of the composer's contemporaries and later composers such as Louis Spohr. The latter, de Marliave noted, went so far as to declare the piece to be no less than 'the artist's masterpiece and the summit of possible achievement in the quartet genre'. This was too much for de Marliave who responded: 'Time has changed this sweeping opinion and the movement is now considered a fluent but not remarkably interesting work: brilliant but [with] superficial colouring [and] passing emotions.'[clxxxix] In support of Spohr, Kerman comments: 'Louis Spohr considered Beethoven's Quartet in F to be the ideal model in its genre; as an academic classicist par excellence, Spohr holds little interest for musicians today, but he was no mean connoisseur of the classical style, and something of a specialist in formal models.'[cxc]

Beethoven's *Death Centenary* (1927) prompted many re-evaluations of the composer's works. The instrumentalist Rebecca Clarke singled out for comment the F major String Quartet, as perceived from the perspective of the performer. Concerning the interpretation of the first movement, she wrote: 'Great accuracy is necessary ... in which the abrupt and pithy subject is continually tossed from one player to another, so that the joints must dovetail very neatly; and they must be played with the same tone colour in order to prevent the whole from sounding disjointed.'[cxci]

The second movement is headed *Adagio affettuoso ed appassionato* – 'slow tempo with tender feeling and with passion'. In this regard, Beethoven was here combining two somewhat disparate expressions: the term *affettuoso* deriving from the eighteenth century and *appassionato* belonging to the nineteenth. Radcliffe comments: '[These] unusually elaborate directions suggest that Beethoven felt himself to be writing a specially emotional piece of music.' Remarking more generally on the composer's adoption of a minor key for this movement, he makes the further observation: 'Haydn and Mozart wrote surprisingly few slow movements in minor keys, especially in their later works; those by Beethoven are more numerous and almost all of exceptional quality.' He cites the very sombre ad passionate *Largo e mesto* from the D major Piano Sonata, Op. 10, No. 3. Contemporaneous with the F major Quartet, this music has been described as 'one of the great tragic utterances in early Beethoven' in which 'struggle' and 'resignation' intertwine within sonata form to yield the effect of 'light dispelling darkness'.[cxcii] Radcliffe adds: 'The *Adagio* of this F major Quartet has something of the same passion, but is considerably more restrained.' In his summation he pronounces the *Adagio* to be 'the most striking part of the Quartet ... a fine specimen of Beethoven's early style in its more Italianate vein, with suggestions of Mozart, but with bolder outlines and stronger emphasis.'[cxciii]

The atmosphere prevailing has been likened to that of 'an operatic scena, nocturnal and Italianate, with the first violin, joined later by the cello, singing in a *bel canto* lament over a softly pulsating accompaniment'.[cxciv] Jones likens the passage to a dialogue between the two instruments with evocations of a duet of the kind to be found in the slow movements of Haydn's String Quartet Op. 20, No. 2 and Mozart's *Hunt* Quartet, K. 458.[cxcv] At every turn there is 'a frank avowal of a romantic impulse ... the romanticism of Beethoven's early period'.[cxcvi] The music is 'self-consciously affecting' but perhaps undermined by 'an element of sentimentality'.[cxcvii] The first violin dominates over a soft dynamic level requiring Beethoven to call for *ppp* (*pianissimo*) 'very soft' — a rare example of such a designation in his scores.[cxcviii] The mood is also sometimes troubled with some of the nervous energy and concentration of the first movement casting their spell over the *Adagio affettuoso ed appassionato*.[cxcix] Here we catch a glimpse of the future nineteenth-century Beethoven 'in characteristic explosions of dynamic force and lightning flashes of rapid notes'.[cc] Perhaps the young Franz Schubert was influenced here by the music's turbulence when he came to write his great String Quintet in C major, D. 956?[cci]

We recall the F major Quartet had its creation origins in the form of a gift to the clergyman-violinist Karl Amenda. This connection assumes particular significance in relation to the mood prevailing in the second movement. It may possess a poetic-Shakespearian association as we learn from Beethoven's biographer Alexander Thayer. He recalls an occasion when Beethoven played through a piano reduction of the *Adagio* for Amanda. In his account Thayer sets aside his typical formal style and describes the movement as 'glorious'. He relates that at the close of his performance Beethoven asked Amenda: 'What thought had been awakened by it?' Amanda responded: 'It pictured for me the parting of two lovers.' 'Good!' remarked Beethoven: 'I thought of the scene in the burial vault in *Romeo and Juliet*.'[ccii]

Musicologists have justification for approaching such

anecdotes with caution, given the manner in which the creation origins of Beethoven's work have been mythologised. It is known, for example, that when Anton Schindler asked Beethoven the meaning permeating his Piano Sonata in D minor, Op. 31, No. 2 – *The Tempest* – the composer is alleged to have responded: 'Just read Shakespeare's *Tempest.*' This is now considered to be one of Schindler's fabrications. With regard to Amenda's alleged recollections, William Hadow was of the view: 'It is dangerous to lay any emphasis on such statements as this. Even when they are seriously made – and Beethoven was not always serious – they convey no more than a very general hint of very limited application.' Hadow continues: 'Music cannot be translated into terms of anything other than itself; and all we can safely say here is that the opening melody is of extraordinary passion and poignancy, and that the manner of writing is largely in duet.'[cciii] Lam mediates: 'Even without such evidence, [as the *Romeo and Juliet* anecdote] a dramatic element could be recognised in this very beautiful piece, which has an emotional expansiveness that never appears in Beethoven's purely personal slow movements ... It was not until the *Eroica* that Beethoven surpassed the tragic eloquence of this *Adagio.*' Lam is one who also finds a connection with Beethoven's writing and its influence on his young contemporary: 'Schubert remembered, in the slow movement of his C major Quintet, the moving effect of this figure when given to the cello.'[cciv] Cooper cites compelling evidence in favour of the anecdote: 'Among the sketches to this movement are [the remarks] "il prend le tombeau" ... "il se tue" and "les derniers soupirs".' Cooper surmises: 'There is no proof that these refer to [Shakespeare's] play but the comments certainly fit the situation.'

Jones lends credence to Amenda's account by recalling the large number of string quartets that were issued in

Vienna in the 1780s and 1790s and which were arrangements of vocal numbers from popular operas and oratorios; Gluck, Mozart and Salieri contributed to the genre. Beethoven himself wrote several sets of piano variations that he adopted from popular melodies of the day.[ccv] Jones concludes: 'Given the prevalence of this market, now completely forgotten, it is not surprising that ... Karl Amenda should have remarked that the movement seemed to him to portray the parting of two lovers.'[ccvi] Of related interest is that in the first version of the Quartet, Beethoven marked the second movement simply as *Adagio molto*. Only in his later revisions did he modify this to *Adagio affettuoso ed appassionato* — which may be taken as a measure of his desire to indicate to the performer that the music should be interpreted tenderly and expressively.

These qualities were not lost to the reviewer writing about the music in the 22 November issue of the *Berliner Allgemeine musikalische Zeitung*: 'What beautiful melancholy and elegiac depth animate the fantasy-like *Adagio* in D minor, and how impudently and teasingly does the rondo, in contrast, bubble forth in jovial humour!'[ccvii] A century later, de Marliave expressed similar thoughts: '[Nothing] so deeply felt had hitherto (1800) ever come from the composer's pen ... Among Beethoven's slow movements, this has only one precursor, the *Largo* of the Sonata in D, Op. 10, No. 3; later movements, born of similar inspiration (the slow movements of the quartet in F major, Op. 59, and of the quartet in E flat, Op. 74), are to crystalize its memory.'[ccviii] Contemporaneously Romain Rolland maintained: 'The *Adagio* is very beautiful, and one can feel in it the future Beethoven.'[ccix] Bekker likened the *Adagio affettuoso ed appassionato* to 'a most moving song of sorrow such as only Beethoven could accomplish when he turned to the grave D minor key'.[ccx] We give the last words here to Joseph Kerman: 'This D-minor

Adagio affettuoso ed appassionato is one of the most accomplished things that Beethoven had yet written, one of the very best things. Few movements among the Op. 18 Quartets so reward study, and testify so strongly to his now formidable ability in melodic draughtsmanship, his control of form [and] his mastery of the string-quartet medium.'[ccxi]

The third movement is headed *Scherzo* – one of four such designations in the Op. 18 set. Beethoven invariably adopted this expression to signify its original Italian etymological meaning suggestive of humour and high spirits.[ccxii] In the F major Quartet, the *Scherzo* replaces the Classical minuet and is signified to be performed *Allegro molto* – 'in a lively tempo, very swift'. Lam justifies Beethoven's rejection of the conventional minuet form on the grounds 'after the romantic intensity of the slow movement a minuet would be too formal'. Equally, he recognizes that a straightforward scherzo would be 'too inconsequential'. By introducing a chromatic element, and shifting bar accents, Lam considers a kind of unrest is achieved 'that links it with the seriousness of the first half of the quartet'. Of the composer's craftsmanship he enthuses: 'Technically it is beyond praise, the work of an absolute master of composition.'[ccxiii]

More than one commentator has detected the influence of Haydn in the third movement, in the manner of its 'high-spirited humour and its capricious syntax'.[ccxiv] Commenting on Beethoven's adoption of the scherzo form at this period, Jones observes: 'Beethoven's piano sonatas and string trios from the 1790s have a number of one-in-a-bar scherzos which, in turn, might have prompted three similar movements in Haydn's Op. 76 and Op. 77.'[ccxv] Humour is evident in the Trio section with its 'striking rhythmic and textural passages',[ccxvi] 'leaping octave passages ... a trait significant of vitality[ccxvii], and 'high speed witticisms of many kinds ... chromatic distortions ... abrupt stops and starts that contribute to the humorous effect'.[ccxviii] Affinities have been found here with the *Menuetto* section of the contemporaneous Symphony No.1, described as 'its twin'[ccxix] but 'more subtle and light footed'[ccxx].

Joseph de Marliave considered this scherzo of Beethoven's first manner gives a hint 'at the sparkling tonal audacities that the artist is later to mould into this form'.[ccxxi] Looking ahead to Beethoven's final statements in the medium, Bernhard Jacobson contends: 'The *Scherzo* is perhaps the most roundedly successful movement — its weird, thrusting rhythms look still further forward ... to the spectral, frightening scherzo of Op. 135, written in 1826 ... the galumphing octave unisons that lead into the trio section are quintessential Beethoven.'[ccxxii]

Beethoven designated the fourth movement of the Amenda version of the F major string quartet *Allegretto* — 'a moderately quick tempo' — but in the revised edition he changed this to a full blown *Allegro* — 'lively-brisk' — thereby to more fully covey the energy and vitality that characterizes the music. The *Allegro* 'leaps upon the ear without warning or preparation'. It appears to have similarly sprung from the composer's imagination, since the opening motif appeared at an early stage in the sketches in a close approximation to its final form. The movement is at once for Beethoven 'a natural outlet for imaginative vigour',[ccxxiii] in which he maintains to a remarkable degree 'a sense of cumulative verve and vitality',[ccxxiv] and a 'relaxed and brilliant sense of a maturely dispersed knot of feeling'.[ccxxv] The manner is close in feeling to that found in some of the composer's early piano sonatas. For example, the animated finale of the Piano Sonata Op. 2, No. 1 (1793–95/96) has been described as 'a work of youthful violence with its many indications of fortissimo and its brilliant arpeggios'[ccxxvi] — the first of Beethoven's 'stormy finales'.[ccxxvii] In the Piano Sonata C minor, Op. 10, No. 1 (1796–98), Beethoven marked *prestissimo* throughout the entire movement. Here, as in the F major Quartet, the layout is concise and possessed of energy and intensity. Harold Truscott believes an even stronger connection is to be found in the work's closing pages with the main theme of the finale of the C minor Trio, Op. 9. He remarks: 'The idea seems to have been still with Beethoven when he wrote the main theme of the finale of the F major String Quartet, Op. 18, No. 1.' He adds: 'In fact, since the dates of composition of the Three Trios and the Op. 18 Quartet overlap, it is possible that one idea suggested the other.'[ccxxviii]

In the composition of his first string quartets, Beethoven's debt to Mozart has been mentioned (see String Quartets, Op. 18, Nos. 1–6). Robert Winter suggests the writing for violin was influenced by the opening of Mozart's D-major Quartet, K. 499. He comments: 'The personality is if course quite different – earth and fire as against Mozart's air ... This movement has tremendous verve and surprisingly few rests ... counterpoint becomes the tool of wit.'[ccxxix] Moreover: 'All through the Quartet the interest is most skilfully divided between the players.'[ccxxx]

---

[i] In 1787 Beethoven had spent a short time in Vienna where he received some instruction from Mozart. He had to terminate his studies and return to Bonn when he learned his mother was terminally ill – she died soon afterwards of consumption. See: Thayer-Forbes, 1967, p. 89.

[ii] Theodore Albrecht, 1996 Vol. 1, Letter No. 13g, pp. 22–3.

[iii] For a reproduction of Beethoven's Album, open at the pages showing Waldstein's text together with his silhouette, see: Hans Conrad Fischer, and Erich Kock, 1972, p. 107.

[iv] Beethoven's early relationship with Haydn, in the context of his visits to London, is outlined in *Musical Visitors to Britain*, David Gordon, 2005, pp. 93-4.

[v] For an account of Ferdinand Waldstein and his relationship with Beethoven, see: Elliot Forbes, editor, 1967, pp. 91–2 and p. 351; Peter Clive, 2001, pp. 385–7; and Eric Blom, 1938, p. 148.

[vi] Peter Clive, 2001, p. 247.

[vii] Emily Anderson, editor and translator, 1961, Vol. 1, Letter No. 6, p. 9.

[viii] See: Beethoven-Haus, Bonn website.

ix Barry Cooper, 1991, p. 69.
x Emily Anderson, editor and translator, 1961, Vol. 1, Letter No. 8, p. 12.
xi Thayer-Forbes, 1967, p. 144 and Theodore Albrecht, translator and editor, 1996, Vol. 1 Letter No. 16, pp. 32–4. For a commentary on this extended and eloquent letter, with remarks concerning the compositions mentioned therein, see also: H. C. Robbins Landon 1959, pp. 141–2.
xii Theodore Albrecht, translator and editor, 1996, Vol. 1 Letter No. 17, pp. 34–5.
xiii For a discussion of these circumstances see: Beethoven House, Digital Archives, Document, Sammlung H. C. Bodmer. HCB Mh 42.
xiv Peter Clive, 2001, p. 307.
xv Johann Baptist Schenk, as recorded by Oscar George Theodore Sonneck, *Beethoven: impressions of contemporaries*, 1927, pp. 15–16.
xvi Peter Clive, 2001, p. 302.
xvii Salieri's pupils included Johann Nepomuk Hummel, Mozart's son Franz Xavier Mozart and Franz Schubert.
xviii Joseph Kerman, 1967, pp. 4–5.
xix The original account is given by Ferdinand Ries: *Impressions of Beethoven*, in: Oscar George Theodore Sonneck, 1927, p. 49.
xx Elliot Forbes, editor, 1967, pp. 149–50. See also: Philip G. Downs, 1992, pp. 559–60.
xxi Barry Cooper, 2000, pp. 78–9.
xxii *Ibid*.
xxiii Igor Stravinsky, 1972, p. 256.
xxiv Cited in: Robert Winter and Robert Martin, editors, 1994, p. 150.
xxv Christian Schubart outlined his views in: *Ideen zu einer Aesthetik der Tonkunst* (1806). Beethoven was interested in Schubart's writings, particularly his theory in which he characterised the musical keys with feelings and ascribed to them a certain 'psyche'. For example, he considered A-flat minor implied 'difficult struggle' and 'wailing lament' and B minor suggested 'patience' and 'calm awaiting one's fate'. In comparison, C major was the key with the connotation 'completely pure'. For an account of Schubart's theories and Beethoven's attachment to them, see: Anton Schindler, 1860, English edition: Donald MacArdle, 1966, pp. 366-7.
xxvi As expressed by Leon Botstein, *Music, culture and society in Beethoven's Vienna*, in: Robert Winter and Robert Martin, editors, 1994, pp. 91–2.
xxvii The *AmZ* quotation is derived from: Paul Griffiths, 1983, p. 85.
xxviii Robert Winter and Robert Martin, editors, 1994, pp. 3–4.
xxix As remarked and amplified by Paul Yarbrough in his Liner notes to *Beethoven's String Quartets*, Alexander String Quartet.
xxx Leon Plantinga, 1984, pp. 30–31.
xxxi See Richard Kramer, *On the autograph of Beethoven's String Quartet in F major*, Op. 59, No. 1 in: Christoph Wolff and Robert Riggs, *The string quartets of Haydn, Mozart and Beethoven: studies of the autograph manuscripts: a conference at Isham Memorial Library*, March 15–17, 1979, 1980, p. 230.
xxxii Joseph Kerman, 1967, p. 82.
xxxiii The phrase quoted is derived from Stephanie Schroeder, Liner notes to the recording of the Beethoven string quartets by the Alexander Quartet.

xxxiv Philip Downs, 1992, p. 588.

xxxv Basil Lam, 1975, p. 12.

xxxvi As further evidence of Beethoven's early development in writing for string instruments, mention should be made of his recasting of the String Octet ([posthumously published as Op. 103) as the String Quintet, Op. 4. This was undertaken some time in early 1791, probably when he was composing the C major Piano Sonata, Op. 2, No. 3. Writing of this Gerald Abraham remarks how a comparison of the two versions 'shows considerable light on his development as an instrumental composer during [these] formative years'. He elaborates: 'The Quintet is by no means an arrangement of the Octet ... it is in many aspects a new work. Everything has become more plastic: stiff formulae are softened; the texture is lightened in weight but enriched with polyphony ... The harmony had become richer ... All in all, it is hardly an exaggeration to say that the difference between the Octet and the Quintet represents the whole difference between the *al fresco*, serenade music that was just going out of fashion and the new finely wrought quartet style of Haydn with its openwork texture.' Gerald Abraham, *Beethoven's chamber music*, In: *The age of Beethoven, The New Oxford History of Music, Vol. VIII*, Gerald Abraham, editor, 1988, pp. 260–5.

xxxvii H. C. Robbins Landon, 1977, p. 502.

xxxviii This creative period of Beethoven's life is considered in some detail by: Thayer-Forbes, 1967, Chapters XIII and XIV; Wilfrid Mellers, 1957; Denis Matthews, 1985; and Glenn Stanley, 2000. Beethoven's letter to his publisher Franz Hoffmeister also sheds light on the many compositions he had in hand at this time, see: Emily Anderson, 1961, Vol. 1, Letter No, 41, pp. 42–3.

xxxix See, for example, David Wyn Jones, in: Robin Stowell, editor, *The Cambridge companion to the string quartet*, 2003, p. 211.

xl Robert Simpson, *The chamber music for strings*, in: Denis Arnold and Nigel Fortune, editors, *The Beethoven companion*, 1973, pp. 242–4.

xli Thayer-Forbes, 1967, pp. 166–8.

xlii Ferdinand Ries as recounted in: Oscar George Theodore Sonneck, *Beethoven: impressions of contemporaries*, 1927, pp. 74–5.

xliii Paul Bekker, 1925, pp. 295–6.

xliv H. C. Robbins Landon, 1977, p. 503.

xlv Paul Bekker, 1925, p. 296.

xlvi Franz Wegeler, *Remembering Beethoven: the biographical notes of Franz Wegeler and Ferdinand Ries*, 1988, p. 75.

xlvii Gerhard von Breuning, 1874, English edition, 1992, pp. 98–9. Diabelli made the gift of the lithograph of Haydn's birthplace when Beethoven was in his last illness.

xlviii Doubtless Mozart would have identified with Samuel Johnson's 1755 lexicographic definition of a patron as: 'Commonly a wretch who supports with insolence, and is paid with flattery.'

xlix Leon Botstein: *Music, culture and society in Beethoven's Vienna*, in: Robert Winter and Robert Martin, editors, *The Beethoven quartet companion*, 1994, pp. 88–9.

l Tia De Nora, 1997, pp. 150–1.

li Barry Cooper, 2000, p. 73.

lii On account of Schuppanzigh's great size, Beethoven nicknamed him *Falstaff*.

liii As recounted in, *Vienna and its musical life*, in, *Haydn: The years of the Creation*, H. C. Robbins Landon, 1977, p. 25.

- As recalled in: Hans Conrad Fischer and Erich Kock, 1972, pp. 29–30.
- This annuity was set as 4000 florins, the equivalent of an upper-middle class income. However, personal misfortunes to Kinsky and Lobkowitz, combined with inflation, soon undermined its purchasing power.
- Anton Felix Schindler, *Beethoven as I knew him*, edited by Donald W. MacArdle and translated by Constance S. Jolly from the German edition of 1860, 1966, p. 50.
- Cited in: Piero Weiss and Richard Taruskin, 1984, p. 325.
- The quotations from the *AmZ* are derived from Wayne M. Senner, Robin Wallace and William Meredith, editors, *The critical reception of Beethoven's compositions by his German contemporaries*, 1999, Vol. 1.
- By way of further illustration of money values, at the period when Lichnowsky conferred his 600 florins on Beethoven, the following are typical: A clerk working for a nobleman could earn 550 florins in 1821, rising to 2,000 after twenty years of service. A teacher could earn as much as 700. A postal worker received 400 and a senior civil servant with the title of secretary 2, 500 florins. The concertmaster (conductor) of the opera received 2,400. Inflation progressively reduced the value of these sums. In later life, Beethoven paid his female servants around 130 florins a year. In comparison, a count had an income from 30,000 to 100,000 florins a year. In 1824, Beethoven offered the publisher Schott's & Sons the Ninth Symphony for 1,000 florins and the String Quartet Op. 127 for 125 florins. A concert ticket cost about 1 florin. An entire opera score typically cost 11 florins. String quartet parts were available on loan form music libraries for a relatively small charge. Derived from Leon Botstein, *Music, culture and society in Beethoven's Vienna* in: Robert Winter and Robert Martin, editors, *The Beethoven quartet companion*, 1994, p. 86.
- Emily Anderson, editor and translator, 1961, Vol. 1, Letter No. 51, pp. 57–62.
- *Ibid*, Letter No. 16, pp. 22–3.
- Theodore Albrecht, translator and editor, 1996, Vol. 1 Letter No. 34, pp. 63–4.
- Emily Anderson, editor and translator, 1961, Vol. 1, Letter No. 44, pp. 47–8.
- H. C. Robbins Landon, 1992, p. 79.
- Robert Winter and Robert Martin, editors, 1994, p. 30.
- From the recollections of Carl Czerny, see: Paul Badura-Skoda, editor, 1970, p. 4. Czerny conveyed his father's recollections of Gelineck to Beethoven's early biographer Otto Jahn.
- Peter Clive, 2001, p. 52.
- Emily Anderson, editor and translator, 1961, Vol. 1, Letter No. 9, pp. 13–15. As themes for his piano variations Beethoven would often adapt melodies derived from popular operas of the day.
- Thayer-Forbes, 1967, p. 262.
- Joseph Kerman, 1967, pp. pp. 7–8.
- See website text: *Beethoven's string quartets; The first six quartets, Op. 18*.
- Just how much Förster influenced the style and manner of Beethoven's early writing for the string quartet is debated. Some commentators do, however, consider Förster's compositions to be Beethovenish in character.
- Thayer-Forbes, 1967, pp. 261–2.
- William Henry Hadow, 1926. The words quoted derive from Hadow's *Introduction*.
- Modern-day musicologists have reservations as to the extent to which Förster's

^{lxxv} string quartets exerted a direct influence on Beethoven's own writing for the genre. For example, H. C. Robbins Landon considers, despite the proximity of these works to Beethoven's Op. 18, 'it is unlikely Beethoven benefitted from them'. See: *Haydn: the years of The Creation, 1796–1800, 1977*, p. 50. Joseph Kerman observes: 'There remains only the possibility that at certain soirées and rehearsals the young master may have picked up one tip or another from Förster in respect to minor technical details' — *The Beethoven quartets*, 1967, pp. 11–12.

lxxvi Peter Clive, 2001, p. 208 and p. 329.

lxxvii Thayer-Forbes, 1967, p. 228.

lxxviii For a contemporary portrait of Zmeskall, combined with biographical information concerning him and his connection with Beethoven, see: Beethoven House, Digital Archives, document Ley, Band VII, 178a.

lxxix A portrait of Karl Holz is reproduced in facsimile in the Beethoven House, Digital Archives, B 837.

lxxx A portrait of Joseph Mayseder is reproduced in facsimile in the Beethoven House, Digital Archives, B 618.

lxxxi Joseph de Marliave, *Beethoven's quartets*, 1961 (reprint), p. 46.

lxxxii Quoted by Robert Winter in, *Performing Beethoven quartets in their first century* in: Robert Winter and Robert Martin, editors, 1994, p. 37. Reichardt, however, deplored the manner in which Schuppanzigh 'beat the time with his foot'!

lxxxiii Thayer-Forbes, 1967, p. 228.

lxxxiv As remarked by Joseph Kerman in: *Beethoven quartet audiences: actual, potential*, ideal in: Robert Winter and Robert Martin, editors, *The Beethoven quartet companion*, 1994, p. 10

lxxxv Thayer-Forbes 1967, pp. 264–5. See also Peter Clive, 2001, p. 122.

lxxxvi The instruments in question are illustrated in: Robert Winter, and Robert Martin editors, 1994.

lxxxvii Remarking on Beethoven's contact with the Schuppanzigh Quartet, Hadow comments: '[Part] of the reason [Beethoven progressed as he did] may well be that he had at his disposal a [more] complete group of executive artists such as were not gathered together even at Eisenstadt.' William Henry Hadow, 1926. (*Introduction*).

lxxxviii Peter Clive, 2001, pp. 212–13.

lxxxix H. C. Robbins Landon, 1977, p. 505.

xc As discussed in Robert Winter and Robert Martin, editors, *The Beethoven quartet companion*, 1994, p. 150.

xci Carl Czerny remarks: 'Of the first six Violin Quartets, that in D major, No. 3 in print was the very first composed by Beethoven. On the advice of Schuppanzigh he called that in F major No. 1, although it was composed later. Ferdinand Ries confirms this: 'Of his Violin Quartets, Op. 18, he composed that in D major first of all. That in F major, which now precedes it, was originally the third.' Derived from Elliot Forbes, editor, *Thayer's life of Beethoven*, 1967, p. 261.

xcii This historical summary is derived from: Beethoven House, Digital Archives, Document, Composition, Op. 18 String Quartets.

xciii The artist Donna Dralle has created an imaginary study in pencil and watercolour titled *Beethoven stitching a notebook*. See: http://www.graphixnow.com/fine_art/images/fine_art_pgs/lvbsew.jpg

xciv See: Joseph Kerman, *Beethoven's early sketches* in: Paul Henry Lang, editor,

1971, pp. 13–36. Kerman, quoting Dr. Hans Schmidt of the Beethoven Archive Bonn, suggests nearly 400 sketch sources of various kinds have to date been identified, consisting variously of single sheets, bifolia (double sheets), bound sketchbooks and miscellaneous gatherings. Of his predisposition to set his thoughts down in draft form, Kerman concludes: 'Beethoven seems to have experienced a compulsion to get things down on paper – not only musical monographs, but also drafts of all kinds – he had a veritable commitment to the graphic act.' For a facsimile illustration of a typical two-page bifolium, of the kind Beethoven carried around with him, see: Beethoven House, Digital Archives, Library Document, Sammlung H. C. Bodmer, HCB BSK 16/24. See also: Beethoven Haus Bonn, Digital Archive *Research* and Barry Cooper, 1990, p. 77.

xcv Edward T. Cone, editor, *Roger Sessions on music: collected essays*, 1979, p. 45. The Italian musicologist Professor Giovanni Biamonti has made numerous audible recordings of many of Beethoven's sketches titled *The Unheard Beethoven*.

xcvi Gustav Nottebohm, 1979, pp. 4–7.

xcvii Alan Tyson, *Sketches and autographs*, in: Denis Arnold, and Nigel Fortune, editors. *The Beethoven companion*, 1973, pp. 443–58.

xcviii Paul Henry Lang, 1997, p. 242.

xcix Barry Cooper, 1990, p. 79.

c Most of the leaves that were removed from Grasnick 1 have subsequently been traced and identified. Two of these 'sketch leaves' are illustrated as: Beethoven House, Digital Archives, Document, Sammlung H. C. Bodmer. HCB Mh 64. Other sketches are contained on leaves that did not belong to larger sketchbooks. Specimens are now held in the Bibliothèque National as MS 71 and MS 89. Additional sources are known as Bonn Mh 64 and Mth 65. See: Douglas Porter Johnson, editor, 1985, p. 72 and p. 78 and William Kinderman, editor, 2005, pp. 323–4.

ci Douglas Porter Johnson, editor, 1985, p. 87.

cii *Ibid* pp. 89–98: Autograph 19E also includes sketches for the Violin Sonata, Op. 23; Piano Variations, Op. 34; and the Piano Concerto in C minor, Op. 37.

ciii *Ibid* pp. 101–6.

civ Stephanie Schroeder, Programme notes to the Alexander String Quartet.

cv The rather complex history of the gestation of the Op 18 String Quartets is admirably summarised by Beethoven's biographer Alexander Thayer. We quote here from Thayer's summation of the works' chronology: '[The] composition of the Quartets was begun in 1798, that in D, the third, being first undertaken. This was followed by that in F and soon after, or simultaneously. Work was begun on that in G, which was originally deigned as the second; but, as with that in F, was completed earlier; this was designated as the second by Beethoven and that in G became in point of time the third. The Quartet in F was finished in its original shape by 25 June 1799, on which day he gave it to Amenda; he revised it later.' [Thayer refers the reader to the Beethovenhaus for the original version.] Thayer continues: 'He then wrote the one in A (now No. 5), intending it to be the fourth; in this he seems to have made use of a *motif* invented at an earlier period. The Quartets in B-flat and C minor followed, the latter being, perhaps, the last. The definitive elaboration of the Quartets then appeared in two sets from the press of Mollo. It is likely that the first three, at least, were in the hands of the publisher before the end of 1800, as proved by the letter to Hoffmeister [see main text]. The first three appeared in the summer of 1801 and were advertised as on sale by Nägeli in Zurich already in July; they were mentioned in the *Allgemeine musikalische Zeitung* on 26 August ... In October of the same year the last three appeared and Mollo advertised them in the *Wiener Zeitung* of 28 October.' Elliot Forbes, editor, *Thayer's life of Beethoven*, 1967, pp. 262–6.

cvi William Kinderman, editor, 2005, p. 324.

cvii Prince Lobkowitz's notes of authorisation to his cashier to make the required payments to Beethoven for the String Quartets Op. 18, still survive and are preserved in the Lobkowitz family archives. The first of these was for the Quartets Op. 18, Nos. 1–3 and is dated 7 October 1799; Beethoven made acknowledgement the following week. Lobkowitz's second payment, for the Quartets Op. 18, Nos. 4–6, was made in early October 1800 to which the composer once more made acknowledgement on 18 October. See, Theodore Albrecht, 1996 Vol. 1, Letters Nos. 29, 30, 31 and 32, pp. 54–62.

cviii Barry Cooper, 2000, p. 93.

cix H. C. Robbins Landon, 1977, pp. 503–5. Landon elaborates: 'No doubt the younger generation much preferred Beethoven's language and considered Op. 18 the greatest achievement [to date] in the field of the quartet.' He further suggests: 'Haydn's Op. 77 may even have seemed something of an anti-climax after the great spiritual heights of Op. 76.' He conjectures: 'What would ... have been [Haydn's] feelings as he noticed a certain condescension on the part of the younger "pro-Beethoven aristocracy" A certain arrogance on the part of Beethoven himself?'

cx Emily Anderson, editor and translator: 1961, Vol. 1, letter No. 47, pp. 50–2.

cxi *Ibid*, Vol. 1, Letter No. 48, pp. 52–4. A date suggested for this letter is June 1801. For a facsimile reproduction of this letter, together with the transcription of the text in the original German, see: Beethoven House, Digital Archives, Document, Sammlung H. C. Bodmer, HCB Br 267.

cxii For a facsimile reproduction of the Title Page, see: Beethoven House, Digital Archives, Document C 18/45.

cxiii Emily Anderson, editor and translator, 1961, Vol. 1, Letter No. 57, pp. 73–4. This letter dates from 8 April 1802 and is reproduced in facsimile on the Beethoven House, Digital Archives, Document NE 197. In this, Beethoven's reference to the mistakes in the String Quartets Op. 18, Nos. 4–6 are described as 'wriggling about like fish in the water'.

cxiv Maynard Solomon, 1977, p. 100.

cxv See, for example, the Introduction to Jáno Kárpáti, *Bartók's chamber music*, 1994.

cxvi Paul Griffiths, 1983, p. 81.

cxvii H. C. Robbins Landon, 1977, p. 502.

cxviii Bernhard Jacobson Liner notes to: *Ludwig van Beethoven; The early string quartets*, Op. 18, Alban Berg Quartet, EMI, 1981.

cxix William Henry Hadow, 1926. The words quoted are derived from the Introduction, pp. 7–8.

cxx H. C. Robbins Landon, 1977, p. 285.

cxxi David Wyn Jones in: Robin Stowell, editor, *The Cambridge companion to the string quartet*, 2003, p. 211.

cxxii Philip Radcliffe, 1978, p. 15.

cxxiii See: Beethoven House, Digital Archives, Document NE 119, NE22.

cxxiv See also Richard Kramer, *On the autograph of Beethoven's String Quartet in F major*, Op. 59, No. 1 in: Christoph Wolff and Robert Riggs, *The string* quartets of Haydn, Mozart and Beethoven: studies of the autograph manuscripts: a conference at Isham Memorial Library, March 15–17, 1979, 1980, p. 230.

[xxxv] Douglas Johnson: *1794–1795: Beethoven's early development* in: Alan Tyson, editor, *Beethoven studies 3*, 1982, p. 2.

[xxxvi] William Kinderman, editor, 2005, p. 13. Other authorities remark in similar fashion, as for example: 'Almost certainly, Beethoven had planned the six pieces as a set from the beginning, presumably with Mozart's six Quartets dedicated to Haydn and with several of Haydn's own six-headed opuses as his models.' Source: Robert Winter and Robert Martin, editors, 1994, p. 150.

[xxxvii] William Henry Hadow, 1926, derived from Introduction, pp. 7–8.

[xxxviii] Maynard Solomon, 1977, p. 101.

[xxxix] William Kinderman, editor, 2005, p. 55.

[xxx] Joseph Kerman, 1967, pp.11–12.

[xxxi] Bernhard Jacobson Liner notes to: *Ludwig van Beethoven; The early string quartets*, Op. 18, Alban Berg Quartet, EMI, 1981.

[xxxii] William Kinderman, editor, 2005, p. 14.

[xxxiii] H. C. Robbins Landon, 1977, pp. 511–12.

[xxxiv] For a commentary on Beethoven's constructional procedures, within the format of sonata form, see: William Henry Hadow, 1926, notes to pp. 11–12.

[xxxv] Bernhard Jacobson Liner notes to: *Ludwig van Beethoven; The early string quartets*, Op. 18, Alban Berg Quartet, EMI, 1981.

[xxxvi] H. C. Robbins Landon, 1977, pp. 511–12.

[xxxvii] William Henry Hadow, 1926, pp. 7–8.

[xxxviii] Tully Potter in: Robin Stowell, editor, *The Cambridge companion to the string quartet*, 2003, p. 43.

[xxxix] Robert Winter and Robert Martin, editors, 1994, p. 122 and pp. 137–8.

[cl] As quoted in: David Blum, *The art of quartet playing: the Guarneri Quartet in conversation with David Blum*, 1986, p. 98.

[cli] David Blum, *The art of quartet playing: the Guarneri Quartet in conversation with David Blum*, 1986, pp. 157-8.

[clii] For a discussion of the reception of Beethoven's music in the *AmZ*, see: Robin Wallace, *Beethoven's critics: aesthetic dilemmas and resolutions during the composer's lifetime*, 1986.

[cliii] Wayne M. Senner, Robin Wallace and William Meredith, editors, 1999, Vol. 1, p. 153 and Robert Winter and Robert Martin, editors, *The Beethoven quartet companion*, 1994, p. 68. In particular see: Leon Botstein: *Music, culture and society in Beethoven's Vienna* at pp. 91–2.

[cliv] Theodore Albrecht, 1996 Vol. 1, Letter No. 114, pp. 177–8.

[clv] Wayne M. Senner, Robin Wallace and William Meredith, editors, 1999, Vol. 1, pp. 153–4. This review is also cited in, Joseph de Marliave, *Beethoven's quartets*, 1925 (reprint 1961), pp. 47–8.

[clvi] H. C. Robbins Landon, *Haydn: chronicle and works – Haydn, the late years, 1801–1809*, 1977, pp. 408–9.

[clvii] Louis Spohr, *Louis Spohr's autobiography*, London: Longman, Green, Longman, Roberts, & Green, 1865, pp. 122–3.

[clviii] Romberg considered the Op. 18 String Quartets to be 'absurd' and the Razumovsky Quartets to be 'unplayable'.

[clix] Wayne M. Senner, Robin Wallace and William Meredith, editors, 1999, Vol.

1, pp. 157–8.

ᵈ Derived from: Robert Winter, *Performing Beethoven quartets in their first century*, in, Robert Winter, and Robert Martin, editors, *The Beethoven quartet companion*, 1994, pp. 43–4.

ᵈⁱ Joseph de Marliave, 1925 (reprint 1961), pp. 48–9.

ᵈⁱⁱ Anton Felix Schindler, *Beethoven as I knew him*, edited by Donald W. MacArdle and translated by Constance S. Jolly from the German edition of 1860, 1966, pp. 111–12.

ᵈⁱⁱⁱ Joseph de Marliave, 1925, (reprint 1961), pp. 22–3.

ᵈⁱᵛ Arthur Shepherd, 1935, p. 25.

ᵈᵛ Joseph Kerman, 1967, pp. 85–6.

ᵈᵛⁱ Philip Radcliffe, 1978, pp. 44–5.

ᵈᵛⁱⁱ Bernhard Jacobson Liner notes to: *Ludwig van Beethoven; The early string quartets*, Op. 18, Alban Berg Quartet, EMI, 1981.

ᵈᵛⁱⁱⁱ H. C. Robbins Landon, 1977, pp. 504–5.

ᵈⁱˣ Joseph Kerman, 1967, pp. 85–6.

ᵈˣ William Kinderman, editor, *The string quartets of Beethoven*, Urbana, 2005, p. 54.

ᵈˣⁱ Michael Broyles, 1987, p. 47.

ᵈˣⁱⁱ Philip Radcliffe, 1978, p. 45.

ᵈˣⁱⁱⁱ Robert Simpson: *The chamber music for strings* in: Denis Arnold and Nigel Fortune, editors, *The Beethoven companion*, 1973, pp. 248–9.

ᵈˣⁱᵛ Basil Lam, 1975 p. 14.

ᵈˣᵛ Quoted in: Barry Cooper, 2000, pp. 80–1. See also Elliot Forbes, 1967, p. 261.

ᵈˣᵛⁱ Wilhelm Altmann, *Preface* to Eulenberg miniature score, 1911.

ᵈˣᵛⁱⁱ Beethoven House, Digital Archives, Document, BH 84. The Amenda version of the F major Quartet has been recorded by a number of artists including the Pro Arte Quartet issued by Laurel 116.

ᵈˣᵛⁱⁱⁱ Joseph Kerman, *Beethoven quartet audiences: actual, potential, ideal* in: Robert Winter and Robert Martin, editors, *The Beethoven quartet companion*, 1994, pp. 8–9.

ᵈˣⁱˣ Emily Anderson, 1961, Vol. 1, Letter No, 53, pp. 63–5. For a facsimile reproduction of this letter, together with the transcription of the text in the original German, see: Beethoven House, Digital Archives, Document, Sammlung H. C. Bodmer, HCB BBr 1.

ᵈˣˣ Robert Simpson: *The chamber music for strings* in: Denis Arnold and Nigel Fortune, editors, *The Beethoven companion*, 1973, p. 244.

ᵈˣˣⁱ Paul Bekker, 1925, pp. 310–11.

ᵈˣˣⁱⁱ Barry Cooper, 2000, p. 92.

ᵈˣˣⁱⁱⁱ Joseph Kerman, 1967, p. 32.

ᵈˣˣⁱᵛ Wayne M. Senner, Robin Wallace and William Meredith, editors, *The critical reception of Beethoven's compositions by his German contemporaries*, Lincoln: University of Nebraska Press, in association with the American Beethoven Society and the Ira F. Brilliant Center for Beethoven Studies, San José State University, 1999, Vol. 1, pp.153–4.

ᵈˣˣᵛ *Ibid*, 1999, Vol. 1, pp. 156–7. In the earlier concert season of 1824 we have further evidence of the growing popularity of Beethoven's string quartets. The February issue of the *Berliner Allgemeine musikalische Zeitung* for this year includes a review of a concert held in Berlin in which quartets by Haydn,

Mozart and Beethoven were performed. The reviewer cites 'one [Beethoven] quartet in particular ... received distinguished applause'. Unfortunately the work in question is not identified. Such was the popularity of the piece, however, it had to be played again at two further concerts. The reviewer adds a characteristic Beethovenian-style remark: 'Mozart may suit the fiery temperament of the players less than Beethoven's bold, often bizarre fantasy. But the energy and romanticism that is expressed in most tone paintings of this genius, who has retreated into himself and carries within himself a world of musical notes, does excite feeling less than Mozart.' Cited in the same source as the foregoing at p. 59.

[clxxvi] The concert in question took place on 11 February 1849. As derived from Joseph de Marliave, 1961 (reprint), pp. 48–9.

[clxxvii] Pamela J. Willetts, 1970, pp. 55–8.

[clxxviii] Marion Scott, 1940, p. 253.

[clxxix] William Henry Hadow, 1926, p. 14.

[clxxx] William Kinderman, editor, *The string quartets of Beethoven*, 2005, p. 14.

[clxxxi] Joseph Kerman, 1967, p. 32.

[clxxxii] Bernhard Jacobson Liner notes to: *Ludwig van Beethoven; The early string quartets*, Op. 18, Alban Berg Quartet, EMI, 1981.

[clxxxiii] Basil Lam, 1975, p. 13.

[clxxxiv] David Wyn Jones in: Robin Stowell, editor, *The Cambridge companion to the string quartet*, 2003, p. 211.

[clxxxv] Barry Cooper, 1990, p. 130.

[clxxxvi] The expression here is that of Joseph Kerman's in: Robert Winter and Robert Martin, editors, *The Beethoven quartet companion*, 1994, p. 151.

[clxxxvii] Arthur Shepherd, 1935, p. 11.

[clxxxviii] Marion Scott, 1940, p. 253.

[clxxxix] Joseph de Marliave, 1961 (reprint), pp. 5–6.

[cxc] Joseph Kerman, 1967, p. 30.

[cxci] Rebecca Clarke, *The Beethoven quartets as a player sees them*, in: *Musical Times. Special Issue*: Vol. VIII, No. 2, 1927, pp. 178–90.

[cxcii] Adapted from: William Kinderman, 1997, p. 42 and William Kinderman *Beethoven* in: *Nineteenth-century piano music* in: Larry R. Todd, editor, 2004, pp. 56-7.

[cxciii] Philip Radcliffe, 1978, p. 27. Tovey used almost identical words to those of Radcliffe in his estimation of the *Adagio*, describing it as 'one of Beethoven's early great tragic movements alongside that of the Sonata Op. 10, No. 3'. See: Donald Francis Tovey, 1944, p. 119.

[cxciv] Conrad Wilson, 2003, p. 16.

[cxcv] David Wyn Jones in: Robin Stowell, editor, *The Cambridge companion to the string quartet*, 2003, p. 211.

[cxcvi] Arthur Shepherd, 1935, p. 12.

[cxcvii] Bernhard Jacobson Liner notes to: *Ludwig van Beethoven; The early string quartets*, Op. 18, *The Alban Berg Quartet*, EMI, 1981.

[cxcviii] See: Barry Cooper, 2000, p. 93.

[cxcix] See: Robert Simpson: *The chamber music for strings* in: Denis Arnold and Nigel Fortune, editors, *The Beethoven companion*, 1973, pp. 248–9.

[cc] Nicolas Slonimsky, 2000, p. 158. Beethoven makes use of the extremely rare 128th note values.

[cci] As suggested by Robert Winter, and Robert Martin, editors, 1994, p. 154.

[ccii] Elliot Forbes, editor, *Thayer's life of Beethoven*, 1967, p. 261.
[cciii] William Henry Hadow, 1926. (*Introduction*).
[cciv] Basil Lam, 1975, p. 15.
[ccv] By way of illustration: WoO 65, twenty-four variations on Vincenzio Righini's aria *Venni Amore*; WoO 66, thirteen variations on Carl Dittersdorf's aria *Es war einmal ein altar Mann*; WoO 67, eight variations for four hands on a theme by Count Waldstein; WoO 68, twelve variations on a theme from Jacob Haibel's ballet *La nozza disturbate* — a dozen or so more could be listed.
[ccvi] David Wyn Jones in: Robin Stowell, editor, *The Cambridge companion to the string quartet*, 2003, p. 211.
[ccvii] Wayne M. Senner, Robin Wallace and William Meredith, editors, *The critical reception of Beethoven's compositions by his German contemporaries*, Lincoln: University of Nebraska Press, in association with the American Beethoven Society and the Ira F. Brilliant Center for Beethoven Studies, San José State University, 1999, Vol. 1, pp.156–7.
[ccviii] Joseph de Marliave, 1961 (reprint), pp. 5–6. De Marliave points out passages later in the music that he finds have similarities with the *Andante* in the Second Symphony, at the close of which he states 'one feels the weight of an endless grief'.
[ccix] Rolland, Romain, 1917, p. 179.
[ccx] Paul Bekker, 1925, p. 311.
[ccxi] Joseph Kerman, 1967, p. 41.
[ccxii] Donald Tovey is frequently cited for being the authority for the statement that Beethoven always used the word *scherzo* in its etymological sense. For example, see: Nicolas Slonimsky, 2000, p. 158.
[ccxiii] Basil Lam, 1975, p. 15.
[ccxiv] See, for example, the remarks of Arthur Shepherd, 1935, p. 12 and Robert Winter and Robert Martin, editors, *The Beethoven quartet companion*, 1994, p. 154.
[ccxv] David Wyn Jones in: Robin Stowell, editor, *The Cambridge companion to the string quartet*, 2003, p. 212.
[ccxvi] William Kinderman, editor, *The string quartets of Beethoven*, Urbana, 2005, p. 54. Michael Broyles, 1987, p. 54.
[ccxvii] Marion Scott, 1940, p. 253.
[ccxviii] Barry Cooper, 2000, pp. 93–4.
[ccxix] Joseph Kerman. 1967, p. 43.
[ccxx] Phillip Radcliffe, 1978, p. 28.
[ccxxi] Joseph de Marliave, 1961, pp. 5–6.
[ccxxii] Bernhard Jacobson Liner notes to: *Ludwig van Beethoven; The early string quartets*, Op. 18, *The Alban Berg Quartet*, EMI, 1981.
[ccxxiii] Joseph de Marliave, 1961 (reprint), pp. 5–6.
[ccxxiv] Arthur Shepherd, 1935, p. 13.
[ccxxv] Robert Simpson *The chamber music for strings* in: Denis Arnold and Nigel Fortune, editors, *The Beethoven companion*, 1973, p. 249.
[ccxxvi] Charles Rosen, 2002, p. 124. Rosen also draws attention to Beethoven's insistent use of the minor mode as a pre-figuration of the sonatas of Chopin, Schumann and Liszt.
[ccxxvii] Maynard Solomon, 1977, p. 102.
[ccxxviii] Harold Truscott, 1968, p. 27. Gerald Abraham also shares Truscott's

        opinion, see: Gerald Abraham, *Beethoven's Chamber Music*, in: *The Age of Beethoven, The New Oxford History of Music, Vol. VIII*, Gerald Abraham, editor, 1988, pp. 282–3.
[ccxxix] Robert Winter, and Robert Martin, editors, 1994, p. 154.
[ccxxx] Phillip Radcliffe, 1978, p. 29.

STRING QUARTET IN F MAJOR, OP. 18, NO. 1

'As the work stands it is gratifying to the performer and offers pleasant not over-difficult problems to the listener, and shows the skill of the composer in handling the quartet instruments, among which the violin is still given the most prominent place.'

Paul Bekker, *Beethoven*, 1925, p. 311.

'The Quartet in F is the biggest and in obvious ways the most impressive [of the Op. 18]. Its first and last movements, besides lasting appreciably longer than corresponding movements in the other quartets, make a more brilliant effect — the first by means of thematic manipulation, the last by proliferating form. The second movement, if not quite the longest slow movement, is the only one in the minor mode and by far the most emotional. The *Scherzo* ... runs the fastest and runs the farthest in harmonic range.'

Joseph Kerman, *The Beethoven Quartets*, 1967, p. 30.

'Ultimately, individual works of art are all that exist, and that is how they are to be experienced ... We cannot get out of Op. 18, No.1 what Beethoven put into it if we listen to it with the ears we use for the *Grosse Fuge* or even the *Razumowsky* Quartets. And it is what the composer put into each work that is what we should try to find, rather than damaging the concentration of our perception by telling ourselves what it was that he was not yet ready to say.'

Robert Simpson, *The Chamber Music for Strings* in: Denis Arnold and Nigel Fortune, *The Beethoven Companion*, 1973, p. 242.

'The young master who could command such resources [as here evident] had no need to imitate even Haydn or Mozart, and to adopt an attitude of patronage to this quartet is mere impertinence ... Perhaps because it was completely composed twice over, this quartet is the most varied in expression, and the most masterly in overall design, of the six works comprising Op. 18.'

Basil Lam, *Beethoven String Quartets*, 1975, pp. 14–18.

In our overview of the String Quartets Op. 18, Nos. 1–6 we remarked that Beethoven placed the F major Quartet, No. 1 at the head of the series since it is 'the grandest and most immediately impressive'.[i] We recall the influence of Beethoven's friend, the violinist Ignaz Schuppanzigh, regarding his suggested ordering of the compositions. In the case of the F major Quartet he encouraged Beethoven to give it first place for being 'the most brilliant' and, on the surface, 'the most impressive piece'. Furthermore, its first movement and finale are the longest movements in this position in the entire opus. In his survey of the composer's musical evolution, Michael Broyles discusses what he describes as the 'stylistic dualism' that is to be found in early Beethoven. This disposes him to find 'pairing' within contemporaneous compositions. He thereby pairs the first of the String Quartets of Op. 18 with the First Symphony, Op. 21.[ii] Philip Radcliffe also draws attention to the parallels to be found within Beethoven's early compositions, citing from this period the Piano Sonata in B-flat major, Op. 22 that he considers has the most in common with Op. 18, No. 1: 'Its Adagio is less poignant than that of the Quartet in F, but the two movements, both in 9/8 time, have the same mixture of flowing Italianate melody with rich and nostalgic harmony of the Teutonic kind.'[iii] In his estimation, Robert Simpson was unequivocal that Op. 18, No. 1 was the strongest and most concentrated of all six works, remarking: 'The F major shows the most perfect mastery of all the early quartets, both in equality of part-writing and succinctness (as well as breadth) of form.'[iv] Basil Lam was so moved by the composition as to enthuse: 'Beethoven's polyphonic treatment is great Beethoven of any period, and reveals the full power of the quartet medium in a way without precedent in any of the masterpieces previously given to it.'[v]

The creation origins of the String Quartet in F major

are intimately associated with the clergyman-violinist Karl Amenda. Beethoven became acquainted with him in 1799 at the chamber-music sessions held in the household of Prince Lobkowitz where Amenda was employed. He soon became Beethoven's closest friend; it is a measure of the closeness of the composer's feelings towards Amenda that he was one of the first to whom Beethoven confided the onset of his deafness. When Amenda had to return to his native Courland, Beethoven made him a gift of the first version of the F major quartet. On 25 June 1799, Beethoven wrote to Amenda inscribing on the first violin part: 'Take this quartet as ... memories of our friendship, and whenever you play it recall the days we spent together and the sincere affection felt for you then and which will always be felt by ... your warm and true friend Beethoven.'[vi] The Quartet remained in the possession of the Amada family to the end of the nineteenth century. In 1904 the possessor of the Quartet, Frau Pastor Anna Kawall née Amenda, allowed the work to be published.[vii] Today the Amenda version of the F major String Quartet survives in the Beethoven House Archives in the form of a set of parts in the hand of a professional copyist.[viii] In this copy the piece is described in Beethoven's hand as 'Quartetto No. II', implying that, at that stage in the Op. 18 compositional sequence, the F-major Quartet was not planned to commence the series.

Reflecting more generally on these circumstances, Joseph Kerman comments: 'The very existence of this music in two forms tells us something about the ambience of the string quartet at that period. It tells us that pieces circulated in what might be called "trial versions", works in progress that would evidently be touched up or recast after being played and discussed by friends and patrons. The "finalization" represented by publication could be left for later.'[ix]

On 1 July 1801, Beethoven wrote to Amenda primarily

to confide in him the realization he was losing his hearing. Towards the end of this moving letter he refers to the F major quartet with the plea: 'Be sure not to hand on to anybody your quartet, in which I have made some drastic alterations. For only now have I learnt how to write quartets.'[x] A comparison of the two versions of the music is illuminating insofar as it reveals Beethoven's capacity for self-criticism and self-improvement. Authorities who have studied the composer's surviving sketches, bear testimony to the rigour with which he revised both the smallest motifs and the largest compositional units, and how to make the music sound in terms of the voicing and scoring for the individual instruments so as to bring the four parts into more equal prominence. Simpson likens Beethoven's revisions to 'an absorbing study in clarification and in the closer articulation of counterpoint and form'.[xi] In his comparison of the details of the two versions of Beethoven's quartet writing, Paul Bekker considers the revisions display 'a freer, more soloistic treatment of the accompanying parts, a clearer individualisation of the violoncello cello part and greater tonal delicacy in the ensemble effects'.[xii] Based on his study of Beethoven's sketches, Barry Cooper draws attention to the changes in texture that he finds 'becomes smoother and more linear' and in which 'motifs are made to stand out more clearly, while fussy accompaniment figures such as oscillating patterns are eliminated'.[xiii] One illustration of this aspect of Beethoven's newfound self-control is that a particular gruppetto figure (a turn motif) that occurs in the first version no fewer than 130 times is reduced to a leaner 104 repetitions in the published version.[xiv]

Beethoven's piano pupil Ferdinand Ries made an arrangement of the Op. 18 String Quartets for piano trio, prompting a review of them in the 16 July 1806 issue of the *Allgemeine musikalische Zeitung:* 'Whoever is concerned with hearing an ingenious composition and making it available for others to hear, let him acquire them, particularly No. 1 (F major), which in the original is also one of the reviewer's favourites of these quartets and which can also be played on the pianoforte much better than No. 2 (G major).' The reviewer commended the quality of the publisher's engraving for being free from errors, adding 'that is not a trifle in such music!'[xv] Twenty years later, the Op. 18 String Quartets had long been assimilated into the concert repertoire. We infer this from a review of the compositions that appeared in the *AmZ's* sister music journal the *Berliner Allgemeine musikalische Zeitung*. In the issue for 22 November 1826 the writer expressed caution concerning the composer's most recent ventures into the genre of quartet writing but found favour in his early works: 'Beethoven showed himself worthy of his forerunners in the first quartet in F major with that genius that we admire in astonishment from the oldest up to his most recent artistic creations, even if we cannot always grasp them and discover the context for the ideas. These older quartets [Op. 18] are nevertheless quite clear, grand, and new in invention, as in the combination of harmonies.' The concertmaster for the quartet series that had prompted this review was Karl Möser, then a leading figure in Berlin's music scene. The reviewer praised him for 'comprehending the spirit of Haydn's humour, Mozart's soul, and Beethoven's sublime genius'.[xvi]

Concerning the early reception of Beethoven's chamber music in France, something of this may be discerned from the following circumstances. In the winter of 1847–8, the violinist Théophile Tilmant founded the *Société de musique classique*. This society played several Beethoven quartets at regular intervals, especially those of Op. 18. In the programme of its opening concert in 1849, the Quartet in F Op. 18 was performed. The critic of the *Revue et Gazette musicale de Paris* recorded: 'The originality of the great symphonic writer already breaks through the influence and manner of Mozart in brilliant flashes; the work was performed with fine ensemble and subtlety of feeling.'[xvii]

In our Preface we have noted that in England *The Beethoven Quartet Society* pioneered the performance of the composer's string quartets. In their very first recital, held in 1845, the players gave a rendering of Op. 18, No.1. Later in the season the entire Beethoven quartet cycle was performed with the exception of the *Grosse Fuge*.[xviii]

Beethoven designates the first movement of the F-major Quartet *Allegro con brio*, a directive to perform the music at 'a fast tempo with spirit'. The opening motif has the power to seize the listener's immediate attention. Perhaps a parallel may be found in the strident opening notes of the String Quartet Op. 95 (*Quartetto Serioso*). Beethoven's manner in the F major has been described variously as; 'beautifully incisive'[xix]; 'crisp ... unforgettable'[xx]; 'the very touchstone of motivic integration in the High Classical style'[xxi]; and 'full of fits and starts based on heady, thematic, rhythmic and harmonic contrast'[xxii]. In his commentary to the recording of the work by *The Alban Berg Quartet*, Bernhard Jacobson draws attention to Beethoven's originality: '[In] idiom and mood, the riveting unison principle theme of the *Allegro con brio* immediately raises Beethoven-ness to a new power.' He invokes the composer's later dramatic quartet opening to which we have just alluded: '[Here] is the same man as we find in the pithier unison opening of the F minor Quartet, Op. 95 of 1810.'[xxiii] The manner in which Beethoven's invests such vigour and animation in the first movement, derived from the pervasive rhythm of the opening theme, disposed Lam to dismiss as 'absurd' the notion that in early Beethoven he was 'cautiously following Haydn and Mozart'. Although Beethoven may not have been following his former teacher 'cautiously', Lam does concede the composer's debt to Haydn is evident; he cites an early version of the opening theme being reminiscent of the older master's Quartet in B flat, Op. 50 No. 1.[xxiv] Likewise, David Wyn Jones finds Beethoven's F major Quartet to be 'the most obviously Haydnesque work in the Op. 18'. He draws attention to the opening movement of Haydn's quartet in D major, Op. 76, No. 2, which, as he observes, 'was a very recent example of this kind of concentrated writing for the medium'. He also suggests the first movement of Haydn's Quartet Op. 50, No. 3 in E flat may also have been a stimulus to Beethoven.[xxv]

A comparison between the published edition of the F major Quartet and that of the Amenda version reveals the extent to which Beethoven modified his thoughts so as to refine the overall proportions of the movement. In this context Cooper draws attention to the frequent deletions Beethoven made in order to achieve the balance he required; we have previously cited, by way of illustration, the curtailment of the number of occurrences of the opening figuration. Other transformations were more Draconian: 'In the first movement of the Quartet Op. 18, No. 1, Beethoven originally planned both halves to be repeated, as is clear from the early version he sent to Karl Amenda; but when he undertook a thorough revision of the quartet the second repeat was cancelled.'[xxvi]

The opening of the first movement that springs forth seemingly so spontaneously caused Beethoven a great deal of trouble as he reshaped his first thoughts to the finished 'sharply defined profile'.[xxvii] Reflecting on its compositional origins — as revealed in the composer's surviving sketches — Arthur Shepherd draws attention to Beethoven's characteristic, and painstaking, striving for simplicity: 'It is difficult to believe that so blithe and naïve a theme, as that which launches this first quartet, is one of those laboriously wrought ideas that found its definite form only after much contemplation.'[xxviii] No fewer than sixteen pages exist in the composer's sketchbooks for the period 1798–9 and 1800 (see our remarks to String Quartets Op. 18, Nos. 1–6). These reveal, in Marion Scott's words, 'Beethoven chiselling his first subject' and then, not satisfied, submitting it to more 'refining and retouching'.[xxix]

Joseph de Marliave offered a somewhat mixed estimation of the F major Quartet's first movement. He regarded it as 'an interesting example of Beethoven's technical brilliance' and of his skill 'in working a theme', a device he considered 'had been carried to perfection by his predecessors'. But in his judgment the music has 'too many passages of unison and harmonic padding ... the young musician [shows] mastery over form [but] at the same time a certain failure of inspiration'. He more generously acknowledged the extent to which Beethoven's creation, regarded as a whole, had moved many of the composer's contemporaries and later composers such as Louis Spohr. The latter, de Marliave noted, went so far as to declare the piece to be no less than 'the artist's masterpiece and the summit of possible achievement in the quartet genre'. This was too much for de Marliave who responded: 'Time has changed this sweeping opinion and the movement is now considered a fluent but not remarkably interesting work: brilliant but [with] superficial colouring [and] passing emotions.'[xxx] In support of Spohr, Kerman comments: 'Louis Spohr considered Beethoven's Quartet in F to be the ideal model in its genre; as an academic classicist par excellence, Spohr holds little interest for musicians today, but he was no mean connoisseur of the classical style, and something of a specialist in formal models.'[xxxi]

Beethoven's *Death Centenary* (1927) prompted many

re-evaluations of the composer's works. The instrumentalist Rebecca Clarke singled out for comment the F major String Quartet, as perceived from the perspective of the performer. Concerning the interpretation of the first movement, she wrote: 'Great accuracy is necessary ... in which the abrupt and pithy subject is continually tossed from one player to another, so that the joints must dovetail very neatly; and they must be played with the same tone colour in order to prevent the whole from sounding disjointed.'[xxxii]

The second movement is headed *Adagio affettuoso ed appassionato* — 'slow tempo with tender feeling and with passion'. In this regard, Beethoven was here combining two somewhat disparate expressions: the term *affettuoso* deriving from the eighteenth century and *appassionato* belonging to the nineteenth. Radcliffe comments: '[These] unusually elaborate directions suggest that Beethoven felt himself to be writing a specially emotional piece of music.' Remarking more generally on the composer's adoption of a minor key for this movement, he makes the further observation: 'Haydn and Mozart wrote surprisingly few slow movements in minor keys, especially in their later works; those by Beethoven are more numerous and almost all of exceptional quality.' He cites the very sombre ad passionate *Largo e mesto* from the D major Piano Sonata, Op. 10, No. 3. Contemporaneous with the F major Quartet, this music has been described as 'one of the great tragic utterances in early Beethoven' in which 'struggle' and 'resignation' intertwine within sonata form to yield the effect of 'light dispelling darkness'.[xxxiii] Radcliffe adds: 'The *Adagio* of this F major Quartet has something of the same passion, but is considerably more restrained.' In his summation he pronounces the *Adagio* to be 'the most striking part of the Quartet ... a fine specimen of Beethoven's early style in its more Italianate vein, with suggestions of Mozart, but with bolder outlines and stronger emphasis.'xxxiv

The atmosphere prevailing has been likened to that of 'an operatic scena, nocturnal and Italianate, with the first violin, joined later by the cello, singing in a *bel canto* lament over a softly pulsating accompaniment'.xxxv Jones likens the passage to a dialogue between the two instruments with evocations of a duet of the kind to be found in the slow movements of Haydn's String Quartet Op. 20, No. 2 and Mozart's *Hunt* Quartet, K. 458.xxxvi At every turn there is 'a frank avowal of a romantic impulse ... the romanticism of Beethoven's early period'.xxxvii The music is 'self-consciously affecting' but perhaps undermined by 'an element of sentimentality'.xxxviii The first violin dominates over a soft dynamic level requiring Beethoven to call for *ppp* (*pianissimo*) 'very soft' – a rare example of such a designation in his scores.xxxix The mood is also sometimes troubled with some of the nervous energy and concentration of the first movement casting their spell over the *Adagio affettuoso ed appassionato*.xl Here we catch a glimpse of the future nineteenth-century Beethoven 'in characteristic explosions of dynamic force and lightning flashes of rapid notes'.xli Perhaps the young Franz Schubert was influenced here by the music's turbulence when he came to write his great String Quintet in C major, D. 956?xlii

We recall the F major Quartet had its creation origins in the form of a gift to the clergyman-violinist Karl Amenda. This connection assumes particular significance in relation to the mood prevailing in the second movement. It may possess a poetic-Shakespearian association as we learn from Beethoven's biographer Alexander Thayer. He recalls an occasion when Beethoven played through a piano reduction of the *Adagio* for Amanda. In his account Thayer sets aside his typical formal style and describes the movement as 'glorious'. He relates that at the close of his performance

Beethoven asked Amenda: 'What thought had been awakened by it?' Amanda responded: 'It pictured for me the parting of two lovers.' 'Good!' remarked Beethoven: 'I thought of the scene in the burial vault in *Romeo and Juliet.*'[xliii]

Musicologists have justification for approaching such anecdotes with caution, given the manner in which the creation origins of Beethoven's work have been mythologised. It is known, for example, that when Anton Schindler asked Beethoven the meaning permeating his Piano Sonata in D minor, Op. 31, No. 2 — *The Tempest* — the composer is alleged to have responded: 'Just read Shakespeare's *Tempest.*' This is now considered to be one of Schindler's fabrications. With regard to Amenda's alleged recollections, William Hadow was of the view: 'It is dangerous to lay any emphasis on such statements as this. Even when they are seriously made — and Beethoven was not always serious — they convey no more than a very general hint of very limited application.' Hadow continues: 'Music cannot be translated into terms of anything other than itself; and all we can safely say here is that the opening melody is of extraordinary passion and poignancy, and that the manner of writing is largely in duet.'[xliv] Lam mediates: 'Even without such evidence, [as the *Romeo and Juliet* anecdote] a dramatic element could be recognised in this very beautiful piece, which has an emotional expansiveness that never appears in Beethoven's purely personal slow movements ... It was not until the *Eroica* that Beethoven surpassed the tragic eloquence of this *Adagio.*' Lam is one who also finds a connection with Beethoven's writing and its influence on his young contemporary: 'Schubert remembered, in the slow movement of his C major Quintet, the moving effect of this figure when given to the cello.'[xlv] Cooper cites compelling evidence in favour of the anecdote: 'Among the sketches to this movement are [the remarks] "il prend le tombeau" ...

"il se tue" and "les derniers soupirs".' Cooper surmises: 'There is no proof that these refer to [Shakespeare's'] play but the comments certainly fit the situation.'

Jones lends credence to Amenda's account by recalling the large number of string quartets that were issued in Vienna in the 1780s and 1790s and which were arrangements of vocal numbers from popular operas and oratorios; Gluck, Mozart and Salieri contributed to the genre. Beethoven himself wrote several sets of piano variations that he adopted from popular melodies of the day.[xlvi] Jones concludes: 'Given the prevalence of this market, now completely forgotten, it is not surprising that ... Karl Amenda should have remarked that the movement seemed to him to portray the parting of two lovers.'[xlvii] Of related interest is that in the first version of the Quartet, Beethoven marked the second movement simply as *Adagio molto*. Only in his later revisions did he modify this to *Adagio affettuoso ed appassionato* — which may be taken as a measure of his desire to indicate to the performer that the music should be interpreted tenderly and expressively.

These qualities were not lost to the reviewer writing about the music in the 22 November issue of the *Berliner Allgemeine musikalische Zeitung*: 'What beautiful melancholy and elegiac depth animate the fantasy-like *Adagio* in D minor, and how impudently and teasingly does the rondo, in contrast, bubble forth in jovial humour!'[xlviii] A century later, de Marliave expressed similar thoughts: '[Nothing] so deeply felt had hitherto (1800) ever come from the composer's pen ... Among Beethoven's slow movements, this has only one precursor, the *Largo* of the Sonata in D, Op. 10, No. 3; later movements, born of similar inspiration (the slow movements of the quartet in F major, Op. 59, and of the quartet in E flat, Op. 74), are to crystalize its memory.'[xlix] Contemporaneously Romain Rolland maintained: 'The *Adagio* is very

beautiful, and one can feel in it the future Beethoven.'[l]
Bekker likened the *Adagio affettuoso ed appassionato* to 'a
most moving song of sorrow such as only Beethoven could
accomplish when he turned to the grave D minor key'.[li] We
give the last words here to Joseph Kerman: 'This D-minor
Adagio affettuoso ed appassionato is one of the most
accomplished things that Beethoven had yet written, one of
the very best things. Few movements among the Op. 18
Quartets so reward study, and testify so strongly to his now
formidable ability in melodic draughtsmanship, his control
of form [and] his mastery of the string-quartet medium.'[lii]

The third movement is headed *Scherzo* — one of four
such designations in the Op. 18 set. Beethoven invariably
adopted this expression to signify its original Italian etymological meaning suggestive of humour and high spirits.[liii] In
the F major Quartet, the *Scherzo* replaces the Classical
minuet and is signified to be performed *Allegro molto* — 'in
a lively tempo, very swift'. Lam justifies Beethoven's rejection of the conventional minuet form on the grounds 'after
the romantic intensity of the slow movement a minuet would
be too formal'. Equally, he recognizes that a straightforward
scherzo would be 'too inconsequential'. By introducing a
chromatic element, and shifting bar accents, Lam considers
a kind of unrest is achieved 'that links it with the seriousness
of the first half of the quartet'. Of the composer's craftsmanship he enthuses: 'Technically it is beyond praise, the work
of an absolute master of composition.'[liv]

More than one commentator has detected the influence
of Haydn in the third movement, in the manner of its
'high-spirited humour and its capricious syntax'.[lv] Commenting on Beethoven's adoption of the scherzo form at this
period, Jones observes: 'Beethoven's piano sonatas and
string trios from the 1790s have a number of one-in-a-bar
scherzos which, in turn, might have prompted three similar

movements in Haydn's Op. 76 and Op. 77.'[lvi] Humour is evident in the Trio section with its 'striking rhythmic and textural passages',[lvii] 'leaping octave passages ... a trait significant of vitality[lviii], and 'high speed witticisms of many kinds ... chromatic distortions ... abrupt stops and starts that contribute to the humorous effect'.[lix] Affinities have been found here with the *Menuetto* section of the contemporaneous Symphony No.1, described as 'its twin'[lx] but 'more subtle and light footed'[lxi].

Joseph de Marliave considered this scherzo of Beethoven's first manner gives a hint 'at the sparkling tonal audacities that the artist is later to mould into this form'.[lxii] Looking ahead to Beethoven's final statements in the medium, Bernhard Jacobson contends: 'The *Scherzo* is perhaps the most roundedly successful movement — its weird, thrusting rhythms look still further forward ... to the spectral, frightening scherzo of Op. 135, written in 1826 ... the galumphing octave unisons that lead into the trio section are quintessential Beethoven.'[lxiii]

Beethoven designated the fourth movement of the Amenda version of the F major string quartet *Allegretto* — 'a moderately quick tempo' — but in the revised edition he changed this to a full blown *Allegro* — 'lively-brisk' — thereby to more fully covey the energy and vitality that characterizes the music. The *Allegro* 'leaps upon the ear without warning or preparation'. It appears to have similarly sprung from the composer's imagination, since the opening motif appeared at an early stage in the sketches in a close approximation to its final form. The movement is at once for Beethoven 'a natural outlet for imaginative vigour',[lxiv] in which he maintains to a remarkable degree 'a sense of cumulative verve and vitality',[lxv] and a 'relaxed and brilliant sense of a maturely dispersed knot of feeling'.[lxvi] The manner is close in feeling to that found in some of the composer's early piano sonatas.

For example, the animated finale of the Piano Sonata Op. 2, No. 1 (1793–95/96) has been described as 'a work of youthful violence with its many indications of fortissimo and its brilliant arpeggios'[lxvii] – the first of Beethoven's 'stormy finales'.[lxviii] In the Piano Sonata C minor, Op. 10, No. 1 (1796–98), Beethoven marked *prestissimo* throughout the entire movement. Here, as in the F major Quartet, the layout is concise and possessed of energy and intensity. Harold Truscott believes an even stronger connection is to be found in the work's closing pages with the main theme of the finale of the C minor Trio, Op. 9. He remarks: 'The idea seems to have been still with Beethoven when he wrote the main theme of the finale of the F major String Quartet, Op. 18, No. 1.' He adds: 'In fact, since the dates of composition of the Three Trios and the Op. 18 Quartet overlap, it is possible that one idea suggested the other.'[lxix]

In the composition of his first string quartets, Beethoven's debt to Mozart has been mentioned (see String Quartets, Op. 18, Nos. 1–6). Robert Winter suggests the writing for violin was influenced by the opening of Mozart's D-major Quartet, K. 499. He comments: 'The personality is if course quite different – earth and fire as against Mozart's air ... This movement has tremendous verve and surprisingly few rests ... counterpoint becomes the tool of wit.'[lxx] Moreover: 'All through the Quartet the interest is most skilfully divided between the players.'[lxxi]

---

[i] William Kinderman, editor, *The string quartets of Beethoven*, Urbana, 2005, p. 54.

[ii] Michael Broyles, 1987, p. 47.

[iii] Philip Radcliffe, 1978, p. 45.

[iv] Robert Simpson: *The chamber music for strings* in: Denis Arnold and Nigel Fortune, editors, *The Beethoven companion*, 1973, pp. 248–9.

[v] Basil Lam, 1975 p. 14.

[vi] Quoted in: Barry Cooper, 2000, pp. 80–1. See also Elliot Forbes, 1967, p. 261.

[vii] Wilhelm Altmann, *Preface* to Eulenberg miniature score, 1911.

[viii] Beethoven House, Digital Archives, Document, BH 84. The Amenda version

of the F major Quartet has been recorded by a number of artists including the Pro Arte Quartet issued by Laurel 116.

[ix] Joseph Kerman, *Beethoven quartet audiences: actual, potential, ideal* in: Robert Winter and Robert Martin, editors, *The Beethoven quartet companion*, 1994, pp. 8–9.

[x] Emily Anderson, 1961, Vol. 1, Letter No, 53, pp. 63–5. For a facsimile reproduction of this letter, together with the transcription of the text in the original German, see: Beethoven House, Digital Archives, Document, Sammlung H. C. Bodmer, HCB BBr 1.

[xi] Robert Simpson: *The chamber music for strings* in: Denis Arnold and Nigel Fortune, editors, *The Beethoven companion*, 1973, p. 244.

[xii] Paul Bekker, 1925, pp. 310–11.

[xiii] Barry Cooper, 2000, p. 92.

[xiv] Joseph Kerman, 1967, p. 32.

[xv] Wayne M. Senner, Robin Wallace and William Meredith, editors, *The critical reception of Beethoven's compositions by his German contemporaries*, Lincoln: University of Nebraska Press, in association with the American Beethoven Society and the Ira F. Brilliant Center for Beethoven Studies, San José State University, 1999, Vol. 1, pp.153–4.

[xvi] *Ibid*, 1999, Vol. 1, pp. 156–7. In the earlier concert season of 1824 we have further evidence of the growing popularity of Beethoven's string quartets. The February issue of the *Berliner Allgemeine musikalische Zeitung* for this year includes a review of a concert held in Berlin in which quartets by Haydn, Mozart and Beethoven were performed. The reviewer cites 'one [Beethoven] quartet in particular ... received distinguished applause'. Unfortunately the work in question is not identified. Such was the popularity of the piece, however, it had to be played again at two further concerts. The reviewer adds a characteristic Beethovenian-style remark: 'Mozart may suit the fiery temperament of the players less than Beethoven's bold, often bizarre fantasy. But the energy and romanticism that is expressed in most tone paintings of this genius, who has retreated into himself and carries within himself a world of musical notes, does excite feeling less than Mozart.' Cited in the same source as the foregoing at p. 59.

[xvii] The concert in question took place on 11 February 1849. As derived from Joseph de Marliave, 1961 (reprint), pp. 48–9.

[xviii] Pamela J. Willetts, 1970, pp. 55–8.

[xix] Marion Scott, 1940, p. 253.

[xx] William Henry Hadow, 1926, p. 14.

[xxi] William Kinderman, editor, *The string quartets of Beethoven*, 2005, p. 14.

[xxii] Joseph Kerman, 1967, p. 32.

[xxiii] Bernhard Jacobson Liner notes to: *Ludwig van Beethoven; The early string quartets*, Op. 18, Alban Berg Quartet, EMI, 1981.

[xxiv] Basil Lam, 1975, p. 13.

[xxv] David Wyn Jones in: Robin Stowell, editor, *The Cambridge companion to the string quartet*, 2003, p. 211.

[xxvi] Barry Cooper, 1990, p. 130.

[xxvii] The expression here is that of Joseph Kerman's in: Robert Winter and Robert Martin, editors, *The Beethoven quartet companion*, 1994, p. 151.

[xxviii] Arthur Shepherd, 1935, p. 11.

[xxix] Marion Scott, 1940, p. 253.

[xxx] Joseph de Marliave, 1961 (reprint), pp. 5–6.

xxxi Joseph Kerman, 1967, p. 30.

xxxii Rebecca Clarke, *The Beethoven quartets as a player sees them*, in: *Musical Times. Special Issue*: Vol. VIII, No. 2, 1927, pp. 178–90.

xxxiii Adapted from: William Kinderman, 1997, p. 42 and William Kinderman *Beethoven* in: *Nineteenth-century piano music* in: Larry R. Todd, editor, 2004, pp. 56-7.

xxxiv Philip Radcliffe, 1978, p. 27. Tovey used almost identical words to those of Radcliffe in his estimation of the *Adagio*, describing it as 'one of Beethoven's early great tragic movements alongside that of the Sonata Op. 10, No. 3'. See: Donald Francis Tovey, 1944, p. 119.

xxxv Conrad Wilson, 2003, p. 16.

xxxvi David Wyn Jones in: Robin Stowell, editor, *The Cambridge companion to the string quartet*, 2003, p. 211.

xxxvii Arthur Shepherd, 1935, p. 12.

xxxviii Bernhard Jacobson Liner notes to: *Ludwig van Beethoven; The early string quartets*, Op. 18, *The Alban Berg Quartet*, EMI, 1981.

xxxix See: Barry Cooper, 2000, p. 93.

xl See: Robert Simpson: *The chamber music for strings* in: Denis Arnold and Nigel Fortune, editors, *The Beethoven companion*, 1973, pp. 248–9.

xli Nicolas Slonimsky, 2000, p. 158. Beethoven makes use of the extremely rare 128th note values.

xlii As suggested by Robert Winter, and Robert Martin, editors, 1994, p. 154.

xliii Elliot Forbes, editor, *Thayer's life of Beethoven*, 1967, p. 261.

xliv William Henry Hadow, 1926. (*Introduction*).

xlv Basil Lam, 1975, p. 15.

xlvi By way of illustration: WoO 65, twenty-four variations on Vincenzio Righini's aria *Venni Amore*; WoO 66, thirteen variations on Carl Dittersdorf's aria *Es war einmal ein altar Mann*; WoO 67, eight variations for four hands on a theme by Count Waldstein; WoO 68, twelve variations on a theme from Jacob Haibel's ballet *La nozza disturbate* – a dozen or so more could be listed.

xlvii David Wyn Jones in: Robin Stowell, editor, *The Cambridge companion to the string quartet*, 2003, p. 211.

xlviii Wayne M. Senner, Robin Wallace and William Meredith, editors, *The critical reception of Beethoven's compositions by his German contemporaries*, Lincoln: University of Nebraska Press, in association with the American Beethoven Society and the Ira F. Brilliant Center for Beethoven Studies, San José State University, 1999, Vol. 1, pp.156–7.

xlix Joseph de Marliave, 1961 (reprint), pp. 5–6. De Marliave points out passages later in the music that he finds have similarities with the *Andante* in the Second Symphony, at the close of which he states 'one feels the weight of an endless grief'.

l Rolland, Romain, 1917, p. 179.

li Paul Bekker, 1925, p. 311.

lii Joseph Kerman, 1967, p. 41.

liii Donald Tovey is frequently cited for being the authority for the statement that Beethoven always used the word *scherzo* in its etymological sense. For example, see: Nicolas Slonimsky, 2000, p. 158.

liv Basil Lam, 1975, p. 15.

lv See, for example, the remarks of Arthur Shepherd, 1935, p. 12 and Robert Winter and Robert Martin, editors, *The Beethoven quartet companion*,

1994, p. 154.
- lxi David Wyn Jones in: Robin Stowell, editor, *The Cambridge companion to the string quartet*, 2003, p. 212.
- lxii William Kinderman, editor, *The string quartets of Beethoven*, Urbana, 2005, p. 54. Michael Broyles, 1987, p. 54.
- lxiii Marion Scott, 1940, p. 253.
- lxi Barry Cooper, 2000, pp. 93–4.
- lx Joseph Kerman. 1967, p. 43.
- lxi Phillip Radcliffe, 1978, p. 28.
- lxii Joseph de Marliave, 1961, pp. 5–6.
- lxiii Bernhard Jacobson Liner notes to: *Ludwig van Beethoven; The early string quartets*, Op. 18, *The Alban Berg Quartet*, EMI, 1981.
- lxiv Joseph de Marliave, 1961 (reprint), pp. 5–6.
- lxv Arthur Shepherd, 1935, p. 13.
- lxvi Robert Simpson *The chamber music for strings* in: Denis Arnold and Nigel Fortune, editors, *The Beethoven companion*, 1973, p. 249.
- lxvii Charles Rosen, 2002, p. 124. Rosen also draws attention to Beethoven's insistent use of the minor mode as a pre-figuration of the sonatas of Chopin, Schumann and Liszt.
- lxviii Maynard Solomon, 1977, p. 102.
- lxix Harold Truscott, 1968, p. 27. Gerald Abraham also shares Truscott's opinion, see: Gerald Abraham, *Beethoven's Chamber Music*, in: *The Age of Beethoven, The New Oxford History of Music, Vol. VIII*, Gerald Abraham, editor, 1988, pp. 282–3.
- lxx Robert Winter, and Robert Martin, editors, 1994, p. 154.
- lxxi Phillip Radcliffe, 1978, p. 29.

STRING QUARTET IN G MAJOR, OP. 18, NO. 2

'Throughout his life ... G major is [Beethoven's] favourite vehicle for the expression of serenity and happiness: the G major Piano Concerto the Piano Sonata, Op. 14, No. 2. The last Violin Sonata. Are all instances, and the light that shines from them irradiates in full measure the perfect spring-day loveliness of the present quartet.'

Hadow, William Henry, *Beethoven's Op. 18 Quartets*, 1926. p. 23.

'The Quartet in G is Beethoven's wittiest composition in the genre. As such it immediately recalls Haydn, and in view of the almost deferential bow to Mozart in the next quartet, the A-major, Op.

> 18, No. 5, it may be tempting to interpret this one as a parallel, prior act of homage to the older composer.'

Joseph Kerman, *The Beethoven quartets*, 1967, p. 44.

> 'The composer of this delightful entertainment was no revolutionary ... he was always ready to compose works of classical objectivity designed to give pleasure to connoisseurs.'

Basil Lam, *Beethoven string quartets*, 1975, p. 18.

> 'Of all the Op. 18 quartets the G major comes nearest to the eighteenth century in its urbanity. But, without attaining to the profundity of the greatest works of Haydn and Mozart, it can stand firmly on its own feet as a most delightful and refreshing work, in no way inferior to its bolder and more forward-looking companions.'

Philip Radcliffe, *Beethoven's string quartets*, 1978, pp. 32–3.

A measure of the character of the String Quartet in G major, Op. 18, No. 2 is that for many years it was popularly known as the *Compliment Quartet*. It derived this nickname from the manner in which its opening phrases were considered to resemble a polite greeting, typical of an exchange between two refined eighteenth-century elegants.[i] This is not so fanciful as it may today appear. At the period of the work's composition (1798–99), the string quartet held sway in the intimate environment of the salon where the interplay between the four instruments had the authority and interest of informed conversation. In the G major

Quartet, however, Beethoven is not content to be merely conversationally polite. He is 'overtly witty and dry ... essentially epigrammatic'[ii] and 'witty and gracious'[iii] in what is 'a deliciously happy work' full of 'a merry character'.[iv]

Of the six String Quartets Op. 18, the G major is the one that most evidently looks back to the eighteenth century with its conversational and genial 'talkative' quality.[v] In its composition, was Beethoven perhaps recalling passages in Haydn's String Quartet Op. 33 in the same key?[vi] The music has Haydnesque spirit flavoured with Beethoven's sense of irony. But is the composer quite ready to step into his old teacher's shoes? 'It has a certain humour, if rather stilted, as though Beethoven was trying to squeeze himself into Haydn's mindset.'[vii] It is 'less ambitious' than its predecessor and 'less varied in content' but, notwithstanding, 'it is a work of great beauty and gaiety'.[viii] Joseph Kerman viewed the G-major Quartet as being 'a transitional work par excellence'. He praised the creation for its 'technical experiments' and Beethoven for his earnestness: 'In one work [the F major] the composer is looking for vehemence and passion, in the other [the G major] for sustained humour ... What is very evident in each is a new boldness of invention, a surer grasp of the medium, and a deepening sophistication about musical means.'[ix]

The F major Quartet was originally planned to be the third in the set of six; Beethoven marked it *Quartetto III*. He worked on the composition in 1799 and revised it in the summer of 1800. No sketches survive for the first draft of the piece but Beethoven's later working is preserved in the so-called *Grasnick* 2 Sketchbook, at pp.15–18 and pp. 20–32, and the *Autograph* 19e at pp. 20–25.[x] Based on his study of these sources, Barry Cooper considers Beethoven revised the G major Quartet as thoroughly as he did the F major. He cites significant structural adjustments to the text.

For example, the second movement was originally conceived as a continuous *Adagio* but was later amended with an *Allegro* insertion 'creating an unusual form'. Of the closing pages, Cooper states: 'The Finale too was thoroughly overhauled, with part of the development coda being almost completely rewritten.'[xi]

With the interests of the performer in mind, Rebecca Clarke mused: 'The second quartet, in G, demands still greater precision than the first, for it is conceived throughout in a vein of naïve and brittle gaiety, even the middle section of the *Adagio*. Here every note stands out with disconcerting clearness, and the slightest deviation from exact intonation or rhythm is at once apparent.'[xii]

It is from the German-speaking countries that the G major Quartet derived its nickname. There, it became known as the *Komplimentierungs-Quartet*. It has been suggested this may be loosely translated as 'quartet of bows and curtseys'.[xiii] In similar fashion, English performers in the distant past might refer colloquially to Haydn's String Quartet in G, Op. 33, No. 5 as the 'How d-you do' Quartet. More seriously, this composition might well have sowed the seeds in the mind of Beethoven for his own creation.[xiv] Alison Bullock is content to describe the opening of the first movement as 'an exaggeratedly courtly flourish'.[xv] Donald Tovey characterises it as the Quartet's 'delicious opening theme' that, he observes, 'is continued in epigrams and in two-bar rhythm'.[xvi]

The first movement is prescribed the tempo *Allegro* — to be played quickly and bright. Endorsing the idea that the opening resembles a conversational rejoinder, Phillip Radcliffe likens the series of phrases that follow to 'a delightful and convincing sentence'.[xvii] This is one of the Op. 18's 'most finely wrought movements'.[xviii] The Italian musicologist Professor Giovanni Biamonti identified the opening passage in its sketch form, as preserved in the *Grasnick* 1 Sketchbook that is now held by the Staatsbibliothek Preussischer Kulturbesitz, Berlin. From this he made one of his many Beethoven audio recordings as listed in his *Catalogo Tematico* (Audio Catalogue).[xix]

The first violin's opening flourish establishes 'a mood of airy lightness and Mozartian grace'.[xx] The pace is 'relaxed ... cadences are regular' and Beethoven 'revels in melodic detail'.[xxi] Arthur Shepherd found 'vernal freshness' in the opening melody and with it a certain analogy with the theme of the Violin Sonata in F major, Op. 24, familiarly known as the *Spring* Sonata.[xxii] The character of the music disposed William Hadow to reflect in similar terms with reference to other of the composer's works: 'Throughout his life ... G major is [Beethoven's] favourite vehicle for the expression of serenity and happiness: the G major Piano Concerto, the Piano Sonata, Op. 14, No. 2 and the last Violin Sonata ... all [are] instances, and the light that shines from them irradiates in full measure the perfect spring-day loveliness of the present quartet.'

The opening *Allegro* reveals Beethoven assimilating Haydn's 'comedy of manners'[xxiii] whilst at the same time imposing 'an occasional dramatic thrust that is unmistakably Beethovenian'.[xxiv] 'For all its courtliness of bearing, the first movement's comedy of manners builds up a formidable head of steam.'[xxv] 'The first section of the first movement is very Haydnesque, but the ways in which the theme is manipulated and the music's texture and sonority [are] deepened are pure Beethoven, the serious composer underlying the surface humour.'[xxvi]

In his estimation of the G major String Quartet, Joseph de Marliave quotes Theodor Otto Helm, a leading figure in Viennese musical life in the nineteenth century and a prominent music critic for fifty years. In Beethoven musicology he is remembered for his pioneering *Beethovens Streichquartette* (1885). Writing of the *Allegro*, Helm enthuses: 'The principal subject ... brings before one's imagination a brilliant scene in some eighteenth-century *salon*, with all the ceremonious display and flourish of courtesy typical of the period.' As the music progresses: 'The doors of the drawing room swing open to usher in the arriving guests, met with bows and gracious words of greeting.' Reflecting on this imagery, de Marliave conceded it as being 'rather fantastic'.[xxvii] In his response to Helm's fanciful imaginings, the American musicologist Arthur Shepherd was more candid. He accepted the music's stylistic affinity with Haydn's powdered-wig elegance, but dismissed Helm's style of writing about it as 'hifalutin'![xxviii]

In the Amenda version of the Quartet, the second movement had a more complex structure than in the published edition. Beethoven designated this simply as *Largo* – a very slow tempo. He reworked it in the summer of 1800 making substantial changes to his original conception and heading the movement *Adagio cantabile* – to be played slowly and in a singing style. The evolution of the majestic opening theme appears to have given Beethoven some difficulty. Twelve versions are evident in the sketches – typical of the composer's painstaking manner in which an apparently simple theme was born of more complex origins.[xxix] [xxx] The result is a three-part design in which the *Adagio cantabile* is developed 'in measured intimacy of feeling' eventually to be interrupted with a 'cheerful' and 'dance-like *Allegro*' that in turn yields to the elegiac feeling of the opening that Beethoven's marks *Tempo 1*. Stephanie Schroeder believes these changes in mood, and in particular the manner of the *Allegro's* abrupt interceding, must have had 'a dazzling effect' at their first hearing.[xxxi]

In the more decorative passages of the movement, 'an

atmosphere of tension and mystery' is introduced. Beethoven may here have been recalling Haydn's Op. 20 Quartets of 1772 and their 'profound expressiveness' and 'earnest and elaborate fugal finales'.[xxii] Perhaps, in establishing the movement's 'grave tone, formal manner and elegant embellishment', Beethoven was also influenced by the construction and layout of Haydn's C-major Quartet, Op. 54, No. 2, particularly with respect to its alternating slow-fast-slow passages.[xxiii][xxiv] De Marliave found the whole movement 'graceful and pleasing, after the manner of Haydn'. He also considered the manner of its 'grave beauty', broken by the 'vigorous *Allegro*', to be suggestive of the slow movement of the composer's Piano Sonata Op. 27, No.1. He cannot resist quoting Theodor Otto Helm once more who invited the listener to imagine 'a troop of irresponsible youths making hits at their old master, the wise philosopher to whom they listened in patience only for a time.' Extending this imagery, de Marliave describes the subsequent cello passage as 'a solemn exhortation'.[xxv] It has also been proposed Beethoven's decorative writing has a decidedly Mozartian character.[xxvi]

The third movement reveals itself first in scherzo form and later as an allegro. Although designated *Scherzo*, its 'wittily pointed ... frisky theme' is almost a minuet in tempo whose theme is derived from the slow-movement melody but 'irreverently divested of its heaviness'.[xxvii] In its lightness it has been compared with the *Scherzo* of the Piano Sonata in A, Op. 2, No. 2, which predates the G major Quartet by just a few years.[xxviii] It is 'more elaborate in texture' with its 'good humour more unclouded' and without any suggestion of its companion's 'gruffness'. 'This *Scherzo* is not, perhaps, quite as bold and original as that of the F major Quartet ... but it is a most delightful movement which fits perfectly into the generally gay atmosphere of the whole work.'[xxix] Kerman praises the *Scherzo* as 'perhaps the cleverest that Beethoven had yet written' as well as being 'one of the most amusing'.[xl] Kinderman is more cautious. He finds Beethoven employing 'a rhetoric bristling with Haydnesque devices' such as what he calls 'suspicious repeats' and 'rising scale patterns'. Haydn, Kinderman asserts, handles such musical devices 'with finesse', whereas Beethoven 'makes his point more bluntly'.[xli]

The *Allegro* is a form of minuet, once more revealing a debt to Haydn.[xlii]

The final verdict on the merits of the third movement is unequivocal: 'sedate ... slightly unpredictable ... 'more bows and curtseys ... in the Haydnesque mould';[xliii] 'impish and bouncing'; [xliv] and a Beethoven movement that 'breathes more genuine *scherzoso* feeling than any other of the early quartet-scherzos.'[xlv]

In his working-out of a piece, Beethoven would typically set down his thoughts intermittently in sketch form — often over a period of time — in the process, turning his mind from one composition to another. In his study of the composer's sketches, Cooper suggests this was so in the case of the G major Quartet, in which ideas for the *Scherzo* were conceived alongside those for the *Largo* and *Finale*.[xlvi] Sketches for the fourth movement may derive from ideas Beethoven worked on from as early as the spring of 1799.[xlvii] Commenting on these, Richard Kramer reflects: 'They leave an erratic chart to the swift processes of mind. Some relationships are exaggerated, others neglected. Ambiguities form and dissolve elusively.'[xlviii] In its construction, the music hovers between rondo and sonata form.[xlix] The moods and shape here recall the first movement: 'Rhythms and symmetries abound, but there is plenty of opportunity for humour and surprise ... Altogether, this exuberant finale represents the young Beethoven at his most wittily inventive.'[l]

The closing pages are headed *Allegro molto quasi Presto*. The spirit of Haydn is invoked 'tersely and wittily'[li] in a manner that would have been immediately apparent to those of the composer's contemporaries familiar with the older master's musical language. 'It would hardly be surprising to see Beethoven in his first quartets seriously influenced by the one great master who was steadily flooding Vienna with such pieces — fourteen of them ... in the decade of the 1790s (Opp. 71, 74, 76 and 77).'[lii] Beethoven himself described this movement as *aufgeknopft* — 'unbuttoned'. The spirit of gaiety is maintained suggestive of the manner prevailing at a convivial event when 'the champagne has been round'.[liii] Although the music belongs to the world of a comedy of manners, it reveals 'a more formidable temper ... a superior version of the First Symphony'.[liv] Roman Rolland thought traces of Niccolò Paganini could be detected in the violin work, not surprising given the manner in which he had 'cast his glamour over Europe'.[lv] Perhaps, twenty years later, the 'hammering insistence' on the chord of D major at the end of the exposition would influence the youthful Mendelssohn when he was composing his Overture *A Midsummer Night's Dream* Overture?[lvi]

As suggested by Philip Radcliffe, 1978, pp. 31–2.

String Quartet in G major, Op. 18, No. 2

---

[i] Marion Scott, 1940, p. 254. Scott adds: 'Old William Gardiner of Leicester was right when he discerned in the young Beethoven's music "an intellect that opened a new world to him".' William Gardiner (1770-1853) was an English composer best known for his hymns but who is remembered in Beethoven circles for being one of the first to promote his music in England — from possibly as early as 1794.

[ii] Robert Simpson *The chamber music for strings* in: Denis Arnold and Nigel Fortune, editors, *The Beethoven companion*, 1973, p. 247.

[iii] William Kinderman, editor, *The string quartets of Beethoven*, 2005, p. 3.

[iv] Marion Scott, 1940, p. 253.

[v] Robert Winter, and Robert Martin, editors *The Beethoven quartet companion*, 1994, p. 156.

[vi] As suggested by William Kinderman, editor, *The string quartets of Beethoven*, 2005, p. 53.

[vii] Alison Bullock, *Notes to the BBC Radio Three Beethoven experience*, Tuesday 7 June 2005, www.bbc.co.uk/radio3/Beethoven.

[viii] Phillip Radcliffe, 1978, p. 29.

[ix] Joseph Kerman, 1967, pp. 52–3.

[x] William Kinderman, editor, *The string quartets of Beethoven*, 2005, pp. 323–4.

[xi] Barry Cooper, 2000, pp. 92–3. Associated with these sketches are ideas for the Piano Sonata in B flat, Op. 22 – evidence of Beethoven's inclination to work on a number of compositions at once. See Thayer-Forbes, 1967, pp. 262–3.

[xii] Rebecca Clarke *The Beethoven quartets as a player sees them*, writing on the occasion of Beethoven's Death Centenary in: *Musical Times. Special Issue*: Vol. VIII, No. 2, 1927, pp. 178–90.

[xiii] Robert Winter, and Robert Martin, editors *The Beethoven quartet companion*, 1994, p. 158.

[xiv] Joseph Kerman, 1967, p. 45.

[xv] Alison Bullock *Notes to the BBC Radio Three Beethoven experience*, Tuesday 7 June 2005, www.bbc.co.uk/radio3/Beethoven.

[xvi] Donald Francis Tovey, 1944, p. 94.

[xvii] Philip Radcliffe, 1978, p. 29.

[xviii] Gerald Abraham, 1968, pp. 282–3.

[xix] The Catalogue entry is Biamonti midi file 1978, No. 188.

[xx] Denis Matthews, 1985, p. 129.

[xxi] Michael Broyles, 1987, p. 47.

[xxii] Arthur Shepherd ,1935, p. 14.

[xxiii] Joseph Kerman, 1967, p. 44.

[xxiv] William Kinderman, editor, *The string quartets of Beethoven*, 2005, pp. 54–5.

[xxv] Bernhard Jacobson Liner notes to: *Ludwig van Beethoven; The early string quartets*, Op. 18, *The Alban Berg Quartet*, EMI, 1981.

[xxvi] Alison Bullock, *Notes to the BBC Radio Three Beethoven experience*, Tuesday 7 June 2005, www.bbc.co.uk/radio3/Beethoven.

[xxvii] Joseph de Marliave, 1961 (reprint), pp. 14–15.

[xxviii] Arthur Shepherd, 193, p. 14.

[xxix] See William Kinderman, editor *The string quartets of Beethoven*, 2005, p. 19 and note 13. Kinderman cites Beethoven exploring alternative ideas for the *Adagio* theme as drafted in the so-called *Scala Leaf* that originally formed part of the reconstructed *Autograph* 19e Sketchbook.

[xxx] Philip Radcliffe, 1978, p. 30.

[xxxi] Stephanie Schroeder, *Programme notes* to the Alexander String Quartet.

[xxxii] Leon Plantinga, 1984, pp. 30–31 and Philip Radcliffe, 1978, pp. 30–1. Radcliffe adds: 'There is some decorative writing [in Beethoven's *Adagio cantabile*] not unlike that in the slow movement of Mozart's K. 387 in the same key. Beethoven's texture is less subtle and varied than that of the Mozart movement, but is massive and dignified.'

[xxxiii] As proposed by Robert Winter, and Robert Martin, editors *The Beethoven quartet companion*, 1994, p. 158.

[xxxiv] Arthur Shepherd, 1935, p. 15.

[xxxv] Joseph de Marliave, 1961 (reprint), pp. 14–15.

[xxxvi] Philip Radcliffe, 1978, p. 18.

[xxxvii] Bernhard Jacobson Liner notes to: *Ludwig van Beethoven; The early string*

quartets, Op. 18, *The Alban Berg Quartet*, EMI, 1981.
[xxxviii] Basil Lam. 1975, p. 20.
[xxxix] Philip Radcliffe, 1978, pp. 31–2.
[xl] Joseph Kerman 1967, p, 51.
[xli] William Kinderman, 2005, p. 55.
[xlii] Joseph de Marliave, 1961 (reprint), pp. 14–15. He illustrates his observation with examples of Haydn's quartet writing.
[xliii] Alison Bullock, *Notes to the BBC Radio Three Beethoven experience*, Tuesday 7 June 2005, www.bbc.co.uk/radio3/Beethoven.
[xliv] Robin Golding, *Liner Notes to* The Lindsey Quartet, *Beethoven String Quartets*.
[xlv] Joseph Kerman, 1967, pp. 44–5.
[xlvi] Barry Cooper, 1990, p. 118.
[xlvii] See: Sieghard Brandenburg, *The First version of Beethoven's G major String Quartet, Op. 18, No.2, Music and Letters*, lvii, 1977, p. 150.
[xlviii] Richard Kramer in: Alan Tyson, editor, *Beethoven studies 3*, 1982, pp. 35–42.
[xlix] Philip Radcliffe (1978, pp. 31–2.) describes the final movement as being 'in full sonata form' but Basil Lam (1975, p. 20–1) is more ambivalent: 'Like the Finale of the first quartet, this spirited piece is neither rondo nor sonata; in broad outline it is a sonata scheme ...'.
[l] Robert Winter and Robert Martin, editors: The Beethoven quartet companion, 1994, p. 159.
[li] Dennis Matthews, 1985, p. 129.
[lii] Joseph Kerman, 1967, pp. 44–5.
[liii] Arthur Shepherd, 1935, p. 16.
[liv] Basil Lam, 1975, p. 20.
[lv] Romain Rolland, 1917, p. 180.
[lvi] As suggested by Philip Radcliffe, 1978, pp. 31–2.

STRING QUARTET IN D MAJOR, OP. 18, NO. 3

'This beautiful quartet ... already points to the maturity of [Beethoven's] second period, especially in the first movement.'

Romain Rolland, *Beethoven and Handel*, 1917, p. 180

'Remembering that this was the first quartet Beethoven wrote, one is not surprised to find more traces here than in the five others of Op. 18 of the direct influence of Haydn and Mozart. Rigid adherence to form, correct balance of movement with movement, traditional conventions of tempo and rhythm, all the rules of classical art are perfectly observed.'

Joseph de Marliave, *Beethoven's Quartets*, 1925, (reprint 1961), p. 17.

> 'What a lovely work! And what a number of ideas from it have been used by other composers; Mendelssohn having taken the minuet subject bodily and phrases from the first movement, and Schubert having utilized freely one of the figures of the last movement in the first movement of his great D Quartet [*Death and the Maiden*].'

Charles L. Graves, *Hubert Parry: His life and Works*, Vol. 1, 1926, p. 164.

> 'There is in the D major, less subservience to stereotyped pattern and figure. Externally there are many points of adherence to the Haydn-Mozart formulae ... On the other hand, one has not far to look to discover bold strokes betokening the individuality that was predestined to enlarge the potentialities of the quartet medium.'

Arthur Shepherd, *The String Quartets of Ludwig van Beethoven*, 1935, p. 17.

> 'The piece shows signs both delicate and rude of Beethoven's determination to spike his quartet with formal contrapuntal devices.'

Joseph Kerman. *The Beethoven Quartets*, 1967, p. 16.

> 'Except for a sudden surge of energy in the finale, it is the gentlest, most consistently lyrical work in the set. It seems to begin in mid-thought and in

a singularly enchanting way.'

Robert Winter and Robert Martin, editors, *The Beethoven Quartet Companion*, 1994, p. 159.

Beethoven commenced work on the String Quartet in D major, Op. 18, No. 3 in the summer or autumn of 1798 and completed it either later in the year or in January 1799. He may have revised the composition sometime in 1800.[i] In our introductory remarks to the Op 18 String Quartets, Nos. 1—6, we have remarked that the genesis of their creation can be traced through the surviving pages of the so-called Grasnick Sketchbooks that derive their name from the collector of autograph scores Friedrich August Grasnick. Sketches for the D major Quartet are found in Grasnick 1 (pp. 11—19) and Grasnick 2 (pp. 31—2). Additional ideas for the composition are worked on a sketchleaf now preserved in the Glinka Museum in Moscow with further drafts contained in the Landsberg 7 Sketchbook (p. 1 and p. 111), named after the collector of manuscripts Ludwig Landsberg.[ii] The evidence from these sources confirms that the D major Quartet was the first of the series of six on which Beethoven worked continuously.[iii]

Bernhard Jacobson describes the work as accepting 'a more-or-less conventional overall movement plan'.[iv] In her pioneering *Master Musicians* study, Marion Scott refers to the composer's first efforts at quartet writing as being 'more tentative in workmanship than the others, but no less loveable'.[v] The third quartet is distinguished by the fact that each movement, except the third, is in sonata form.[vi] Denis Matthews comments on Beethoven's 'effects of utmost economy' felt in what he describes as the music's 'long-breathed themes'.[vii] Beethoven 'rejoices for the most part in smooth euphony ... consciously serious and smoothly architectural'.[viii] Beethoven's personality, however, emerges in 'the harmonic procedures' he adopts, 'the ordering of tonalities' and, most strikingly, 'unexpected modulatory digressions [that] provide an admirable foil for the more conventional structural features'.[ix] 'Gaiety ... characterises the Quartet in D major, as is to be expected from the choice of key, though a pensive and sentimental strain is woven into the work, and the *Andante* in B flat major is definitely lyrical.'[x]

The German composer and musicologist Adolf Bernhard Marx considered the D major Quartet to be the composer's 'most perfect achievement' within his capacity for writing in the quartet style at the outset of his composing for the genre.[xi] The later German music theorist Hugo Riemann was no less supportive in his praise for the work, singling out for special mention its 'boldness of conception' and 'the unforced nature of its development'.[xii] Contemporary feelings towards the String Quartet Op. 18, No. 3 are perhaps best captured in the views expressed by Philip Radcliffe: 'It has never been one of the most popular, and contains nothing as deeply emotional as the *Adagio* of the Quartet in F major, No.1, or the prophetic quality of the *Melinconia* section of No. 6. But it is full of a beauty of a quiet and thoughtful kind, which becomes more apparent the better the work is known.'[xiii]

The first movement is an allegro that looks back to Haydn; authorities have traced the older composer's influence to the development and recapitulation sections of his String Quartet Op. 33.[xiv] The opening unsupported phrases of the first violin are also held to be reminiscent of Haydn's String Quartet, Op. 50, No. 6 that shares the same key and the 'quiet sustained harmonic background' recalls the first movement of his *Sunrise* Quartet in B-flat major from Op. 76.[xv] The movement may not be 'fast on its feet nor subtle in its gestures' but is possessed of phrases that have a 'determined march' that are 'excellently realized'.[xvi] The atmosphere that prevails 'has an admirable continuity, spontaneous ease [and] delightful unexpected modulations'.[xvii]

Although Beethoven may look back to classical, Haydnesque precedents in his D major Quartet, he is never subservient to its stereotyped 'patter and figuration' that has aptly been described as *Zapf Musik* – 'pigtailed music'.[xviii] The music's inner expressiveness is pure Beethoven. More so is the way in which he experiments with the listener's expectations, as, for example, in the manner in which the movement opens with two long unaccompanied notes on the first violin that soar upwards.[xix] Beethoven also departs from classical orthodoxy by beginning the *Allegro* theme on the dominant of the key and not the tonic, as prescribed by eighteenth-century theorists. Although a modern-day audience may not readily perceive such a departure from classical orthodoxy, such a gesture would have sounded audacious to the ears of the composer's more musically principled listeners.[xx] Basil Lam protests at the criticism that detects immaturity in the D major Quartet, the opening of which he considers to be 'no less characteristic of the composer than the fiery pathos of [String Quartet] No. 4 or the *Sonata Pathétique*'. He asserts: 'Neither Haydn or Mozart had begun a quartet quite in this way, with movement scarcely defined by the decorative violin figure over the sustained harmony of the lower parts.'[xxi]

Beethoven marks the second movement *Andante con moto* – literally, 'slowly but with motion'. It has been suggested a more fitting interpretation, given the nature of the music, would be 'moving, but really moving', in other words 'anything but slow'.[xxii] The melody is given to the second violin, calling for 'restraint and broadness of playing'.[xxiii] 'Serenity, contemplativeness and nobility pervade the movement ... which pursues its course with impressive deliberateness.'[xxiv] Beethoven exploits a simple theme that, it has been remarked, 'in the hands of an inferior composer, could easily have seemed pedestrian and commonplace, but is here treated with great sensitiveness [and] episodic passages of great delicacy'.[xxv] Joseph Kerman is fulsome in his estimation of Beethoven's string writing and construction: 'Long, serious, and very carefully worked, it is the densest of all the slow movements of Op. 18 with the exception of the pathetic D-minor *Adagio* of the Quartet in F ... This *Andante* ... is blessed by one of the happiest lyric ideas of Beethoven's early period. For once he seems relaxed in slow melodic utterance, warm, simple, sentimental, neither intimidated by Haydn and Mozart nor tediously marking out his independence of them.'[xxvi] Basil Lam's observations here are also of interest and worthy of citation in full: 'This broadly planned rondo has something of the romantic solemnity of the *Largo* in the Piano Sonata Op. 7, though Beethoven is now mature enough to contrast this emotional seriousness with something more *grazioso*, a lesson he learned from Mozart that he continued to absorb to the end of his life.'[xxvii]

The expressive range is wide in this movement, prompting suggestions its tender eloquence may perhaps be regarded as 'a first step in the direction that will lead, twenty-five years later, to the *cavatina* in Op. 130'.[xxviii] Moreover, in its spaciousness this slow movement anticipates the composer's later more extended style of string-quartet writing. It is innovatory insofar as it is more expansive than any typical string-quartet adagio of Haydn or Mozart. Thereby, Beethoven makes the slow movement, with its extended development, the central apex of the whole work.[xxix]

We take leave of this movement with a recollection of its interpretation by the fifteen-year old Adrian Bolt. On 30

April 1904 he heard the celebrated Joachim String Quartet play three of the Quartets Op. 18 together with the Quartets Op. 135 and Op. 59, No. 2. Formed in 1869 by Joseph Joachim, the Quartet was in London to mark their leader's Diamond Jubilee commemorating his first appearance in the capitol when, as a mere twelve-year old, he had played Beethoven's Violin Concerto with Mendelssohn conducting — Joachim supplied his own cadenzas! Of the rendering of the D major Quartet, Bolt later wrote in his diary: 'I still remember the slow movement in Beethoven's op.18. No. 3 when Haliř's second violin rose to the surface above the first violin for four bars and let us hear a beautiful cantabile which came from him at no other time.'[xxx]

Beethoven is content to designate the third movement simply as *Allegro* — a procedure he adopts in other of his works.[xxxi] It is typically referred to as being a cross between a minuet and a scherzo, in certain passages also embodying the 'emotionalising of the dance form'; Mozart's G minor String Quartet, K. 478 has been cited as a possible source of influence.[xxxii] The lineage is essentially that of the minuet, with, as just remarked, more harking back to Mozart than Haydn.[xxxiii] It is in the outer sections of the movement, with their 'dramatic off-beat accents and unexpected shifts of harmony', that draw the music nearer to 'the world of the genuine Beethovenian scherzo'.[xxxiv] In its construction the movement follows the classical form with alternating major (minuet) and minor (trio) sections. Notwithstanding Beethoven's dependence on role models, de Marliave, with others, detects 'the piece has a veiled grace of distinctly original cast.'[xxxv] The origins of the movement's jaunty melody have been traced to the Landsberg 7 Sketchbook where, at p. 170, seventeen identifiable bars are outlined.[xxxvi]

Radcliffe reminds us: 'The more obviously great qualities of Beethoven's music have tended to blind people to his capacity for the flowing, comparatively relaxed lyrical mood of which this movement is a characteristic and delightful specimen.'[xxxvii] Here, in the third movement, we have 'a spotlessly groomed little piece whose one interest seems to be in making itself inconspicuous'.[xxxviii] It is 'tersely effective ... along the lines of the First Symphony'[xxxix] as it delights in bathing 'in the bright world of D major'.[xl] More seriously, Lam was of the opinion: '[The] third movement ... could almost belong to one of the late quartets, with its undertone of pathos and its elusive rhythms.'[xli]

Whereas the third movement hovers between the manner of a minuet and a scherzo, the fourth movement is unambiguously designated *Presto* – to be played 'at a rapid tempo'. 'This *Presto* forms the logical conclusion to the work and the climax of the spirit of *joie de vivre* which flows through the second movement and inspires the intimate contentment of the other two.'[xlii] Perhaps, when composing this piece, Beethoven was recalling the finale of Mozart's D-minor Quintet, K 593?[xliii] Robert Simpson, however, considered this comparison to be unfavourable on the grounds that from the outset Beethoven sets out 'bigger lines and already shows a more comprehensive sense of movement that his senior'.[xliv] As the four instruments vie with each other, the spirit of the tarantella is invoked with its anticipations of the finale of the *Kreutzer* Sonata Op. 47 and that of the Piano Sonata Op. 31, No. 3.[xlv]

In his estimation of the final movement, Hadow found Beethoven looking back to the lively dance form of the baroque period: 'The present finale is Beethoven's idea of a gigue, a breathless whirl of scattering triplets and streaming melodies which Tam o' Shanter might well have envied. There is no other piece of music which flies so fast or which is so complete and triumphant a sense of escape.'[xlvi] '[The] subjects tear along in a sublimated gigue'[xlvii] with 'an energetic duo for the two violins'.[xlviii] Although the influence of Mozart in this movement has been cited, contrary opinion favours Haydn as a source. The first movement of his so-called *Clock* Symphony and the last movement of the *Military* Symphony are suggested for reasons of their 'springing energy' ... 'high spirits' ... and an occasional 'touch of ferocity' that are tempered by 'almost uncanny stillness'.[xlix] The *presto* finale reveals Beethoven at his jolliest: 'It is a veritable *tour de force* of gay badinage.'[l] But it also has its more striking pages. These may have made an impression on the youthful Schubert in the working-out of passages in his own String Quartets, D 810 and D 887, and Beethoven himself may have subconsciously remembered the movement's powerful development section years later when at work on the *Grosse Fuge*, Op. 133.[li]

Indications in the sketchbooks suggest the thematic material, as we now know it, did not, in Arthur Shepherd's memorable phrase, 'spring forth whole and radiant, like Minerva from the brain of Jove'.[lii] Beethoven apparently worked on the *presto* finale quite some time after completing the preceding three movements, and only after 'changes of heart and a great deal of labour' as he wrestled with new challenges of instrumental virtuosity and contrapuntal technique.[liii] Drafts for the first violin part and that for the cello appear at p. 3 of the Grasnick 1 sketchbook and have been realized in audio form by Professor Biamonti.[liv]

For three movements the music flows along more-or-less serenely and graciously until the exhilarating scramble of the finale — 'such fun to play' enthuses Rebecca Clarke in her *Beethoven Centenary* study of the composer's writing for the string quartet.[lv] 'The end, based on the three-note phrase from the exposition-development juncture, is a delightful joke. Haydn must have been pleased to be so skilfully emulated.'[lvi]

[i] Barry Cooper (2000, p. 78) gives the start-date for Op. 18, No. 3 as the summer of 1798, remarking 'it was virtually completed by the end of the year'. William Kinderman (2005, p. 323) suggests Beethoven commenced work on the composition in the autumn of 1798, completing it in January 1799 with revisions later in 1800.

[ii] William Kinderman, editor, 2005, pp. 323–4. See also: Beethoven House, Digital Archives, Document, Sammlung H. C. Bodmer. HCB Mh 64.

[iii] Robert Winter and Robert Martin, editors, 1994, p. 150 and Joseph de Marliave, 1925 (reprint 1961), p. 17.

[iv] Bernhard Jacobson Liner notes to: *Ludwig van Beethoven; The early string quartets*, Op. 18, Alban Berg Quartet, EMI, 1981.

[v] Marion M. Scott, 1940, p. 254.

[vi] Robin Golding discusses the construction of the D major Quartet in his Liner Notes to The Lindsey String Quartet, *Beethoven's String Quartets*.

[vii] Denis Matthews, 1985, p. 129.

[viii] Robert Simpson, *The chamber music for strings* in: Denis Arnold and Nigel Fortune, editors, 1973, p. 244–5.

[ix] Arthur Shepherd, 1935, p. 17.

[x] Paul Bekker, 1925, p. 311.

[xi] As quoted by Joseph de Marliave, 1925 (reprint 1961), pp. 17–18.

[xii] As quoted by Therese Muxeneder, Liner Notes to *Beethoven String Quartets*, Arte Nova Classics.

[xiii] Philip Radcliffe, 1978, p. 23.

[xiv] See, for example, Therese Muxeneder, Liner Notes to *Beethoven String Quartets*, Arte Nova Classics.

[xv] Philip Radcliffe, 1978, p. 23.

[xvi] Joseph Kerman, 1967, p. 20.

[xvii] Philip Radcliffe, 1978, pp. 23–4.

[xviii] The phrase in question here is derived form Arthur Shepherd, 1935, p. 17.

[xix] Two examples of Beethoven's originality are cited by William Kinderman, editor, 2005, p. 55 and Misha Donat, *Notes to the BBC Radio Three Beethoven experience*, Monday 6 June 2005, www.bbc.co.uk/radio3/Beethoven

[xx] As discussed by Joseph de Marliave, 1925 (reprint 1961), p. 18.

[xxi] Basil Lam, 1975, pp. 22–3.

[xxii] Robert Winter and Robert Martin, editors, 1994, p. 162.

[xxiii] The view of Romain Rolland, 1917, p. 180.

[xxiv] Arthur Shepherd, 1935, p. 17.

[xxv] Philip Radcliffe, 1978, p. 24.

[xxvi] Joseph Kerman, 1967, pp. 20–1.

[xxvii] Basil Lam, 1975, p. 23.

[xxviii] Robert Winter and Robert Martin, editors, 1994, p. 162.

[xxix] See Joseph de Marliave, 1925 (reprint 1961), p. 20 and Arthur Shepherd, 1935, p. 17.

[xxx] Adrian Bolt writing in *My Own Trumpet* as recalled by Michael Kennedy in: *Adrian Boult*, 1987, p. 20.

[xxxi] As discussed by Philip Radcliffe, 1978, p. 25.

[xxxii] Denis Matthews, 1985, pp. 129–30.

[xxxiii] Arthur Shepherd, 1935, p. 17.
[xxxiv] Misha Donat *Notes to the BBC Radio Three Beethoven experience*, Monday 6 June 2005, www.bbc.co.uk/radio3/Beethoven
[xxxv] Joseph de Marliave, 1925 (reprint 1961), p. 18.
[xxxvi] These have been recorded by Professor Biamonti in his *Audio Catalogue* 234 (1800). He offers the alternative possibility the sketches may refer to the Violin Sonata, Op. 24.
[xxxvii] Philip Radcliffe, 1978, p. 24.
[xxxviii] Joseph Kerman, 1967, p. 20.
[xxxix] Bernhard Jacobson Liner notes to: *Ludwig van Beethoven; The early string quartets*, Op. 18, Alban Berg Quartet, EMI, 1981.
[xl] Robert Winter and Robert Martin, editors, 1994, p. 162.
[xli] Basil Lam, 1975, p. 24.
[xlii] Joseph de Marliave, 1925 (reprint 1961), pp. 21–2.
[xliii] As suggested by Robert Winter and Robert Martin, editors, 1994, p. 163.
[xliv] Robert Simpson, *The chamber music for strings* in: Denis Arnold and Nigel Fortune, editors, 1973, pp. 244–5.
[xlv] As remarked by Misha Donat, *Notes to the BBC Radio Three Beethoven experience*, Monday 6 June 2005, www.bbc.co.uk/radio3/Beethoven
[xlvi] William Henry Hadow, 1926. p. 38.
[xlvii] Marion M. Scott, 1940, p. 254.
[xlviii] Denis Matthews, 1985, p. 129.
[xlix] Philip Radcliffe, 1978, p. 25.
[l] Arthur Shepherd, 1935, p. 17.
[li] As maintained by Basil Lam, 1975, p. 24.
[lii] Arthur Shepherd, 1935, p. 17.
[liii] Joseph Kerman, 1967, p. 25.
[liv] Professor Biamonti, *Audio Catalogue* 187 (1798).
[lv] Rebecca Clarke, *The Beethoven quartets as a player sees them, Musical Times*, Special issue [Beethoven's Death Centenary], Vol. VIII, No. 2, 1927.
[lvi] Robert Winter and Robert Martin, editors, 1994, p. 163.

STRING QUARTET IN C MINOR, OP. 18, NO. 4

'Among the Op. 18 quartets, the C minor Quartet with its mournful earnestness stands as sole witness of an outlook on life, a restless dissatisfaction, the very opposite of the cheerful sense of concord with the world and mankind expressed in the other five.'

Paul Bekker, *Beethoven*, 1925, p. 313.

'This quartet is the most polished work of Op. 18 and one of the most advanced in style of Beethoven's early manner. It possess the depth of lyrical feeling and the dramatic power of another work of contemporary date, the Op. 13 Piano Sonata also written in C minor. Like that

> it might also be called the *Pathétique*.'

Joseph de Marliave, *Beethoven's Quartets*, 1925 (reprint 1961), p. 22.

> 'As Beethoven employs G major for moods of tenderness and serenity, so he seems to employ C minor for those of strength or vehemence or sternness. The present quartet may in this matter be compared with the C minor Violin Sonata, the finale of the C minor Trio, with the Sonata *Pathétique*, with the last piano sonata, and especially the Fifth Symphony. Indeed, one of the most wonderful passages of the symphony is here partly anticipated.'

William Henry Hadow, *Beethoven's Op. 18 Quartets*, 1926. p. 40.

> 'So far as the C minor Quartet is concerned, much harm has been done by the expectations aroused by Beethoven's famous "C minor mood", as if there were such a thing in a generalised sense. C minor often incites Beethoven to blunt energy, but never to the same mood twice ... [The] point is that most criticisms of Op. 18, No. 4, miss its sardonic humour by expecting a C minor Titan.'

Robert Simpson, *The Chamber Music for Strings*, in: *The Beethoven Reader*, 1971, pp. 246–7.

> 'One could expect something remarkable when for the first time Beethoven chose the pathetic-

laden "key of destiny" for a string quartet. Even
the opening theme shows that once again he was
opening a hidden doorway of his art.'

Heinz Becker, Liner Notes to, *Beethoven: The String Quartets*, The Amadeus Quartet, Deutsche Grammophon, 1974.

'The Quartet in C minor is the most vigorous of the six and makes the most direct appeal.'

Philip Radcliffe, *Beethoven's String Quartets*, 1978, pp. 33.

'The Quartet in C minor, Op. 18, No. 4 is less assured stylistically, but of still greater interest in the way it carries forward Beethoven's experimentation with movement roles. It is indeed, the first of several cyclic works in which he comes close to reversing the traditional characters of the slow movement and the dance movement.'

Bernhard Jacobson, Liner Notes to: *Ludwig van Beethoven; The Early String Quartets*, Op. 18, Alban Berg Quartet, EMI, 1981.

'Here is one of Beethoven's earliest C-minor essays, though it is preceded by three strong and interesting works, the Piano Trio, Op. 1, No. 3 (1794), the String Trio, Op. 9, No. 3 (1798), and the Piano Sonata, Op. 10, No. 1 (1796–98).'

Robert Winter and Robert Martin, editors, *The Beethoven Quartet Companion*, 1994, p. 163.

> 'Mozart rather than Haydn may be sensed ... in the background to the standard one work in the minor key in the set, No. 4 in C minor. That key was already Beethoven's favoured minor tonality, prompted by his admiration for C minor movements by Mozart such as the Piano Sonata K. 457 and the Piano Concerto K. 491.'

David Wyn Jones in: Robin Stowell, editor, *The Cambridge Companion to the String Quartet*, 2003, p. 212.

The C minor String Quartet, Op. 14, No. 4 is the only one of the set of six in a minor key. Moreover, Beethoven assigns no fewer than three of its four movements to this key with the *Scherzo* being in C major. 'Coming in the midst of the other five works of this set — all in major tonalities — the C minor of the fourth brings us in touch with the fateful reverberations that become more and more resonant with the onrushing years.' Paul Bekker sensed in the C minor quartet 'a gnawing inner dissatisfaction; a desire to meet and overcome difficulties; the spur of ambition and the longing for victory'.[i] C minor is the key of the *Pathétique* Piano Sonata and the Fifth Symphony and, in popular culture, associated with the defiant, resolute composer whose countenance glares out from the scowling portraits ready, in his own words, 'to seize fate by the throat'.[ii]

In his selection of the keys of C minor and C major, Beethoven was in part harking back to the tradition of the formulas of the earlier suites and partitas.[iii] Nearer to his own time it was customary for a composer, in a set of six string quartets, to arrange one in a minor key. In the case of Op. 18, No. 4: 'Beethoven yet again chose C minor, as if in a deliberate attempt to associate himself with that key in public consciousness.'[iv] In choosing a minor key, Beethoven was also following the precedents of Haydn and the D-minor String Quartet of his Op. 76, and Mozart in the case of the D-minor String Quartet in his set of six dedicated to Haydn. Joseph Kerman remarks: 'C minor was the key that Beethoven chose ... His affection for this tonality in the early years amounted to a mania that was not really played out until the Piano Sonata in C minor, Op. 111 of 1822.'[v]

In Heinz Becker's memorable phrase, 'this quartet lacks the contemplative island of a slow movement'.[vi] It has been observed that when Beethoven dispenses with a slow movement it is for reasons that the work as a whole is light-hearted — the Eighth Symphony and Piano Sonata, Op. 31, No. 3 being such examples.[vii] The mood of the String Quartet, Op. 18, No. 4 is, however, altogether more determined and serious, possessed of 'dark colouring ... passion ... richer and more massive in texture than the other of the Op. 18 Quartets'.[viii] Critics of Beethoven's workmanship draw attention to the manner in which he 'goes in for crunching homophony'.[ix] For others, there is 'little sign of the refining art that had elevated the first [quartets] of the series'. At the same time it is acknowledged 'the outer movements abound in rough-hewn textures and orchestral effects' with touches of 'sardonic humour' making the composition as a whole 'a peculiar hybrid'.[x]

Some commentators believe the C-minor Quartet may have its genesis early in Beethoven's career, perhaps going back to the period when he lived in Bonn.[xi] It is known that he brought drafts for compositions with him when he arrived in Vienna in 1792, some of which he subsequently reworked.[xii] In this regard, the position concerning the C-minor Quartet is uncertain since no preliminary sketches have been identified. Bekker comments: 'It is noteworthy that we possess no studies for the Quartet in C minor. This rather suggests that it was separated from the others by time as well as by the character of its contents.' He supported the opinion of the German music theorist Hugo Riemann who reasoned the composition was a revision of an older work now lost and may therefore be regarded, in terms of Beethoven's creative output, as a supplementary piece to the C minor Piano Sonatas, Op. 10 and Op. 13, the C minor Pianoforte Trio, Op. 1 and the C minor String Trio, Op. 9.[xiii]

Ideas for the C minor Quartet may have been worked in a sketchbook presumed lost; this may also have contained sketches for the Septet, Op. 20, the First Symphony, Op. 21 and the Third Piano Concerto, Op. 37.[xiv] The Grasnick 2 sketchbook contains drafts of what may be early sketches for the first movement of the C minor Quartet (see String Quartets, Op. 18, Nos. 1–6).[xv] Beethoven probably worked on the piece from the summer to the autumn of 1799.[xvi] An aspect of Beethoven's construction has given rise to an anecdote that is worthy of reiteration. Beethoven's pupil Ferdinand Ries relates that he had occasion to look through the manuscript of the C minor Quartet and discovered two pure fifth progressions. Later, when out on a walk with the composer, he remarked on these pointing out that parallel fifths were disapproved of by the learned pedagogues of the day and were considered to be a departure from conventional compositional refinement. Beethoven responded: 'Now, and who has forbidden them?' To Ries's answer that the grammatical failing was forbidden by Friedrich Marburg, Johann Kirnberger, Johann Joseph Fux, and other theorists, Beethoven defiantly declared: 'And I allow them!'[xvii]

In point of fact, in his student days Beethoven practised strict counterpoint diligently, using as a guide Fux's *Gradus ad Parnassum* – 'Steps to Parnassus'. Nicolas Slonimsky comments: 'But strict counterpoint never appealed to Beethoven, although he felt great admiration for master contrapuntists of his day. In actual composition Beethoven made use of counterpoint as he saw fit, without being much concerned about strictness of the interval or the pedantry of the science. He humanized counterpoint.'[xviii] Reflecting on the Ries anecdote, Arthur Shepherd concludes: 'It seems, almost, that Beethoven was making sport of Ries, for the fifths in question move in contrary direction and are apparent to the eye only [on reading the score], and certainly not to the ear.'[xix] Moreover, the fifths in question are separated by rests.

As the nineteenth century progressed, piano arrangements of instrumental works grew in popularity, 'signalling a gradual shift from a string-based musical culture to a keyboard-based one'.[xx] It is from this circumstance that a measure of the popularity of the String Quartet, Op. 18, No.4, at the period in question, can be derived. On 15 November 1820, the *Allgemeine musikalische Zeitung* published an estimation of a four-hand arrangement of the work, created by Ferdinand Ries. The reviewer considered the endeavour 'splendid in every regard.' Of particular interest are the reviewer's general observations: '[This] is the one out of the six earlier ones (still the dearest of all for not just a few people) for which we owe this master our gratitude. That precisely Beethoven's quartets, as well arranged as they are, must lose more on the pianoforte than those of many other masters, especially even Mozart's, is due to the subject and style.' The *AmZ* contributor enthused: 'Performers will find in this, as in other Beethoven quartets arranged in this manner, diverse instruction, ingenious entertainment, and fine enjoyment.'[xxi]

In 1884, the Concert Hall of the old *Gewandhaus* in Leipzig was reopened after a period of reconstruction; the original facilities dated back to 1781 and had been developed from a building used by cloth merchants. In the year of its opening, a recital of string quartets was given, prompting the reviewer to remark: 'It is difficult to decide whether the performers celebrated their mastery most in the C minor Quartet of Beethoven [Op. 18, No. 4], the G major Quartet of Haydn [Op. 33, No. 5 or Op. 77, No. 1] or the G major Quartet of Mozart [K. 387].'[xxii]

Nearer to our own time, a recollection from the diary of the American composer, pianist and musicologist Dika Newlin connects us with the music under consideration. In 1939 she attended Arnold Schoenberg's composition class at the University of California, Los Angles. She recalls how Schoenberg expected his students to be able to read and play from published scores. On the day in question (25 October) the subject for study chosen by him was Beethoven's Op. 18 String Quartet, No 4; he wanted the class 'to become proficient in the key of C minor'.[xxiii]

Beethoven designated the first movement *Allegro ma non tanto*, indicating he wanted the passage to be played *allegro* 'but not too much so'. His adoption in this movement of the key of C minor is somewhat paradoxical, being a key he usually reserved for drama and tension. The opening movement is not lacking in dramatic moments, particularly at the start, but when it gets under way the main thematic material is flowing and lyrical. 'In some ways Op. 18, No. 4 is the least typically C minor, the least stern, the least ferocious of the early pieces in that key; the first movement is, however, music of passion and urgency.'[xxiv]

In our discussion of the creation origins of the String Quartets, Op. 18, Nos. 1–6, we have drawn attention to the influence on Beethoven's string quartet writing by the Silesian-born composer and theorist Emanuel Aloys Förster. It was at his house where the youthful Beethoven heard performances of chamber music and it is from Förster that he may have received lessons in quartet writing. Several string quartets and quintets by Förster were published, a number of which are considered by authorities to possess Beethoven-like features that Beethoven himself may have assimilated into his own style. In particular, the first movement of a quartet in F minor by Förster, published in 1799, is considered to have 'strong affinities with that of Beethoven's C minor Quartet from Op.18'.[xxv] A more distant, and potent, source of influence may have been the first movements of Mozart's String Quartet in G minor, or his String Quintet in G minor.[xxvi] Joseph de Marliave draws attention in the string writing to Beethoven's adoption of muffled *tremoli* as being among the first evidence of the adoption of this technique of string playing in the quartet repertoire — he also cites Haydn's precedent in the String Quartet No. 30 in G minor.[xxvii] Hugo Riemann believed a close thematic connection can be found between the first movement of the C minor Quartet and that of the composer's Duo for viola and cello, the so-called *mit zwei obligaten Augengläsern — Duo 'with two eyeglasses obbligato'*.[xxviii] This dates from around 1796–7, the time-period in question, although it was not published until 1912.[xxix]

The Austrian music critic and writer Theodor Otto Helm was a leading figure in Viennese musical life for more than fifty years; he is remembered today for his pioneering *Beethoven's Streichquartette* (Leipzig, 1910). Writing in 1885, he considered the C minor Quartet to be a worthy counterpart to Beethoven's *Pathétique* Piano sonata set in the same key. Regarding the Quartet, he wrote: '[I] ask the reader just to cast a glance at the music ... and earnestly ask himself whether a quartet movement by Haydn or Mozart can display such a broad and unified, forward-driving melody?'[xxx] In his endorsement of the music, de Marliave invokes nineteenth-century style rhetoric: 'Charged with infinite longing and burning energy, it seems to well up from the depths of the soul in an urgent prayer for deliverance ... The passionate voice rises from bar to bar, pausing once as though to take a breath.'[xxxi] The movement is possessed of 'high seriousness'[xxxii] and 'confronts us with the Beethoven of the tragic portraits'.[xxxiii] *Sturm und Drang* permeate the opening whose contours recall the *Pathétique* Piano Sonata of 1799.[xxxiv] 'The opening passage is one of the first examples of Beethoven's melodic gift, broad and powerful, expressive and yet uncomplex. Neither in Haydn nor Mozart could a period so virile be found, so profoundly imaginative and emotional.'[xxxv] It proceeds in a 'motoric manner' that to some ears is suggestive 'of the language of the Mannheim school of composers' rewarding the listener with a 'judiciously varied interplay of long and rather sumptuous melodic lines'.[xxxvi]

Although the Op. 18, No, 4 String Quartet is widely recognized for being 'the most obviously Beethoven' of the Op. 18 set,[xxxvii] the composer's workmanship is not without its critics. Basil Lam complains: 'It makes a point of presenting formulae of the driest kind', but, he acknowledges '[Beethoven] holds the listener's attention by a pervasive unexpectedness in bar-rhythms'.[xxxviii] In Alison Bullock's estimation: 'The opening of the first movement immediately suggests inexperience: its main melody, with straight quaver accompaniment, is in an entirely conventional, Classical style; the whole movement has an air of impatience but is otherwise nothing but orthodox in form and expression.'[xxxix] David Wyn Jones remarks: 'While Beethoven was to produce several piano sonatas of character, in C minor (including the Sonata *Pathétique* composed shortly before Op. 18) and a piano concerto too [No. 1, Op. 15], his one quartet in C minor disappoints. The opening of the first movement is artificially bolstered by energising turn figures, *sforzando* markings and triple stopped chords.'[xl]

In the opinion of William Kinderman: 'Ultimately, the roughness of this movement seems to arise from an imbalance between the passionate force of Beethoven's "C minor mood" and his ability to mediate or control this idiom in the artistic form as a whole.' He compares the opening movement with that of the opening of the *Pathétique* Sonata that he considers shares similarities in rhythm, register and rhetoric but which are more convincing in the Sonata than in the Quartet whose rhetoric Kinderman finds 'somewhat overblown'.[xli] In Beethoven's defence, Barry Cooper challenges commentators who pronounce the nature of the music as 'weak' or even 'crude'. He mediates: 'Beethoven seems here to be deliberately writing music that is uncomfortable ... perhaps his intention was to heighten the contrast with the other quartets?'[xlii]

The second movement is headed *Andante scherzoso quasi Allegretto* and takes the place of the traditional slow movement. Beethoven adopted a similar procedure in his String Trio, Op. 9, No. 2 signalling a willingness, thereby early in his career, to dispense with strictly formal musical conventions.[xliii] Although Beethoven adopts the term *scherzo*, what we have in essence is 'a contrapuntally playful scherzo'.[xliv] It is 'distinctly harmless' and has little in common with the manner of a more typical boisterous Beethovenian scherzo; here, the players are required to 'tiptoe through the pianissimo staccato tunes'.[xlv] Kerman suggests in this movement Beethoven 'was working for droll simplicity of procedure' and was 'throwing in his lot with the *Teutsche* of the Viennese ballrooms'. That said, he finds evidence of 'quite an original conception' in the music's fugal-style opening.[xlvi] Although the designation *scherzo* may be somewhat arbitrary, as Shepherd comments: 'Its tempo indication *Andante scherzoso quasi Allegretto*, modifies the characteristic rapid tempo of the usual scherzo ... moreover it is entirely cast in fugal style which in turn is adapted to the sonata design ... What more impressive evidence of technical mastery could one look for!'[xlvii]

Professor Giovanni Biamonti believes the composer's sketches reveal 'a proud yet contemplative torso' for the *Andante*, 'almost painfully beautiful in its simplicity and spiritual longing'. It consists of two sections, the first consisting of eight bars and the second of sixteen, both repeated in full score. Biamonti remarks: 'Discontented where the music was taking him — to harmonic explorations that would have seemed shocking for the time — Beethoven abandoned these fragments and started once more from scratch.'[xlviii] Gerald Abraham finds the *Andante scherzoso* to be 'Haydnish' in character with hints about it of the composer's First Symphony.[xlix] De Marliave is more explicit: 'The *Andante scherzoso* is, both in rhythm and design, extraordinarily like that of the *Andante* of the First Symphony.'[l] In the same spirit Leon Plantinga views the *Andante scherzoso* as a counterpart to the First Symphony, particularly regarding 'its particularly attractive counterpoint'. He also cites the pioneering influence of Haydn: 'It had first been invested with these associations in Haydn's remarkable Quartets Op. 20 (1772) with their profound expressiveness and (in three of them) earnest and elaborate fugal finales.'[li]

In his discussion of the movement's construction, Jones identifies it as being 'a scherzo in full sonata form in which the constituent paragraphs all begin with points of imitation'. He adds: 'While the effect is certainly whimsical and engaging, the craftsmanship shows the pedagogic training that Beethoven had undergone a few years earlier with Haydn and Albrechtsberger.'[lii] Donald Tovey offers the generalisation: '[The] occasional displays of counterpoint in Beethoven's early works are far more then merely competent. They are unquestionably brilliant.' As an exemple he cites the triple counterpoint that, in his words, 'adorns the recapitulation' of the *Andante scherzoso*.[liii] On another occasion Tovey wrote: '[From] his well-known technical struggles in his years of pupillage, the easy inference has been drawn that Beethoven never was a great master of counterpoint.' He exonerates the composer on the grounds: 'The fact is that Beethoven's counterpoint becomes rough only under dramatic and emotional stress.' He asserts: 'No Doctor of Music could do better triple counterpoint than that in the *Andante* of the String Quartet in C minor, Op. 18, No. 4.'[liv]

As noted in our opening remarks, in the String Quartet Op. 18, No. 4 the *Andante scherzoso* replaces what might more typically be a deeply felt slow movement of the kind Beethoven composed for the contemporary *Pathétique* Piano Sonata. In Alison Bullock's summation: 'The *Andante* ... indicates a spark of free thought: it is not really a slow movement at all. The marking *scherzoso* gives the clue to its real nature, a spiky, Haydnesque piece that sounds like a minuet but is in fact in sonata form. Partly fugal, it occasionally resembles an exercise in counterpoint [a further reminder of Beethoven's studies with Johann Georg Albrechtsberger].'[lv] Lam refers to 'the witty *scherzo*', the counterpoint of which he considers to be 'less urbane than its counterpart in the First Symphony'.[lvi] Metaphorically speaking Denis Matthews describes the movement as 'light footed in fugal style, taking a backward glance at the fugues in Haydn's Op. 20 quartets'.[lvii] Barry Cooper expresses similar thoughts: 'The "slow" movement is a whimsical *scherzo* in C major that affects to be fugal but actually pokes fun at the learned style.'[lviii] Joseph de Marliave's appraisal provides a fitting conclusion to this part of our narrative: 'In the *Andante scherzoso* the artist hides his sorrow under a mask of lively good humour, easing his spirit in the solution of rather trivial academic problems of canon and counterpoint ... [but] the artist prevails over the technician [and] delights in his creative power.'[lix]

The third movement is a *Menuetto* — minuet — in *Allegretto* time. Jones, somewhat ruefully, considers the piece to be no more than 'a very four-square rondo'.[lx] It opens exploiting the identical notes that commence the *Andante scherzoso,* 'thus at once adding to the unity in conception of the work'.[lxi] It is another 'stern C minor movement, characterised by strong chromaticism'.[lxii] The profile of Mozart is once more discernable: 'The *sforzandi*, on alternating notes of the first phrase, being reminiscent of the *Menuetto* of the older G major Quartet [the first of Mozart's set of six dedicated to Haydn].'[lxiii] Although designated as being a minuet, the somewhat urgent atmosphere of the music is more akin to that of a scherzo.[lxiv] In this movement Beethoven returns to 'the emotional world of the first movement'.[lxv] A poignant 'upward-climbing melody'[lxvi] establishes a mood that approaches the pathos 'characteristic of other of Beethoven's C minor movements'.[lxvii] In the case of the present movement, its character is made unruly by its offbeat accents: 'It would be a sweet and lyrical interlude but for the restlessness induced by the first violin's triplets.'[lxviii] Notwithstanding, the *Menuetto* is not without 'an atmosphere of courtly grace' typical of that found in the third movements of a Mozart string quartet but here 'its emotion is veiled and controlled'.[lxix] Basil Lam was fulsome in his praise for this particular movement of Beethoven's String Quartet in C minor, Op. 18, No. 4: 'Only Mozart's G minor Quintet and Schubert's A minor Quartet have minuets comparable for pathetic grandeur with the wonderful third movement.'[lxx]

The fourth and final movement is an *Allegro-prestissimo*. It is in the style of a rondo 'with a muscular refrain that has a faint Hungarian tang'.[lxxi] It is in effect a *rondo alla zingarese* — a rondo 'in the style of gypsy music'. In electing to write in this manner Beethoven was subscribing to a musical idiom that Haydn had made popular in his celebrated *Gypsy Rondo* Trio, No. 39 of 1796. 'The finale is a clean textbook rondo whose gypsy bounce is yet one more reminder of how much Beethoven had learned from his study of Haydn's music.'[lxxii] This vogue of writing in a spirited, tarantella-style would find expression later in the nineteenth century as, for example, in the case of the Piano Quartet, Op. 25 of Johannes Brahms.

In describing the opening of the piece, Theodor Otto Helm resorted to fanciful imagery: 'One imagines four combatants battling against each other, clad in shining armour, armed with sword and shield. At the outset the first violin, the *primus inter pares* among the knightly company, is alone in the arena, a young hero trying his strength with supple limb and sinew; but soon the three other champions enter the lists and the jousting commences.'[lxxiii] If we settle for the more straightforward description of the piece as being a rondo, it can be recognized for being a spirited movement 'that mixes impatience with humour'.[lxxiv] Kerman suggests Beethoven's rondo 'strikes a lighter pose' and possesses less of the 'sparkle' than Haydn's example being 'all clatter and no substance'.[lxxv] Jacobson is more sympathetic and considers the movement 'makes its effect exuberantly enough and the *prestissimo* coda provides a suitably tearaway conclusion in the hands of a quartet willing to dispense with caution'.[lxxvi] In its closing *prestissimo*, Lam discerned 'a degree of aggression' somewhat in the manner of the closing pages of the composer's later String Quartet in E minor of Op. 59.[lxxvii]

The finale, in common with that of the Piano Sonata Op. 10, No. 1, is terse rather than expansive but the challenges it poses to the resources of the string quartet medium 'convey a sense agitation'.[lxxviii] Beethoven exploits the full character of the rustic gypsy melody, allowing the music 'to soar into the very highest register with arresting *fortissimo* strokes'.[lxxix] Charging forward at the fastest possible speed, Beethoven brings his String Quartet Op. 18, No. 4 to an end 'with a witty, epigrammatic close'.[lxxx]

---

[i] Arthur Shepherd, 1935, p. 19. Paul Bekker's words are quoted by Shepherd.

[ii] In point of fact the contemporary portraits of Beethoven, taken from life, convey a relatively composed-looking (excuse the pun) countenance. The glaring eyes, wind-swept hair, resolute jaw etc. are largely superimpositions of later artists and sculptors of the Romantic era.

[iii] As remarked by Marion M. Scott, 1940, p. 254.

[iv] Barry Cooper, 2000, pp. 92–4.

[v] Joseph Kerman, 1967, p. 70.

[vi] Heinz Becker, Liner Notes to, *Beethoven: The string quartets*, The Amadeus Quartet, Deutsche Grammophon, 1974.

[vii] As cited, amongst others, by William Henry Hadow, 1926, pp. 40–1, and Philip Radcliffe, 1978, p. 33.

[viii] Philip Radcliffe, 1978, p. 33.

[ix] Robert Simpson, *The chamber music for strings* in: Denis Arnold and Nigel Fortune, editors, *The Beethoven companion*, 1973, p. 247.

[x] Denis Matthews, 1985, p. 130.

[xi] Alison Bullock *Notes to the BBC Radio Three Beethoven experience*, Tuesday 9 June 2005, www.bbc.co.uk/radio3/Beethoven

[xii] Robert Winter, and Robert Martin, editors, *The Beethoven quartet companion*, 1994, pp. 163–4.

[xiii] Paul Bekker, 1925, p. 312.

[xiv] Barry Cooper, 2000, p. 92 and 1990, p. 67.

[xv] William Kinderman, 2005, pp. 323–4. The source referred to is British Library, Ms 29997.

[xvi] *Ibid*.

[xvii] Ferdinand Ries, cited in: Oscar George Theodore Sonneck, *Beethoven: impressions of contemporaries,* 1927, pp. 49–50. See also, Elliot Forbes, 1967, p. 367.

[xviii] Nicolas Slonimsky, 2000, p. 157.

[xix] Arthur Shepherd, 1935, p. 20.

[xx] Robert Winter and Robert Martin, editors, *The Beethoven quartet companion*, 1994, p. 33.

[xxi] Wayne M. Senner, Robin Wallace and William Meredith, editors, *The critical reception of Beethoven's compositions by his German contemporaries*, 1999, Vol. 1, pp. 153–4. The authors also draw attention to four-hand arrangements of the String Quartets Nos. 1–3 (1817) and the String Quartet No. 5 (1821) by Friedrich Mockwitz, a contemporary pianist known for his many arrangements of chamber and orchestral works.

[xxii] Quoted in Robert Winter, and Robert Martin, editors, *The Beethoven quartet*

xxii *companion*, 1994, p. 46
xxiii Dika Newlin, 1980, pp. 123–4.
xxiv Robert Winter and Robert Martin, editors, *The Beethoven quartet companion*, 1994, pp. 163–4.
xxv Philip Radcliffe, 1978, p. 178.
xxvi *Ibid*, p. 33.
xxvii Joseph de Marliave, 1925 (reprint 1961), p. 25 and footnote 1.
xxviii Gerald Abraham, *Beethoven's Chamber Music*, in: *The Age of Beethoven, The New Oxford History of Music, Vol. VIII*, Gerald Abraham, editor, 1988, p. 280.
xxix Beethoven wrote the Duo for his friend and cello player Baron Nikolaus Zmeskall von Domanovez who held the post of Secretary in the Hungarian Chancellery and who rendered many services to the composer. In one of his numerous letters to Zmeskall, Beethoven teased him for his short-sightedness, saying: '*Je vous suis biento obligé pour votre faiblesse des votres yeux*' – 'I am most obliged for the weakness of your eyes.' This may be the origin of the humorous title that has been conferred on the Duo.
xxx William Kinderman, editor, 2005, p. 3.
xxxi Joseph de Marliave, 1925 (reprint 1961), pp. 23–4.
xxxii Basil Lam, 1975, p. 25.
xxxiii Arthur Shepherd, 1935, p. 19.
xxxiv Denis Matthews, 1985, p. 130.
xxxv Joseph de Marliave, 1925 (reprint 1961), pp. 23–4.
xxxvi Bernhard Jacobson Liner notes to: *Ludwig van Beethoven; The early string quartets*, Op. 18, Alban Berg Quartet, EMI, 1981.
xxxvii Gerald Abraham, *Beethoven's Chamber Music*, in: *The Age of Beethoven, The New Oxford History of Music, Vol. VIII*, Gerald Abraham, editor, 1988, pp. 282–3.
xxxviii Basil Lam, 1975, p. 25.
xxxix Alison Bullock, *Notes to the BBC Radio Three Beethoven experience*, Tuesday 7 June 2005, www.bbc.co.uk/radio3/Beethoven
xl David Wyn Jones in: Robin Stowell, editor, *The Cambridge companion to the string quartet*, 2003, pp. 212–13.
xli William Kinderman, editor, 2005, p. 56.
xlii Barry Cooper, 2000, p. 94.
xliii See Maynard Solomon, 1977, p. 101.
xliv Therese Muxeneder, Liner Notes to *Beethoven String Quartets*, Arte Nova Classics.
xlv Robert Winter and Robert Martin, editors, *The Beethoven quartet companion*, 1994, p. 164.
xlvi Joseph Kerman, 1967, p. 69.
xlvii Arthur Shepherd, 1935, p. 20.
xlviii Professor Giovanni Biamonti, *The unheard Beethoven* ('First version of the String Quartet, Op. 18, No. 4'). The composer's revisions are preserved in the British Library *Sketch Miscellany*, Ms 29997.
xlix Gerald Abraham, *Beethoven's chamber music*, in: *The Age of Beethoven, The New Oxford History of Music, Vol. VIII*, Gerald Abraham, editor, 1988, pp. 282–3.
l Joseph de Marliave, 1925 (reprint 1961), pp. 23–4.

li Leon Plantinga, 1984, pp. 30–31.
lii David Wyn Jones in: Robin Stowell, editor, *The Cambridge companion to the string quartet*, 2003, pp. 212–13.
liii Donald Francis Tovey, 1944, p. 97.
liv Michael Tilmouth, editor, *Donald Francis Tovey: The classics of music: talks, essays, and other writings previously uncollected*, 2001, pp. 339–40.
lv Alison Bullock, *Notes to the BBC Radio Three Beethoven experience*, Tuesday 9 June 2005, www.bbc.co.uk/radio3/Beethoven
lvi Basil Lam, 1975, p. 25.
lvii Denis Matthews, 1985, p. 130.
lviii Barry Cooper, 2000, pp. 92–4.
lix Joseph de Marliave, 1925, (reprint 1961), p. 26.
lx David Wyn Jones in: Robin Stowell, editor, *The Cambridge companion to the string quartet*, 2003, pp. 212–13.
lxi Joseph de Marliave, 1925 (reprint 1961), p. 28.
lxii Robin Golding, Liner Notes to The Lindsey String Quartet, *Beethoven's string quartets*.
lxiii Arthur Shepherd, 1935, p. 20.
lxiv As considered to be the case by Alison Bullock, in her *Notes to the BBC Radio Three Beethoven experience*, Tuesday 9 June 2005, www.bbc.co.uk/radio3/Beethoven
lxv Denis Matthews, 1985, p. 130.
lxvi William Henry Hadow, 1926, p. 44.
lxvii Therese Muxeneder, Liner Notes to *Beethoven String Quartets*, Arte Nova Classics.
lxviii Robert Winter and Robert Martin, editors, *The Beethoven quartet companion*, 1994, p. 164.
lxix Joseph de Marliave, 1925 (reprint 1961), p. 28.
lxx Basil Lam, 1975, p. 25. Lam further remarks: 'If much of this Quartet seems to belong to Beethoven's earliest style, the *Menuetto* is far beyond the criticism that seeks for influences or signs of derivation.'
lxxi Robin Golding, Liner Notes to The Lindsey String Quartet, *Beethoven's String Quartets*.
lxxii Robert Winter and Robert Martin, editors, *The Beethoven quartet companion*, 1994, p. 165.
lxxiii As quoted by Joseph de Marliave, 1925 (reprint 1961), p, 29.
lxxiv Alison Bullock, *Notes to the BBC Radio Three Beethoven experience*, Tuesday 9 June 2005, www.bbc.co.uk/radio3/Beethoven
lxxv Joseph Kerman, 1967, p. 63 and pp. 69–70.
lxxvi Bernhard Jacobson Liner notes to: *Ludwig van Beethoven; The early string quartets*, Op. 18, Alban Berg Quartet, EMI, 1981.
lxxvii Basil Lam. 1975, p. 27.
lxxviii *Ibid.*
lxxix William Kinderman, 2005, pp. 56–7.
lxxx Robert Winter and Robert Martin, editors, *The Beethoven quartet companion*, 1994, p. 165.

STRING QUARTET IN A MAJOR, OP. 18, NO. 5

'This quartet is chiefly remarkable for its lovely *Andante* and set of variations on the beautiful theme which has all the feeling of a genuine folksong.'

Romain Rolland, *Beethoven and Handel*, 1917, p. 181.

'The ghost of Mozart hangs heavy over much of this music ... We know that Beethoven greatly admired Mozart's K. 464 on which Op. 18, No. 5, is clearly modelled.'

H. C. Robbins Landon, *Haydn: the Years of 'The creation'*, 1796–800, 1977, p. 505.

'If the Quartet in C minor is the most forceful of the six, the fifth, in A major, is the quietist and most retiring. It has strong affinities with Mozart's quartet in the same key, K. 464, which in all probability served s a model.'

Philip Radcliffe, *Beethoven's String Quartets*, 1978, pp. 37.

'In this quartet ... Beethoven is very much engaged in receiving the spirit of Mozart, though by direct study of scores rather than "at the hands of Haydn". The model is the obvious and wonderful one, Mozart's quartet in the same key of K. 464.'

Robert Winter and Robert Martin, editors, *The Beethoven Quartet Companion*, 1994, p. 165.

'Although Op. 18, No. 5 borrows much from Mozart, its drama, flighty changes of mood and rich texture are unmistakably the work of Beethoven's musical imagination.'

Alison Bullock, *Notes to the BBC Radio Three Beethoven experience*, Tuesday 7 June 2005, www.bbc.co.uk/radio3/Beethoven

Beethoven worked on the String Quartet in A major, Op. 18, No. 5 during June and August 1799, shortly after he had completed the first three quartets in the series of six. The larger portion appears to have been sketched alongside the Septet Op. 20. Remarking on this Joseph de Marliave comments in his typical florid style: 'Most of them [the sketches] are already in a form very like their final shape

... They spring up in delightful confusion and spontaneity; and it is as though Beethoven had picked a flower here and there, to make posies of the same colour and scent.'[i] In our opening discussion of the genesis of the Op. 18 String Quartets, we remarked that a source for the origins of the A major Quartet is the so-called Grasnick 2 sketchbook.[ii] This contains ideas for all four movements. It has been conjectured that a further sketchbook — probably containing sketches for the last two movements of the String Quartet No. 5, together with sketches for the Third Piano Concerto, and possibly the Fourth Quartet — has since been lost.[iii]

The A major Quartet has been variously described as 'a good-tempered if perhaps [a] rather formal work';[iv] 'a perfect type of concerto quartet';[v] a work possessed of 'suave polyphony'; [vi] and having an 'elegant and orthodox nature in which everything seems to fall delightfully into place, [forming] an excellent counterweight to the preceding quartet'.[vii]

As is apparent from our opening epigrammatic quotations, the A major Quartet is perceived as being 'a veritable act of homage to Mozart'.[viii] An anecdote from the recollections of Carl Czerny testifies to Beethoven's admiration for Mozart's string-quartet writing. In his reminiscences to Otto Jahn, Mozart's pioneering biographer, Czerny recounts: 'Beethoven once saw in my house the score of the six quartets by Mozart dedicated to Haydn. He opened the fifth in A and said: "That's what I call a work!" '[ix] Further testimony to Beethoven's estimation of Mozart's string quartet writing is that between the years 1798 and 1800 he copied out Mozart's String Quartet in G major K. 387; some 26 pages of manuscript bear testimony to Beethoven's industry and his wish to better understand his illustrious predecessor's compositional technique.[x] Beethoven also modelled his String Trio in E flat Op. 3 on Mozart's

Divertimento in E flat K. 563. Most significant of all, for its influence on the composition of the A major Quartet, was, as alluded to in the Czerny anecdote, Mozart's fifth Quartet from his Haydn set, K. 464 It is known that Beethoven copied out its last two movements in his act of homage and desire to better understand the art of string quartet writing. Not surprisingly, Op. 18, No. 5 has several features in common with Mozart's. It shares the same key of A major; Beethoven adopted the same sequencing of movements — the introductory *Allegro* is followed by a *Menuetto* that in turn is followed by a slow movement, thereby reversing the typical order; and Beethoven followed Mozart in including a movement with variations — in Mozart's Quartet there are six variations and in Beethoven's Quartet there are five.[xi]

We learn something of the public esteem felt for Beethoven's A major String Quartet in a review of a recital that took place in 1821; this was reported in the *Zeitung für Theatre und Musik*. At this time the composition had long been assimilated into the chamber music repertoire, although by then a chasm separated this work and the composer's most recent creations in the genre — the so called 'late quartets'. The concert programme in question included string quartets by Haydn, Andreas Romberg and, to close, Beethoven's A major Quartet of which the reviewer writes 'and finally a genial performance of one of the most magnificent quartets by Beethoven, in A major, with the beautiful variations in D major and a rondo that is truly a new invention.'[xii]

It was not until after Beethoven's death that his string quartets started to appear in recitals in London. Amongst pioneers in their promotion was the Philharmonic Society. In 1815, Beethoven's former piano pupil Ferdinand Ries had been elected to be one of its directors and played a significant role in the early promotion of his master's works in England. In its February issue of 1828 *The Musical Review* reported a concert in which the String Quartet in A major 'was performed with fine feeling'. Of related interest is that the C minor Quartet from the Op. 18 set was performed at its following concert.[xiii]

With assertive opening chords, Beethoven establishes the Quartet's key of A major and the movement's *Allegro* rhythm. Lam describes the movement as being possessed of 'cheerful unaggressive energy' and being 'amiable' in a manner that would be spoilt by 'intellectual exertions'. He further reflects: 'Artists develop according to their individual patterns of experience, and not in conformity with the external schemes of historicism.' With Mozart's model K. 464 in mind, he states: 'Beethoven's first movement is simpler, more primitive, if you like, than Mozart's'. He characterises Beethoven's style as being 'more straightforward' than Mozart's 'more serious' style.[xiv] Recalling the influence of Mozart's K. 464 – see our prefatory quotations – Philip Radcliffe comments: '[The] two first movements are in many ways very unalike; Mozart's is very closely knit and economical with its material; while Beethoven's is far more capricious and wanders in a pleasant, light-hearted way from one idea to another.'[xv] William Henry Hadow was captivated by Beethoven's music, describing it as 'innocent as a fairy tale by Mozart; full of pure delicate melody and light-handed adventure, the strongest conceivable contrast to the force and turbulence of the last quartet [No. 4].'[xvi]

In his study of Beethoven's preparatory sketches, the American musicologist Arthur Shepherd quotes Robert Schuman's remark: 'Beethoven often found his tunes in the alleys and on the sidewalk [pavement], but he made out of them the most beautiful themes in the world.' He cites a sketch of the principal theme of the first movement that, when compared with the final version, he considers 'shows graphically the composer's characteristic forward leap out of inexpressive and stereotyped confines into the clear air of freedom and plasticity'. With others Shepherd also finds Beethoven paying homage to Mozart.[xvii] The Italian musicologist Professor Giovanni Biamonti has rendered Beethoven's sketches more accessible to students and admirers of the composer by making audio recordings of many fragments of his surviving sketches. In the case of the A major String Quartet an audio file of a sketch, taken from p. 64 of the Grasnick 2 Sketchbook, reveals two eight-bar phrases; these are conjectured to be the beginning of a projected composition movement — perhaps for the A major Quartet?[xviii] Abraham considered the first movement of Op. 18, No. 5 to be one of the most 'finely wrought' of the Op. 18 set alongside that of the G major Quartet, No. 2.[xix]

The second movement is a *Menuetto* followed by a trio section. Bekker considered it to be one of the few of Beethoven's movements, so-named, that is truly a minuet in character.[xx] Commentators are at one in their recognition of the movement's lyrical charm. We offer a selection of their expressions of admiration. 'The most gentle and "feminine" of Minuets.'[xxi] 'This movement breathes an atmosphere of sweet, untroubled tenderness ... inspired by the contemplative spirit of Mozart.'[xxii] 'The Mozartian character of the dance movement, this time no scherzo but a minuet, is more generalized [than Mozart] ... is the most perfectly realized movement of the four, with glinting threads of unison emerging from the texture, flowing counterpoints and a sense of harmonic poise that truly emulates Mozart.'[xxiii] 'In its haunting simplicity the minuet is Mozartian, but the authentic voice of Beethoven can be recognised in the Wordsworth-like plainness of speech, wonderfully characterised (when the first two-bar strain is repeated by all four instruments) in giving of the melody to the tenor voice of the viola.'[xxiv] [xxv] 'The minuet, coming second, seems at first sight to be very naïve and simple, especially when compared to the remarkably subtle and closely wrought Minuet from Mozart's Quartet in A major [K. 464]. But its easy tunefulness conceals much skilful and delightful workmanship, especially in its texture.'[xxvi] Finally, in our summation, we cite Hadow who endorses the thoughts just expressed by drawing attention to the original meaning of the term *minuet*: 'If it be true that Minuet means "the little dance", its name was never more justly applied than here. The whole movement is of gossamer: it might serve for the attendants of Titania or Queen Mab; in its whole course ... there is only one loud bar, and it breaks off suddenly as if it were ashamed of its intrusion.'[xxvii]

The theme heard in the Trio is considered to have affinities with that of the composer's Violin Sonata Op. 30 No. 3, the simplicity of which 'conceals its subtle tonal plan' in its 'folksong-type melody'.[xxviii] It is also thought to recall the melody of the slow movement of Haydn's Symphony No. 88. Concerning this contention, however, Radcliffe cautions: 'But it is very dangerous to attach too much importance to thematic resemblances of this kind, especially in music written at a time when there were so many familiar turns of phrase used by all and sundry. Haydn's tune is slow and majestic, and Beethoven's recollections of it all move at a quicker pace, sometimes with the suggestion of a dance.'[xxix]

The third movement's opening theme is headed *Andante cantabile* and is followed by five variations and a *poco adagio* coda. 'It is genuine Beethoven in its simple, singing theme and the vigorous and distinctly personal variations of which each is a characteristic piece by itself.'[xxx] 'The *Andante cantabile* ... is a wonderful example of Beethoven's skill in preserving and exploiting the individual character of his instruments, both separately and in unison.'[xxxi] An anecdote connects the String Quartet Op. 18, No. 4 with Richard Strauss and reveals his appreciation of the composition. Sometime in Easter 1878 he wrote to his friend the composer Ludwig Thuill. Strauss had attended a quartet soirée about which he wrote: 'Next came an exquisite quartet (A major) by our master Beethoven. Particularly beautiful and interesting [were] the variations (*Andante*) in the third movement. You could tell right away whose composition you had before you.' These remarks appear all the more discerning when we consider that at the time Strauss was just fourteen years old.[xxxii]

The variations form the substance of the movement and may be said to be in keeping with the compositional phase of Beethoven's art at this period. We cite, for example: the Variations for Cello and Piano, WoO 45 (1796–97); the Variations for Piano, Violin and Cello, Op. 44 (1792–96/1804); the Variations for Piano and Cello, WoO 46 (1801–02); and the Variations on Salieri's *La stessa, la stessissima*, WoO 73 (1799). To these works may be added several sets of piano variations. Maynard Solomon argues that at this period, in his slow movements, 'Beethoven was progressing from the external variation manner to more complex and imaginative principles of variation technique'. In support of this he cites: the Trio, Op. 1, No. 3; the String Quartet Op. 18, No. 5; the Septet, Op. 20; the Sonata, Op. 14, No. 2; and the somewhat later first movement of the Sonata, Op. 26.[xxxiii] The variation form was to hold a lifelong fascination for Beethoven, finding expression in the *Appassionata* Piano Sonata, Op. 57, the Violin Concerto, Op. 61, culminating in the monumental *Diabelli* Variations of 1819–23. At the period under consideration the variation form was fashionable, both Haydn and Mozart having written compositions in this style. Haydn made use of the variation form in his *Emperor* String Quartet, Op. 76, No.

3 and mention has been made of Mozart's String Quartet K. 464 with its inclusion of a set of six variations. In his A major Quartet Beethoven was following precedent.

The movement's opening theme has divided opinions amongst musicologists. It has been described as 'simple and song-like'[xxxiv] and possessing 'a quality of elemental simplicity', well suited to serving as a point of departure for a series of melodic transformations.[xxxv] Other commentators, however, have expressed reservations. Hadow was of the opinion the opening theme was not one of the composer's best tunes, dismissing it as 'a six-note descent ... a little too obvious' He accepts that what he describes as 'the beginning of the second clause' is more interesting but considers 'it falls back again into the same enunciation of a truism'.[xxxvi] Whereas Joseph Kerman esteemed Mozart's variation theme as 'pure emotion', he did not consider Beethoven's to be a tune at all but 'an abstract construction' that 'does not warm the movement as a whole'.[xxxvii] Discussing the melodic line Beethoven adopted for the variations, Radcliffe comments: 'There is an obvious parallel between this movement and the variations in Mozart's Quartet in A major.' He then qualifies this remarking: '[In] many ways the two sets are dissimilar. On the whole Mozart set himself the harder problem, as his theme is richer in detail, both melodic and harmonic, than that of Beethoven, and proportionately harder to vary ... they have a wealth of new melodies that are so attractive and spontaneous ... Beethoven [however] keeps far more closely to the simple melodic outline of his theme.'[xxxviii] Matthews makes similar observations but is less trenchant: 'Beethoven followed Mozart in writing a slow movement in variation form, but whereas Mozart's variation-theme is strikingly beautiful in itself, Beethoven chose a basic text, simplified from the sketches into a direct march up and down the D major scale.'[xxxix]

Sketches for a portion of the third movement are said to date from 1794, making them, if this is the case, the earliest known elements of the Op. 18 String Quartets.[xl] Lam suggests a slightly wider time frame of 1794–1795.[xli] Radcliffe believes the third-movement melody may have been intended for a piano rondo in C minor.[xlii] In his pioneering study of the composer's life and work, Alexander Thayer identified sketches in the Grasnick sketchbook for the String Quartet in D major that he describes as being 'near the ultimate form, except for the last movement.'[xliii] De Marliave cites barely legible words written by Beethoven above the sketches for the third movement that contain the word 'pastoral'. Although fragmentary, he considered they provide an 'unmistakable indication of the composer's intention for the movement.'[xliv]

By definition, the variation at its most basic is the development of a melodic phrase that is subsequently enriched in rhythm, tonality and adorned with new figuration. In the D major Quartet, De Marliave believed Beethoven 'raises the character of the variation form to a higher level' erecting 'a new melodic structure' and thereby making each variation 'a new creation with an individual rhythm, melody and expressive power'. He acknowledges Beethoven's debt to Mozart's Quartet in A and Haydn's Emperor Quartet and sees these, and Beethoven's, 'as revealing so fluent a technique it is difficult to choose between them'. He concedes: 'Perhaps Mozart's art is most spontaneous and delicate: [his] variations in D minor have the limpid purity of a Raphael Madonna.' Haydn's variations de Marliave considers 'reach the same degree of clarity with added depth of feeling' and exhibit 'an extraordinary advanced harmonic interest'. Beethoven's achievement he writes 'is at once, more assertive and more virile [and] with him a certain whimsical element touches the serenity of inspiration'.[xlv] Lam describes Beethoven's variations as a whole as 'admirably diverse in textures and instrumental invention [and] follow the structure of the theme with a directness characteristic of Beethoven's variation style'.[xlvi] Tovey thought them to be 'delicious' and detects a 'nursery-rhyme kind of wit' in the melody as it goes up and down a hexachord.[xlvii] All the variations are in the key of D major. Robin Golding provides an overview: 'The first two variations exploit, respectively, the cello and the first violin, the third the viola and the cello. The fourth is serious and chromatic, but its solemnity is quickly brushed aside by the boisterous character of the fifth.'[xlviii]

Variation I is 'a spirited dialogue between the instruments'[xlix] in 'light-heartedly fugal style'[l] as it proceeds 'in a series of imitations that build up from the cello'.[li] In its *fugato* passages, Beethoven's debt to his former teacher Haydn is in evidence. As Plantinga remarks: 'It had first been invested with these associations in Haydn's remarkable Quartets Op. 20 (1772) with their profound expressiveness and (in three of them) earnest and elaborate fugal finales.'[lii] By contrast, Variation II 'tiptoes *pianissimo*'[liii] with the first violin moving in sixteenth-note triplets that 'veritably sparkle'[liv] in what is in the first violin's '*pas seul* — solo dance.[lv] In Variation III 'the woodland murmurs'[lvi] and there is 'a new and attractive luxuriance of colour'.[lvii] The tempo quickens and Beethoven challenges would-be performers with passages in thirty-second notes. In Variation IV, Beethoven allows the performers a moment of respite by reverting to the slower-paced quarter and eighth notes of the main theme but which is cast 'in a mysterious, chromatic version of the original'.[lviii] 'By reason of the conciseness of the motif [it] lends itself perfectly to the rapid intricacies of question and imitative response that primarily constitutes "quartet technique".'[lix] Robust Beethovenian humour holds sway in the closing Variation V. Allison Bullock considers the music here to have the ambience of a marching band 'with the cello playing "oompahs" and the violins trilling like a piccolo'.[lx] In more strictly musicological terms the second violin and viola 'play a jauntily decorated version of the theme' in which the first violin contributes 'jubilant trills and leaps' while the cello adds 'a terrifically energised base, full of staccatos and offbeat accents'.[lxi] After a 'boisterous scamper home' the movement ends 'in a dreamy meditation'.[lxii]

The fourth and final movement is an *Allegro* in which it is widely acknowledged Beethoven owes a debt to Mozart and his previously mentioned String Quartet K. 464. This is evident in the in the movement's introduction where Beethoven, in imitation of Mozart, adopts long note values and sustained melodic passages.[lxiii] It is 'a splendid example of pure quartet writing in which all four parts are equally important'.[lxiv] In the *Allegro* finale Kinderman finds Beethoven nearest to Mozart, especially in the later development of the movement where he detects thematic material borrowed from him and 'demonstrates mastery of counterpoint characteristic of the older master'. Although this may have worked to Beethoven's advantage, in these formative years of his writing for the medium of the string quartet, Kinderman concluded that the composer's modelling himself on Mozart 'muted something of Beethoven's own individual voice'. In support of this contention he quotes Joseph's Kerman: 'It must be counted the least personal of the quartets'.[lxv]

Notwithstanding the above expressed reservations, the closing movement of the A major Quartet has its admirers. From the performers' viewpoint, Rebecca Clarke avowed: 'The fifth Quartet ... a good-tempered, if perhaps a rather formal work, contains in the last movement a little passage which never fails to ravish me completely.'[lxvi] Despite his reservations, Kerman concedes Beethoven had not written many earlier passages in such 'a relaxed and conversational manner' as the present one. He also cites the composer borrowing from himself, comparing the close similarity of measures 217—23 in the String Quartet, with measures 99—102 of the third movement of the Piano Sonata in C minor, Op. 13, the *Pathétique*.[lxvii] Philip Radcliffe also detects 'an augmentation of a tune' that Beethoven had used already, albeit in a more contrapuntal texture, in the *Pathétique* Sonata. [lxviii] Hadow also found similar melodic parallels that Beethoven used in the *Pathétique*. He comments: 'It is an ideally good quartet theme, far better suited to the strings than the piano, and it lends colour to the story that the finale of the Sonata *Pathétique* was originally written as a string trio.'[lxix]

Carl Dahlhaus elevates the musicological discourse in his characteristically recondite manner: 'In the finale of the A major Quartet, the entire movement is governed by a combinatory art which can be interpreted as wit — *witz, esprit* — in the sense of Enlightenment poetics.' He elaborates: 'The word *witz* means the same things as *esprit* in the eighteenth century and the concept was one of the fundamental categories of Enlightenment poetics, applicable to both literature and music.' Dahlhaus argues it was an aesthetic principle fundamental to both Haydn and Beethoven. He cites Beethoven's adoption of inversion, variants, chromatic progression, leaps and occasional 'pedantic conformity to textbook rules'.[lxx] Shepherd expresses thoughts close in spirit to those of Dahlhaus's latter observation: 'Throughout this fifth quartet the craftsman seems more in evidence than the tone poet.' This is most apparent he believes in the final *Allegro* 'wherein one is impressed with the dexterous skill expended upon the interweaving of all the thematic, rhythmic and figural elements'. In Hadow's estimation: 'These show a prime concern for fluency, care-free vigour and brightness of sonority.'[lxxi]

Returning to the influence of Mozart's Quartet K. 464 on Beethoven's quartet writing, Kerman elucidates: 'The piece borrows from one of Mozart's own themes and not surprisingly is Mozartian in spirit ... Nothing could be less *Beethovenian* ... Formal contrapuntal devices are entirely absent, but light, classic counterpoint is everywhere, managed with a fluidity and charm that surpasses even Beethoven's very considerable technique with this kind of thing in the earlier quartets.' Warming to the composer's achievement, Kerman is fulsome regarding later passages in the movement, concerning which he remarks: 'One can think already of the fantastic airy transformations in the finale of the Quartet in E flat, Op. 127.'[lxxii]

Beethoven elected not to close his String Quartet in A major Op. 18, No. 4 with an outward show of strength: 'For all its controlled energy, this movement is not designed for a massive ending, which would be inconsistent with the general feeling of the quartet, and the coda is perfectly contrived in its rise and fall towards the quiet final chord.[lxxiii]

---

[i] Joseph de Marliave, 1925, (reprint 1961), p. 31.

[ii] Douglas Porter Johnson, editor, 1985, p. 87. See also William Kinderman, 2005, pp. 323–4.

[iii] Derived from the historical preface to the miniature score of the A major Quartet in the edition by G. Henle Verlag München.

[iv] Rebecca Clarke, *The Beethoven quartets as a player sees them, Musical Times*, Special issue [Beethoven's Death Centenary], Vol. VIII, No. 2, 1927, pp. 178–90.

[v] Paul Bekker, 1925, p. 311.

[vi] Robert Simpson, 1973, p. 246.

[vii] Barry Cooper, 2000, p. 95.

[viii] Joseph de Marliave, 1961, p. 31.

[ix] Czerny recalled the events in question in 1852, four years before Jahn published his pioneering biography of Mozart on the occasion of his Death Centenary.

i The version of the Czerny anecdote, quoted in the main text, is derived from Basil Lam, 1975, p. 28.
ii See: Beethoven House, Digital Archives, Document NE 119, NE22.
iii The parallels between Mozart's K 464 and Beethoven's Op. 18, No. 5 have attracted considerable comment in Beethoven literature. The following sources are typical: William Kinderman, 2005, p. 53; Basil Lam, 1975, p. 28; and Jürgen Ostmann in the programme notes to The Alexander String Quartet, Art Nova Classics, *Beethoven, String Quartets, Op. 18*.
xii Wayne M. Senner, Robin Wallace and William Meredith, editors, *The critical reception of Beethoven's compositions by his German contemporaries*, 1999, Vol. 1, pp. 154–5.
xiii Derived form Joseph de Marliave, 1925 (reprint 1961), p. 50.
xiv Basil Lam, 1975, p. 28.
xv Philip Radcliffe, 1978, p. 36.
xvi William Henry Hadow, 1926, pp. 40–1.
xvii Arthur Shepherd, 1935, p. 22. To further emphasize his point, Shepherd illustrates the first and completed versions of the main theme of the first movement.
xviii *The unheard Beethoven*, draft of a *presto* in A, Hess 334, Internet source.
xix Gerald Abraham, 1988, pp. 282–3. Abraham also cites the influence of the *Adagio* of E. A. Förster's Quartet, Op. 7, No. 5, published in 1793.
xx Paul Bekker, 1925, p. 311.
xxi Robin Golding, Liner Notes to The Lindsey String Quartet, *Beethoven's String Quartets*.
xxii Joseph de Marliave, 1925, (reprint 1961), p. 34.
xxiii Bernhard Jacobson Liner notes to: *Ludwig van Beethoven; The early string quartets*, Op. 18, Alban Berg Quartet, EMI, 1981.
xxiv Basil Lam, 1975, p. 29.
xxv The repeat of the first twelve measures is fully written out so as to give the viola an opportunity to play the tune. See: Robert Winter, and Robert Martin, editors, *The Beethoven quartet companion*, 1994, p. 165. Paul Bekker, 1925, p
xxvi Philip Radcliffe, 1978, p. 38. Of additional interest is Radcliffe's conjecture: '[It] would be interesting to know whether the [the first phrase] of the Minuet was unconsciously in Beethoven's head when, twenty-six years later, he wrote the "Es muss sein" theme in his Op. 135.'
xxvii William Henry Hadow, 1926, p. 50–1.
xxviii Basil Lam, 1975, pp. 30–29.
xxix Philip Radcliffe, 1978, p. 38.
xxx Anonymous: Preface to the Philharmonia score: *Beethoven's String Quartets, Op. 18*.
xxxi Paul Bekker, 1925, pp. 311–12.
xxxii Bryan Gilliam, 1999, p. 206.
xxxiii Maynard Solomon, 1977, p. 98.
xxxiv Alison Bullock *Notes to the BBC Radio Three Beethoven experience*, Tuesday 9 June 2005, www.bbc.co.uk/radio3/Beethoven
xxxv William Kinderman, 2005, p. 58.
xxxvi William Henry Hadow, 1926, p. 51.
xxxvii Joseph Kerman, 1967, pp. 63–5.
xxxviii Philip Radcliffe, 1978, p. 39.

xxxix Denis Matthews, 1985, pp. 130–1.
xl William Henry Hadow, 1926, p. 48.
xli Basil Lam, 1975, pp. 30–1.
xlii Philip Radcliffe, 1978, p. 39.
xliii See Elliot Forbes, 1967, p. 263.
xliv Joseph de Marliave, 1925, (reprint 1961), p. 32.
xlv *Ibid.*
xlvi Basil Lam, 1975, p. 30.
xlvii Donald Francis Tovey, 1944, pp. 131–2.
xlviii Robin Golding, Liner Notes to The Lindsey String Quartet, *Beethoven's String Quartets.*
xlix Joseph de Marliave, 1925, (reprint 1961), p. 36.
l Philip Radcliffe, 1978, p. 39.
li Robert Winter, and Robert Martin, editors, *The Beethoven quartet companion,* 1994, p. 169.
lii Leon Plantinga, 1984, pp. 30–31.
liii Robert Winter and Robert Martin, editors, *The Beethoven quartet companion,* 1994, p. 169.
liv Romain Rolland, 1917, p. 181.
lv Philip Radcliffe, 1978, p. 39.
lvi Romain Rolland, 1917, p. 181.
lvii Philip Radcliffe, 1978, p. 39.
lviii William Kinderman, 2005, p. 58.
lix Joseph de Marliave, 1925, (reprint 1961), pp. 37–8.
lx Alison Bullock *Notes to the BBC Radio Three Beethoven experience,* Tuesday 9 June 2005, www.bbc.co.uk/radio3/Beethoven
lxi Robert Winter and Robert Martin, editors, *The Beethoven quartet companion,* 1994, p. 169.
lxii Romain Rolland, 1917, p. 181.
lxiii As remarked, for example, by Denis Matthews, 1985, pp. 130–1 and David Wyn Jones in: Robin Stowell, editor, *The Cambridge companion to the string quartet,* 2003, p. 213.
lxiv Basil Lam, 1975, p. 31.
lxv William Kinderman, editor, *The string quartets of Beethoven,* 2005, p. 58.
lxvi Rebecca Clarke, *The Beethoven quartets as a player sees them, Musical Times,* Special issue [Beethoven's Death Centenary], Vol. VIII, No. 2, 1927, pp. 178–90.
lxvii *Joseph Kerman, Beethoven quartet audiences: actual, potential, ideal in: Robert Winter and Robert Martin editors, The Beethoven quartet companion, 1994, p. 12.*
lxviii Philip Radcliffe, 1978, p. 40.
lxix William Henry Hadow, 1926, pp. 53–4.
lxx Carl Dahlhaus, 1991, pp. 61–2.
lxxi Arthur Shepherd, 1935, p. 24.
lxxii Joseph Kerman, 1967, p. 64.
lxxiii Basil Lam, 1975, p. 31.

STRING QUARTET IN B-FLAT MAJOR, OP. 18, NO. 6

'A virtuoso and concerto-like element is strong in the B-flat major Quartet. In feeling, the work broadly resembles the B-flat major Sonata [Op. 22] composed at the same time. The prevailing mood is one of cheerfulness and the *Scherzo* is a glorious piece of musicianly humour. Reaction from these high spirits is represented in the *La Malinconia passage*; the work, however, reaches a joyous close.'

Paul Bekker, *Beethoven*, 1925, p. 312.

'Like the Sonata in the same key, Op. 22, the Sixth Quartet expresses Beethoven's emancipation from the weighty influences of Haydn and

Mozart in terms of a drastic simplification of the thematic idea.'

Basil Lam, *Beethoven String Quartets*, 1975, p. 31.

The Quartet in B-flat major as a whole leaves a curiously mixed impression, but it is possible that Beethoven may have meant it to be the climax of the set. It covers a wide range, and the *Scherzo* and the introduction to the finale are as enterprising and original as anything that he had written at that time.'

Philip Radcliffe, *Beethoven's String Quartets*, 1978, pp. 44.

'It is with the Quartet in B-flat major, Op. 18, No. 6 that Beethoven's early experiments in the reinterpretation of movement roles reach their most substantial and forward-looking result so far.'

Bernhard Jacobson Liner notes to: *Ludwig van Beethoven; The early string quartets*, Op. 18, The Alban Berg Quartet, EMI, 1981.

'Just as he saw to it that Op. 18 opened with something especially strong, so did Beethoven take pains to place a particularly impressive and original work at the end of the collection.'

Robert Winter and Robert Martin editors, *The Beethoven Quartet Companion*, 1994, p. 170.

'As well as beginning the standard set of six quartets with the most impressive work,

Beethoven followed the common eighteenth-century practice of concluding his set with the most light-hearted work.' David Wyn Jones, whom we have just quoted, believes the composition endured a mixed reception in the nineteenth century for being considered inferior to the preceding five quartets. Today, he remarks: 'Commentators are now more willing to appreciate its distinctive qualities, for wit and irony [and for being] as much a part of Beethoven's musical make-up as are the seriousness and pathos that appealed consistently to posterity.'[i][ii] Others who are in agreement include Alison Bullock: 'Op. 18, No. 6 exceeds all expectations in its maturity and above all in its originality;'[iii] and Bernhard Jacobson '[A] work of broad range and prophetic individuality.'[iv]

Op. 18, No. 6 is thought to have been composed last, a view supported by the fact that sketches for it are found alongside those for several other compositions. These include: the large-scale Piano Sonata Op. 22 of 1799–1800 (with which it shares the same key); the A minor Violin Sonata, Op. 23; the G major Piano Variations WoO 77; and revisions for the String Quartets in F major and G major.[v] The summer of 1800 seems most probable for the time of completion of the B-flat Quartet with Beethoven making copies of the String Quartets Nos. 4–6 later in the autumn for his patron Prince Lobkowitz (see our opening survey, *String Quartets, Op. 18, Nos. 1–6.*).[vi] The sketchbook used by Beethoven for the summer of 1800 was originally known as Autograph 19e that is now fragmentary, having been dismembered over the intervening years.[vii] Sketch leaves (12–18 and 29–31), originally belonging to

Autograph 19e, are now held in archives in New York, Bonn and Berlin (SPK, Autograph 193).[viii]

On 10 February 1824 the String Quartet Op, 18, No. 6 was performed at a concert in Berlin that provides a contemporary estimation of its perceived merits — albeit some twenty years after its publication. The concert in question was one of a subscription series; previous concerts had been dedicated exclusively to works by Haydn, Mozart and Beethoven. Of the February concert the reviewer enthused: 'The highest pleasure was afforded by Beethoven's magnificent Quartet in B-flat major, which, having already been offered in the sixth session, was repeated today "at the request of many".' The reviewer concludes: 'The genius of Beethoven flowed here in the most sumptuous abundance, not like a mountain stream bursting through ravines and rocks, but rather like a friendly brook through a blooming meadow.'[ix]

In our opening account of the creation origins of the String Quartets, Op. 18, we have noted that Joseph de Marliave relates how from about 1830 Beethoven's chamber works started to be accepted into the concert repertoire in France. By the mid-nineteenth century his first quartets were supported by concert promoters, albeit rather tentatively, but with a recognition of their qualities. By way of illustration, following a performance of the B-flat Quartet the reviewer for the *Gazette musicale* was disposed to enthuse: 'It is a noble work ... one of those works where imagination and technical skill, depth of feeling and delicacy of treatment strive for the ascendency. This sixth quartet is delightful; the exquisitely contemplative reverie, named by the composer *La Malinconia* [see later], forms a perfect foil for the sparkling rhythm of the finale; it falls upon the ear like the passionate pleading of a faithful lover whose despair is mocked by a coquette's heartless mirth.'[x]

'Opus 18 No. 6 begins with Beethoven's own version of crisp, Haydnesque good humour. Here he explores the pleasures of simplicity. As the music gets off to its cheery, relaxed start, everything is symmetrical, everything rhymes ... The conversational exchange between first violins and cello, later first and second violin, are so simple that their very ease becomes amusing and draws a smile from the listener — and, like it or not, from the players.'[xi] To some ears Mozart's presence can be felt: '[It] is the operatic Mozart that peeps through the stylistic turns of melody and harmony in the first movement of this quartet.' Arthur Shepherd, whom we have just quoted, in turn cites the French composer and musicologist Vincent d'Indy — author of *Beethoven: A critical biography* (1913). D'Indy refers to the B-flat major Quartet's 'operatic cadences [and] the clattering dominant tonic reiterations'. Endorsing d'Indy's observation, Shepherd suggests: 'One would not have to look far to find reminiscences of the sparkling melodies of *Don Giovanni*, a work which Beethoven held in affectionate esteem.'[xii]

The tempo indication is *Allegro con brio*, encouraging the performers to play 'with liveliness of spirit'. Some commentators find the main subject of the first movement has close affinities with the *Allegro* of the Second Symphony, Op. 36 from 1802.[xiii] Others compare the epigrammatic sonata-form construction with the Piano Sonata Op. 22 from 1799.[xiv] Joseph Kerman considers the first movement of the B-flat Sonata, Op. 22 to be 'a twin' for that of the B-flat Quartet, remarking: 'The main themes show interesting similarities ... We might picture the quartet theme as a stiff early draft for the sonata, the powerful dynamic variety of which seems not yet to have evolved from the quartet's blank symmetry and mere galvanic action. In contrast to the sonata, the entre quartet movement is cut in flat swaths, four or six rapid bars in length.' Kerman also recalls Beethoven's variations of the period, namely *La stessa, la stessissima*, based on an *opera buffa* melody of Salieri that he considers 'have some striking points of contact with the Quartet.'[xv]

Dissentient voices find Beethoven falling from grace in this movement: 'Though pleasantly vivacious, this is on the whole the least interesting of the six first movements'[xvi] being distinctly 'old fashioned'.[xvii] Robin Golding describes the 'chattering treatment' of the *gruppetto* figure as 'palpably eighteenth-century in character'.[xviii] Kerman finds the *Allegro con brio* presents 'a strange mixture' in which 'certain things in it seem advanced over the other quartets, but crudities of composition also abound'.[xix] In exoneration of Beethoven, William Henry Hadow invoked the adage 'that occasionally even Homer nods' — even the most exalted may be forgiven for occasional lapses. Of the opening movement to the B-flat String Quartet he remarks: 'There is little that we can say about it: to pry into the weak moments of genius is an impiety from which we may well desire to shrink: it is enough to say that no part of this first movement is on Beethoven's customary levels of thought, and that the greater part is far below them.'[xx]

Others, however, have found positive things to say about the movement. Although it may be conservative in mood and construction, 'the familiar Beethoven spark is there'.[xxi] It is 'full of vitality'[xxii] and 'splendid energy',[xxiii] showing 'a humorous spirit and lightness of tone'.[xxiv] For de Marliave: 'The ease and breadth of the finale in the preceding quartet flows on into the first movement of this, the gay principal theme, so true to "quartet" style recalling Haydn.'[xxv] Jones suggests Haydn's String Quartet Op. 77, No. 1 may have served Beethoven as a model, especially in what he describes as 'the deliberately comic dialogue between the first violin and cello over a simplistic accompaniment'.[xxvi] Commenting on Beethoven's workmanship Basil Lam draws attention to the movement's 'broad expanse of the plainest diatonic harmony ... chord-patterned theme' and 'running scales', which he considers 'to be typical of Beethoven's new harmonic architecture'. Reflecting more generally he adds: '[Beethoven] had by this time written a considerable number of masterly sonata movements, full of bold and unexpected turns of thematic and harmonic development.' He concludes: 'Now he can venture on something still more bold ... a new-found power of expansion.'[xxvii]

The second movement occupies the conventional position and character of a slow movement and is headed *Adagio ma non troppo* – 'slow, but not to be observed too strictly'. It is possessed of 'a gentle and leisurely elegance',[xxviii] 'full of graceful tunefulness, somewhat elaborate in texture, and containing many characteristic touches of expression'.[xxix] It shares with the first movement 'a certain economy in form and expression,'[xxx] being 'a study in the possibilities of naiveté'.[xxxi] 'The *Adagio* ... is simple, but beautifully and perhaps deliberately so, serenade-like in form ... The delicate ornamentation of the melodies shows that, despite its outward simplicity, this is a finely-worked movement.'[xxxii] Here we find Hadow in a more receptive mood: 'Though it is marked *Adagio* it is wholly elegiac in character; quiet meditative music with melodies of "linked sweetness" and long trailing tendrils of accompaniment; a feast of pure delight to player and listener.'[xxxiii] 'Despite its affinity with the typical *Zopf Musik* [pigtail music] of the period, the second movement ... is a marvel of pattern weaving, and represents within its own limited expressional range, an important expansion of the quartet idiom. The superb adjustment of sonorities and the complete community of interest between the four parts throughout the ornate figurations can scarcely be matched in similar movements of Haydn or Mozart.'xxxiv

The atmosphere changes and viola and cello 'punctuate the melody with a stalking figuration'. 'Now the floodgates are open, and Beethoven uses unexpected accents, dissonance, and silence to create one of the most intensely expressive of his early slow movements.'xxxv The atmosphere prevailing prompted de Marliave to reflect: 'At the moment of writing this slow movement, Beethoven must have been enjoying one of the periods of relaxation that he was so rarely to experience in his life. The first theme is unfolded, sinuous and fluent, with supple grace.'xxxvi Although Lam considered the slow movement does not plumb any depths, with its 'divertimento-like relaxed euphony' he acknowledges it has 'a reflective sobriety' that for him evoked recollections of Milton's vision of poetic melancholy *Il Penseroso*.xxxvii

After the serenity and restraint of the second's movement's *Adagio ma non troppo*, Beethoven gives his imagination free reign in the third that he heads *Scherzo-Allegro*. The piece opens 'with the distant sound of horns, and widens to an exuberant outburst of joy'.xxxviii The *Scherzo* heralds 'a radical change of scene and style, and an obsession with syncopations that mock at its three-four time-signature'.xxxix Not satisfied with merely disturbing the decorum of the *Adagio*, Beethoven 'takes naïve pleasure in drastic contrasts' in 'the most humorously aggressive *scherzo* he had yet devised'.xl The musician's individuality is 'all pervasive' in the regularly alternating *staccato* and *legato* and its 'ebullient rhythmic vigour'. 'Of all the quartets of Op. 18, this *Scherzo* is undoubtedly the most original movement.'xli With it: 'Beethoven makes an enormous leap into a totally original manner, one that must have struck many a player and listener in 1801 as rude indeed.'xlii

Hadow finds irony pervades this movement: 'The pleasure we derive from syncopation is due to a kind of irony; a conflict of opposing rhythms, that of the phrase and that of the bar ... The whole rhythm of the present *Scherzo* is built upon this device.'[xliii] It takes us by surprise with its disorienting cross rhythms and 'rhythmic ambiguity'.[xliv] 'The syncopations are so wild that one can almost imagine the composer challenging his audience to make sense of the beat.'[xlv] Radcliffe draws attention to Beethoven's adoption of cross rhythms that he considers are made to sound especially eccentric owing to the use of frequent *sforzandi*. 'This is comedy of a far rougher and more wilful kind than the good-humoured gaiety of the Quartet in G; and it looks ahead to later works and must have sounded very disconcerting to contemporary audiences.'[xlvi]

Arthur Shepherd was in no doubt that in the *Scherzo* Beethoven 'out-distanced' the older masters, including Haydn and Mozart, with his 'bold and pungent rhythmic syntax'. He exclaims: 'Here we have more of the *aufgeknopft* [unbuttoned] Beethoven, taking malicious joy in befogging the listener ... The composer deliberately sets a series of stumbling-blocks by way of misplaced *sforzandi*.'[xlvii] Haydn could never have written 'the almost jazz-like syncopations of the Scherzo'.[xlviii] It is 'especially Beethovenish' and 'shows how the quartet medium makes possible a kind of texture, unplayable on the piano, that would no less surely have defeated any orchestra of the period'.[xlix] In Philip Radcliffe's summation: 'The first three movements of this quartet, taken as a whole, give the impression that the composer, beginning at a comparatively low level of inspiration, seems to gather strength as the work proceeds.'[l]

Beethoven took particular care in the designation of the fourth and final movement of the B-flat major String Quartet, heading it *La Malinconia: Adagio – Allegretto quasi Allegro*. Mindful of the character of the music he had created, he marked the movement with the additional superscription *più gran delicatezza* – 'to be played with the greatest delicacy'. Such an explicit attempt to convey a representation of mood is rare in Beethoven. In his Piano Sonata Op. 13 (1798–9), he had sanctioned the expression *Pathétique*' to convey passion and emotion, characteristic of the 18th-century aesthetic movement's *sturm und drang* – storm and stress. Later, at the opening of the *Pastoral* Symphony, he inscribed the caution 'more the expression of feeling than painting'. Here, in the closing movement of the Quartet, Beethoven was similarly seeking to represent a state of mind – not a specific picture or narrative. As he himself observed: *Mehr Ausdruck der Empfindung als Malerei* – 'And first, it does really suggest melancholy.'[li] The character of the movement was not lost to the reviewer of the music following a concert performance of the Quartet in 1824. Writing in the February issue of the Berlin journal *Der Freymüthige*, he remarked: 'In this work, the maestro has achieved a rare control over himself. Contrary to his custom, he has been brief and clear, and has still not given up his originality for one moment. In the last movement, a gloomy *Adagio*, which exhausts all harmonic devices ... is the crown of the entire piece and leaves the listener with an extremely beneficent impression.'[lii]

In his search for expression in the closing pages of the Quartet Op. 18, No. 6, Denis Matthews conjectures: 'Perhaps Beethoven felt the need to deepen the emotions in the final stage of the last movement of his Op.18 Quartets?' He concludes: 'The result is a dual-character movement that uncannily forecasts the "Muss es sein?" finale of his last quartet of all, Op. 135 in F major, of a quarter-of-a-century later.'[liii] In our discussion of the slow movement of the String Quartet, Op. 18, No. 1, we have seen Beethoven often had images from literature in mind when composing; we recall the influence of the death scene in Shakespeare's *Romeo and Juliet*. With such considerations in mind Philip Downs comments: 'Whether or not he had a definite picture in mind during the composition of Op. 18, No. 6, there is no doubt that *La Malinconia* is intended for social recreation, which, although not the ripest of Beethoven's works for quartet, nevertheless points to the heights to be gained later.'[liv] Barry Cooper (1990) accepts the designation *La Malinconia* may be a true reflection on Beethoven's wishes to impart a certain character of sorrow to the music but cautions: 'It is impossible to be certain whether the movement is just a melancholy one with an illustrative title, or an objective attempt to portray the state of melancholy, or a subjective expression of Beethoven's feelings at the time.'[lv] Later (2000) he elaborates: 'Although Beethoven was prone to bouts of melancholy, the movement should not be regarded as in any way subjective but as a musical portrayal of a state of mind, similar to the *Pathétique*.' He refers to the music-devices Beethoven employs, suggesting he 'stretches the bounds of convention to breaking point'. He cites the 'tortured chromaticism', the adoption of 'remote keys', 'harsh dynamic contrasts', 'obsessive use of turns', and 'ponderous progression of chords' which, he believes, are collectively nothing less than 'one of the most vivid illustrations of a mental state in the whole of music history'.[lvi]

Jones characterises the movement as 'a form of dialogue between two opposites'. This leads him to conjecture: 'Beethoven might well have known a Trio Sonata in C minor (H. 579) by C.P.E. Bach that has the title "Conversation between a Sanguineous and a Melancholicus".' He adds: 'In Bach's Sonata, 'Melancholicus gives up the battle and assumes the manner of the other ... an apt description, too, of the final stages of Beethoven's movement.'[lvii] Writing from the standpoint of the performer, Rebecca Clarke interpreted the movement in a similar manner: 'In the opening of this last quartet, Beethoven obtains a marked contrast of colour, the first four bars being played on the three upper instruments and answered an octave below by the three lower ones; the second violin and viola of course play in both, but the effect is as of two distinct choirs, this being heightened by the crescendo with which the upper instruments usher in the pianissimo of the lower.'[lviii]

Interpreting the music as Beethoven requires makes considerable demands on performers. When in conversation with the musicologist David Blum, Michael Tree, the viola member of The Guarneri Quartet remarked: 'If I had to audition a young quartet I would ask them to play the beginning of this movement. It demands the utmost in sustained ensemble playing. The mood must be there from the very beginning: the music should sound as if it's just lifted out of the air. The turns are always singing and expressive and yet are always *changing* — more rapid and dramatic in forte, more yielding in piano. To bring the breath of life to this simple yet eloquent piece is one of the hardest tasks a quartet can undertake.'[lix]

Shepherd was convinced the music's constantly shifting and unstable harmonies 'unquestionably carry programmatic implications' but he disapproved of the extent to which *La Malinconia*, as he saw it, 'had led commentators into extravagant flights of verbal fantasy'.[lx] Perhaps he was thinking of the style adopted by Joseph de Marliave? Writing about this movement, he first enthuses: 'Earlier musical art contains nothing at all like this famous *Malinconia*, [a] flawless example of symbolism in music: here is mirrored the spirit of the artist, with every shade of joy and sorrow manifested in his creative gift.' He elaborates: 'These tears and sighs, this sinking back upon himself, intermingled with the emotion of a tender inspiration, is unlike the virile strength and fortitude that Beethoven was to express in his later works. It is rather the lonely melancholy of an immature spirit already overtaken by the sorrows of the world, longing hopelessly for joy and love, and shut in upon itself in trembling fear of adversity; the sorrow of a tender heart feeling a nameless distress of mind and spirit'.[lxi]

Although more restrained than de Marliave, modern-day commentators also recognize the depth of feeling with which Beethoven endows his final movement. Alison Bullock considers it to be 'the most original piece in the Op. 18 quartets ... an extraordinary piece of harmonic writing that we may interpret as more mysterious than melancholy — it resembles [anticipates] film music in the way it holds the listener in suspense'.[lxii] Kerman writes: 'This piece cuts drastically across the entire mass of Beethoven's early music, an arresting premonition of achievements to come.'[lxiii] With regard to Beethoven's originality, in Jones's reckoning: 'There is no precedent in the quartets of Haydn and Mozart for the finale of Op. 18, No. 6.'[lxiv] Likewise, William Kinderman: ''The finale is a highly original conception that does not suggest the influence of Haydn or Mozart.' He describes as 'extraordinary' what he calls 'the mysterious chromatic progressions' that are found in *La Malinconia* and describes them as 'masterfully shaped into an integrated dramatic progression.' He also makes a comparison with the mood prevailing in the previously mentioned *Pathétique* Piano Sonata: 'If the gloomy slow introduction [of the String Quartet] suggests a subjective awareness of human suffering, the main *Allegro* section seems to posit resistance to such suffering and a refusal to accept that the condition as permanent and irremediable.'[lxv]

In his consideration of Beethoven's further expressions of melancholy — from the period under consideration — Kinderman cites the *Largo e mesto* of the slow movement of the Piano Sonata in D major, Op. 10, No. 3. This is not only Beethoven's first essay in tragedy, 'but is by far the most tragic piece of music that had ever been written up to that time'.[lxvi] Beethoven so designates the movement to invoke, as in the case of Op. 18, No. 6, a sense of overwhelming pathos and sustained tension. In the same spirit, in our discussion of the slow movement of the String Quartet Op. 18, No. 1, we have seen that Beethoven headed the *Adagio affettuoso ed appassionato* — to be performed 'in a slow tempo with tender feeling and with passion'. Both the Sonata and Quartet movements may be said to share certain stylistic features of *La Malinconia* in terms of its 'sombre tone evocative of tragic resignation ... sensitive use of musical rhetoric [and] a striking rapport of sound with silence — a cessation that carries the implication of death'.[lxvii] In addition, we recall that the F major Quartet had its creation origins in the form of a gift to the clergyman-violinist Karl Amenda and how its *Adagio* has associations with the scene in the burial vault in Shakespeare's *Romeo and Juliet.* Among the Op. 18 surviving sketches, is a page on which Beethoven has inscribed the words *il prend le tombeau ... desepoir ... il se tue ...les derniers soupris* — 'he takes [i.e. enters the tomb] — despair — he kills himself — the last sighs'. Commenting on these expressions, Cooper places them in context: 'Normally any words found amongst Beethoven's sketches for abstract instrumental works are purely musical ones, such as names of keys, tempo marks, or indications of form. Here, however, is a clear sign he had some poetic idea in mind.'[lxviii]

Maynard Solomon characterises the 44 bars of *La Malinconia* as being 'mystical' and the most striking example of Beethoven's newfound flexibility in string quartet writing.[lxix] Jacobson is likeminded, praising the passage for being 'one of Beethoven's most searching pieces of harmonic invention'.[lxx] Robert Winter and Robert Martin write of 'the slow music, groping, full of harmonic mystery, strangely alternating between the hushed and the assertive'.[lxxi] Lam, with others, remarks upon the manner in which the psychological programme of this finale astonishingly prefigures that in others in his last string quartets, notably the first movement of Op. 127 and Op. 130.[lxxii]

In the *Allegretto quasi Allegro* section of the movement, the mood changes from the deepest grief to 'cheerfulness and tightly-sprung agility'. The music invokes the spirit of the popular *Deutscher* dance form but with 'a rhythmically-distanced character that seems to overload such evanescent pleasures of society with warnings of an unyielding, even menacing melancholy'. Stephanie Schroeder, whom we have just quoted, poses the thought: 'Whether Beethoven was already expressing, through his music, his awareness of an inchoate deafness cannot be determined for sure; nevertheless, it would explain indeed the exceptional dramatics of this string quartet.'[lxxiii] Perhaps Beethoven was responding to other more external influences: 'The idea of following a mysterious chromatic introduction by a cheerful quick movement [i.e. passage] may have been suggested to Beethoven by Mozart's Quartet in C major, K. 465.' Philip Radcliffe, our source here, comments how Mozart, at the height of his powers, could solve such a construction perfectly but that Beethoven could not succeed, at this stage in his career, in the same way. He remarks: 'His finale is a lively movement of considerable charm, but, after the extraordinary harmonic adventures of the introduction, it seems to be a disconcerting throwback to a different and more conventional world.'[lxxiv] In this context the distinguished Mozart scholar Alfred Einstein was not particularly impressed by Beethoven's attempt to represent the changing moods of a person afflicted with melancholia. Writing on the subject of the representation of temperament in music, he pronounced the closing passages of the final movement of Op. 18, No. 6 to be 'not one of his most inspired inventions'.[lxxv]

Other commentators are less censorious, recognizing the manner in which 'the spirit of the *Allegretto* finally conquers that of melancholy'[lxxvi] as the music 'dissolves into dance' and 'makes its untroubled way to the end'.[lxxvii] Joseph de Marliave is characteristically fulsome in his endorsement of the spirit of Beethoven's concluding pages: 'After a last pause on the dominant of B flat, the *Malinconia* gives way to the lively and vivid inspiration of the *Allegretto quasi Allegro*, and we are whirled into the gay measure of a country dance, in an irresistible rhythm where cello *sforzandi* mark the accentuated weak beat.' To him the music appears to be saying: 'Take heart, the sun is shining through the clouds. Away with repinings and on with the dance!' In this spirit, it is perhaps fitting we allow de Marliave our concluding remarks: '[It] is possible to read into this moving finale ... both an expression of the first phase of Beethoven's life and a foreknowledge of the last; troubled here by the first presentiment of sorrow in store ... at the same time the artist glances back at the pure joy and tenderness of boyhood.'[lxxviii]

---

[i] David Wyn Jones in Robin Stowell, editor, *The Cambridge companion to the string quartet*, 2003, pp. 212–13.

[ii] Something of the dissatisfaction felt by nineteenth-century commentators is expressed in the views of Philip Radcliffe: 'The sixth, in B-flat major, larger, more varied and more ambitious, leaves a less satisfactory impression, owing to its odd diversity of styles.' Philip Radcliffe, 1978, pp. 40. Robert Simpson found Op. 18, No. 6 to be 'ostentatiously disparate in its content'.

[iii] Alison Bullock, *Notes to the BBC Radio Three Beethoven experience*, Tuesday 7 June 2005, www.bbc.co.uk/radio3/Beethoven

[iv] Bernhard Jacobson, Liner notes to: *Ludwig van Beethoven; The early string quartets*, Op. 18, The Alban Berg Quartet, EMI, 1981.

[v] Richard Kramer in: Alan Tyson, editor, *Beethoven studies 3*, 1982, pp. 35–42.

[vi] Leon Plantinga, 1984, pp. 30–31.

vii Barry Cooper, 2000, p. 92.
viii William Kinderman editor, *The string quartets of Beethoven*, 2005, p. 323. Richard Kramer has reconstructed Beethoven's sketchbook for the summer of 1800 which has been published in a facsimile edition (1996). See: Beethoven House, Digital Archives, Library Document, NE 104.
ix Wayne M. Senner, Robin Wallace and William Meredith, editors, *The critical reception of Beethoven's compositions by his German contemporaries*, 1999, Vol. 1, pp. 155–6.
x As quoted in Joseph de Marliave, 1925 (reprint 1961), p. 50.
xi Robert Winter and Robert Martin, editors, *The Beethoven quartet companion*, 1994, p. 170.
xii Arthur Shepherd, 1935, p. 25.
xiii See, for example Basil Lam, 1975, p. 31.
xiv Denis Matthews is a case in point, see his *Beethoven*, 1985, pp. 131–2.
xv Joseph Kerman, 1967, pp. 71–2.
xvi Philip Radcliffe, 1978, p. 40.
xvii Gerald Abraham, *Beethoven's Chamber Music*, in: *The Age of Beethoven, The New Oxford History of Music, Vol. VIII*, Gerald Abraham, editor, 1988, pp. 282–3.
xviii Robin Golding, Liner Notes to The Lindsay String Quartets, *Beethoven, Op. 18*.
xix Joseph Kerman, 1967, pp. 71–2.
xx William Henry Hadow, 1926, pp. 54–5.
xxi Alison Bullock *Notes to the BBC Radio Three Beethoven experience*, Tuesday 9 June 2005, www.bbc.co.uk/radio3/Beethoven
xxii Romain Rolland, 1917, p. 182.
xxiii Basil Lam, 1975, p. 32.
xxiv William Kinderman editor, 2005, p. 59.
xxv Joseph de Marliave, 1925, (reprint 1961), pp. 40–1.
xxvi David Wyn Jones in Robin Stowell, editor, *The Cambridge companion to the string quartet*, 2003, pp. 212–13.
xxvii Basil Lam, 1975, p. 32.
xxviii Philip Radcliffe, 1978, p. 41.
xxix Romain Rolland, 1917, p. 182.
xxx William Kinderman, 2005, p. 59.
xxxi Robert Winter and Robert Martin, editors, *The Beethoven quartet companion*, 1994, p. 171.
xxxii Alison Bullock, *Notes to the BBC Radio Three Beethoven experience*, Tuesday 7 June 2005, www.bbc.co.uk/radio3/Beethoven
xxxiii William Henry Hadow, 1926, pp. 56–7.
xxxiv Arthur Shepherd, 1935, p. 25.
xxxv Robert Winter and Robert Martin, editors, *The Beethoven quartet companion*, 1994, p. 171.
xxxvi Joseph de Marliave, 1925, (reprint 1961), p. 42.
xxxvii Basil Lam, 1975, p. 32.
xxxviii Joseph de Marliave, 1925, (reprint 1961), p. 43.
xxxix Denis Matthews, 1985, pp. 131–2.
xl Basil Lam, 1975, p. 32.
xli Joseph de Marliave, 1925, (reprint 1961), p. 43.

xlii Robert Winter and Robert Martin, editors, *The Beethoven quartet companion*, 1994, p. 172.
xliii William Henry Hadow, 1926, pp. 58–9.
xliv Barry Cooper, 2000, p. 96.
xlv Alison Bullock, *Notes to the BBC Radio Three Beethoven experience*, Tuesday 7 June 2005, www.bbc.co.uk/radio3/Beethoven
xlvi Philip Radcliffe, 1978, pp. 41.
xlvii Arthur Shepherd, 1935, p. 25.
xlviii Rebecca Clarke, *The Beethoven quartets as a player sees them*, *Musical Times*, Special issue [Beethoven's Death Centenary], Vol. VIII, No. 2, 1927, pp. 178–90.
xlix Basil Lam, 1975, p. 33.
l Philip Radcliffe, 1978, p. 42.
li William Henry Hadow, 1926, pp. 60–1.
lii Wayne M. Senner, Robin Wallace and William Meredith, editors, *The critical reception of Beethoven's compositions by his German contemporaries*, 1999, Vol. 1, pp. 155–6.
liii Denis Matthews, 1985, pp. 131–2.
liv Philip G. Downs, 1992, p. 599.
lv Barry Cooper, 1990, p. 58.
lvi Barry Cooper, 2000, p. 95. Basil Lam offers an alternative suggestion as to the possible source of Beethoven's inspiration. He asks: 'Was ... *La Malinconia* ... perhaps suggested by Dürer's "La Melancolia", so frequently reproduced and widely circulated in Germany?' Basil Lam, 1975, p. 33.
lvii David Wyn Jones in Robin Stowell, editor, *The Cambridge companion to the string quartet*, 2003, pp. 212–13.
lviii Rebecca Clarke, *The Beethoven quartets as a player sees them*, *Musical Times*, Special issue [Beethoven's Death Centenary], Vol. VIII, No. 2, 1927, pp. 178–90.
lix David Blum, *The art of quartet playing*: The Guarneri Quartet in conversation with David Blum, 1986.
lx Arthur Shepherd, 1935, p. 27.
lxi Joseph de Marliave, 1925, (reprint 1961), p. 44.
lxii Alison Bullock, *Notes to the BBC Radio Three Beethoven experience*, Tuesday 7 June 2005, www.bbc.co.uk/radio3/Beethoven
lxiii In support of his contention, Kerman provides detailed, illustrated textual analysis. See Joseph Kerman, 1967, pp. 76–7.
lxiv David Wyn Jones in Robin Stowell, editor, *The Cambridge companion to the string quartet*, 2003, pp. 212–13.
lxv William Kinderman, 2005, pp. 24–5 and p. 59.
lxvi Donald Tovey, 1944, p. 92. Tovey also remarks upon the 'tragic' slow movement of the String Quartet Op. 18, No. 1 as a further example of Beethoven's 'progress in rivalling Mozart in such designs'.
lxvii William Kinderman, 2005, pp. 24–5 and p. 59.
lxviii Barry Cooper, 2000, p. 81. See also William Kinderman, 2005, pp. 24–5.
lxix Maynard Solomon, 1977, p. 101.
lxx Bernhard Jacobson Liner notes to: *Ludwig van Beethoven; The early string quartets*, Op. 18, The Alban Berg Quartet, EMI, 1981.
lxxi Robert Winter and Robert Martin, editors, *The Beethoven quartet companion*, 1994, p. 172.

[lxii] Basil Lam, 1975, p. 33.
[lxiii] Stephanie Schroeder, Programme notes to The Alexander String Quartet, *Beethoven's String Quartets*.
[lxiv] Philip Radcliffe, 1978, p. 43.
[lxv] Quoted by Catherine Dower in: *Alfred Einstein on music: selected music criticisms*, 1991, p. 131. Einstein's views were originally expressed in *The Music Review* of August 1946.
[lxvi] Philip G. Downs, 1992, p. 599.
[lxvii] Robert Winter and Robert Martin, editors, *The Beethoven quartet companion*, 1994, p. 172 — with adaptations.
[lxviii] Joseph de Marliave, 1925, (reprint 1961), p. 44.

STRING QUARTET ARRANGEMENT PIANO SONATA IN E MAJOR, OP. 14, NO. 1

Beethoven's arrangement of the Piano Sonata in E major, Op. 14, No. 1 is not one of the official string-quartet canon; for example Breitkopf and Härtel did not included the composition in their complete edition of the composer's works which they published between 1864 and 1867. Although considered to be an engaging work (see later) its relative neglect in present-day performance has been attributed to the inherent superiority of the composer's recognised quartets, and the fact that the Piano Sonata Op. 14, No. 1 is so established in the repertoire that it has inadvertently displaced the arrangement from the attention of string players.[1] The transcription of Op. 14, No. 1 is not alone. In Beethoven's lifetime perhaps as many as twelve or more of his piano sonatas were transcribed, in whole or in part, for string quartet, though not sanctioned by the composer – most were published anonymously.[ii] Typical of other of the composer's works transcribed for string quartet, by another hand, is the arrangement of his ballet music *The Creatures of Prometheus* – published in 1804 by Artaria of Vienna. Simrock of Bonn brought out another quartet edition in 1831 – a measure of the popularity of the music and an indicator of the demand for such string quartet re-working of fashionable melodies of the day.[iii] When Beethoven was asked to make his own transcriptions, he invariably declined, having little appetite for such an undertaking. When prevailed upon he occasionally entrusted the request to his more reliable piano pupils such as Carl Czerny and Ferdinand Ries. Perhaps Beethoven's most memorable, and poignant transcription, is that he made for four hands of the Great Fugue, *Grosse Fuge*, Op. 133, completed on his deathbed.[iv]

Beethoven expressed his reluctance for making transcriptions in a letter to the publisher Breitkopf and Härtel: 'The *unnatural mania*, now so prevalent, for transferring even *pianoforte compositions* to stringed instruments, instruments which in all respects are utterly different from one another ... for not only would whole passages have to be entirely omitted or altered, but some would have to be added.'[v] In the case of his transcription of the Piano Sonata Op. 14, No. 1 he appears to have set aside his reservations, the reasons for which are unknown. The following circumstances may go some way to explaining how the transcription came into being. Beethoven's biographer Franz Wegeler records that sometime in 1795 the music lover and patron of the arts, Count Anton Apponyi asked Beethoven to compose a quartet for him. Apponyi had encountered Beethoven at one of Prince Lichnowsky's morning concerts and was aware that he had not yet written a work in this genre. He was eager to secure Beethoven's services in this genre as he had similarly commissioned Haydn to compose his sets of string quartets Op. 71 and 74. Despite repeated urgings by Gerhard Wegeler, on Beethoven's behalf, he did not respond to Apponyi's request.[vi] Some have speculated that, with Apponyi's putative commission in mind, Beethoven may have set about sketching a work for string quartet only to change his mind and convert his thoughts into the E major Piano Sonata. Only later did he revert to his original intention of composing a string quartet.

Whatever the precise origins of the transcription, it was duly published in Vienna in 1802 by the Bureau des Arts et d'Industrie also known as the Kunst und Industriekomptoir.[vii] A founder member of this firm was Joseph Sonnleithner who, a few years later, supplied Beethoven with the libretto for his opera *Leonora* (*Fidelio*). The string quartet was the first of Beethoven's works to be published by the *Bureau* and was soon followed by a succession of major compositions in what was to become one of the composer's most creative periods. As was the custom of the day, the quartet was issued in parts for the individual players; remarkably, it was not published in full score until 1910.[viii] Like the original Piano Sonata Op. 14, No. 1, Beethoven dedicated the String Quartet to Baroness Josephine von Braun.

We should refer more correctly to the String Quartet as being an arrangement rather than a note-for-note transcription of the piano score. In making the quartet arrangement, Beethoven had to rewrite parts of the piano sonata to give further consideration to such specific quartet properties as sonority, blending and timbre that differ inherently from those of the pianoforte.[ix] He also had to bear in mind the practical limits of the five-octave keyboard for which the

Piano Sonata was conceived. In the Piano Sonata, the high G sharp and high A that Beethoven required were beyond the compass of the contemporary keyboard; by transposing the key a semitone higher, from E to F, high passages were reinstated for the first violin. Furthermore, Beethoven was also able to give added resonance in the bass by placing the low C within the cello's reach, thereby putting the dominant as low down as possible.[x]

Although, as remarked, Beethoven's string-quartet arrangement has not entered the string-quartet repertoire, it has enduring value as vigorously affirmed by Donald Tovey: 'Beethoven's wonderful arrangement of this Sonata as a String Quartet should be in the hands of every student ... A good rehearsal of it by competent players is a lesson in style such as no other piece can give.' Of the Piano Sonata itself he remarks: 'We have here a unique demonstration of what the pianoforte can do better than strings, what qualities of bowed instruments it can really imitate, what qualities it can suggest without imitating, and in what characteristics it is ... totally opposite to the string quartet.'[xi] Others also acknowledge the virtues of the string-quartet arrangement:

Paul Bekker accepted the arrangement varies considerably from the original and shows 'a more refined taste' and 'better appreciations of the finer effect' in the working of the themes.[xii]

Lewis Lockwood writes: 'There can be no doubt that Beethoven's *arrangement* is no mere transcription, but entails a recasting of the material for quartet.' He remarks on Beethoven's awareness of the innate differences in the sonority properties between the pianoforte of c1798 and the string quartet: 'In the former, light percussiveness ... but no real sustaining possibilities; in the latter, as much sustaining quality as he could ask'. In his transcription, Lockwood notes Beethoven's changes in pitch are such as to accommodate the quartet medium: 'The shift from E major to F major ... capitalizes on the cello and viola open C-string sounds to project resonance.' Of wider significance, Lockwood contends, is that making the quartet arrangement assisted Beethoven's approach to the medium of the quartet at this time, bearing upon his gaining 'a deeper understanding of the quartet-medium's specific properties of sonority, blending, and timbre' — beyond those of the pianoforte — 'and [which later] helped him to employ quartet tone-colour effectively as an indispensable compositional element'.[xiii]

Robert Winter and Robert Martin submit the transcription to a movement-by-movement analysis.

FIRST MOVEMENT:

'Beethoven ... changed the tempo of the first movement from *Allegro* to *Allegro moderato*. It is a gentle piece whose opening theme climbs upward in a slow zigzag, and Beethoven enjoys demonstrating various ways at different speed in which one can present this figuration that lies so comfortably under the pianist's hands (and almost so under the string player's).'

SECOND MOVEMENT:

The author's describes the second movement as 'proto-Schubert, tinged with Danube Valley melancholy'. They add: 'Beethoven's pupil Carl Czerny characterizes it as "partaking of a certain mood of ill humour: and says that its performance should be "serious, lively but not too humorous or playful".'

FINALE:

In the finale, Beethoven again changes the tempo and character direction, this time from *Allegro comodo* to plain *Allegro*. They describe Beethoven's transcription here as 'clever and inventive'. In their summation, Winter and Martin reflect: 'The piano original is one of those gratifying pieces that come off as brilliant but without being notably difficult ... Beethoven's [transcription] changes are calculated to perfection; so much so that this movement is really more interesting in the quartet version.'[xiv]

Writing of Beethoven's musicianship, Philip Radcliffe enthuses how this is done 'with great freedom and sensitiveness' though not, he considers, as drastically as the composer's remodelling of the Octet, Op. 103 for wind instruments as the String Quintet, Op. 4. In the E major transcription, he finds 'the texture of the quartet version is lighter and clearer'. He cites the beginning of the central *Allegretto* where he considers Beethoven 'does not attempt to emulate the rich sound of the piano'. He concludes: 'Apart from it containing only three movements, there is nothing to indicate that it is an arrangement. In certain ways the character of the work has been changed; the subdued, rather wistful lyricism of the Sonata has been turned into something rather more precise and clear-cut, but the result is very delightful and well worth enjoying in its own right, apart from the extraordinary skill with which it has been done.'[xv]

---

[i] A view suggested by Denis Matthews, 1985, pp. 132–3.
[ii] Robert Winter and Robert Martin, editors, *The Beethoven quartet companion*, 1994, pp. 145–8.
[iii] As discussed in: Theodore Albrecht, 1996, Vol. 1, Letter No. 65, pp. 110–13.
[iv] Beethoven originally requested the pianist Anton Halm to make a four-hand pianoforte arrangement of the Fugue but was dissatisfied with the result; Halm had divided the parts in a manner that entailed the crossing of hands. Beethoven subsequently made his own arrangement that was published in 1827 in Vienna

by Matthias Artaria. Remarkably, the composer's manuscript came to light only in 2005 when it was discovered in the Library of the Palmer Theological Seminary, Pennsylvania. It is now in the possession of the Julliard School of Music. For the historical context to the origins of the transcription, see Elliot Forbes, editor, *Thayer's Life of Beethoven, 1967, pp. 975–6.*

v Emily Anderson, 1961, Vol. 1, Letter No. 59, pp. 74-5. The observations of Robert Winter and Robert Martin have a bearing on Beethoven's expressed reluctance to make transcriptions: 'Like any sort of translator, the musical transcribe can be suspended in excessive literalism by reverence or sheer lack of imagination: on the other hand, carelessness, irrepressible creative impulses, irreverence, or an inclination always to know better can lead to risky departures from the original.' See: *The Beethoven quartet companion*, 1994, pp. 145–8.

vi Thayer-Forbes, 1967, p. 262.

vii *Ibid*, p. 323.

viii The origins of the string-quartet arrangement are discussed in: Robert Winter and Robert Martin, editors, 1994, pp. 145-8. The string-quartet parts were discovered in 1903 by Dr. W. Altmann. He created the score that was published in 1910. See: John Shedlock, 1918, p. 29.

ix These considerations are discussed in detail by Lewis Lockwood, in: Sieghard Brandenburgh, editor, 1998, pp. 175-180.

x See, for example: Barry Cooper, 2000, p. 115; Eric Blom 1938, pp. 67-8; and Denis Matthews, 1985, p. 83.

xi Harold Craxton and Donald Francis Tovey, *Beethoven: Sonatas for pianoforte, Piano Sonata in E major, Op. 14, No. 1*, p. 192, [1931].

xii Paul Bekker, 1925, pp. 284–5.

xiii Sieghard Brandenburgh, editor, *Haydn, Mozart, & Beethoven: studies in the music of the classical period*: essays in honor of Alan Tyson, 1998, pp. 177–80.

xiv Robert Winter and Robert Martin, editors, *The Beethoven quartet companion*, 1994, pp.145–8.

xv Philip Radcliffe, 1978, pp. 45–7.

BIBLIOGRAPHY

The author has individually consulted all the publications listed in this bibliography and can confirm that each makes reference, in some way or other, to Beethoven and his works. It will be evident from their titles which of these are publications devoted exclusively to the composer. Others that make only passing reference to Beethoven and his compositions, nevertheless unfailingly bear testimony to his genius and humanity. The diversity of the titles listed testifies to the centrality of Beethoven to western culture and beyond; the mere survey of these should be of itself a rewarding experience for a lover of so-called classical music. The entries are confined to book publications, reflecting the scope of the author's researches. The cut-off date for this was 2007; no works after this date are listed, notwithstanding the author is mindful that Beethoven musicology, and related publication, continue to be a major field of endeavour.

Abraham, Gerald. *Beethoven's second-period quartets*. London: Oxford University Press: Humphrey Milford, 1944.

Abraham, Gerald. *Essays on Russian and East European music*. Oxford: Clarendon Press: New York: Oxford University Press, 1985.

Abraham, Gerald, Editor. *The age of Beethoven, 1790-1830*. London: Oxford University Press, 1982.

Abraham, Gerald. *The tradition of Western music*. London: Oxford University Press, 1974.

Abse, Dannie and Joan. *The Music lover's literary companion*. London: Robson Books, 1988.

Adorno, Theodor W., Translator. *Alban Berg: master of the smallest link*. Cambridge: Cambridge University Press, 1991.

Adorno, Theodor W. *Beethoven: the philosophy of music; fragments and texts*. Cambridge: Polity Press, 1998.

Albrecht, Daniel, Editor. *Modernism and music: an anthology of sources*. Chicago; London: University of Chicago Press, 2004.

Albrecht, Theodore, Translator and Editor. *Letters to Beethoven and other correspondence*. Lincoln, New England: University of Nebraska Press, 3 vols., 1996.

Allsobrook, David Ian. *Liszt: my travelling circus life*. London: Macmillan, 1991.

Anderson, Christopher, Editor and Translator. *Selected writings of Max Reger*. New York; London: Routledge, 2006.

Anderson, Emily, Editor and Translator. *The letters of Beethoven*. London: Macmillan, 3 vols., 1961.

Anderson, Martin, Editor. *Klemperer on music: shavings from a musician's workbench*. London: Toccata Press, 1986.

Antheil, George. *Bad boy of music*. London; New York: Hurst & Blackett Ltd., 1945.

Appleby, David P. *Heitor Villa-Lobos: a bio-bibliography*. New York: Greenwood Press, 1988.

Aprahamian, Felix, Editor. *Essays on music: an anthology from The Listener*. London, Cassell, 1967.

Armero, Gonzalo and Jorge de Persia. *Manuel de Falla : his life & works*. London: Omnibus Press, 1999.

Arnold, Ben, Editor. *The Liszt companion*. Westport, Connecticut; London: Greenwood Press, 2002.

Arnold, Denis and Nigel Fortune, Editors. *The Beethoven companion*. London: Faber and Faber, 1973.

Ashbrook, William. *Donizetti*. London: Cassell, 1965.

Auner, Joseph Henry. *A Schoenberg reader: documents of a life*. New Haven Connecticut; London: Yale University Press, 2003.

Avins, Styra, Editor. *Johannes Brahms: life and letters*. Oxford: Oxford University Press, 1997.

Azoury, Pierre H. *Chopin through his contemporaries: friends, lovers, and rivals*. Westport, Connecticut: Greenwood Press, 1999.

Badura-Skoda, Paul. *Carl Czerny: On the Proper Performance of all Beethoven's Works for the Piano*. Universal Edition: A. G. Wien, 1970.

Bailey, Cyril. *Hugh Percy Allen*. London: Oxford University

Press, 1948.

Bailey, Kathryn. *The life of Webern*. Cambridge: Cambridge University Press, 1998.

Barenboim, Daniel. *A life in music*. London: Weidenfeld & Nicolson, 1991.

Barlow, Michael. *Whom the gods love: the life and music of George Butterworth*. London: Toccata Press, 1997.

Barrett-Ayres, Reginald. *Joseph Haydn and the string quartet*. New York: Schirmer Books, 1974.

Bartos, Frantisek. *Bedrich Smetana: Letters and reminiscences*. Prague: Artia, 1953.

Barzun, Jacques. *Pleasures of music: an anthology of writing about music and musicians*. London: Cassell, 1977.

Bauer-Lechner, Natalie. *Recollections of Gustav Mahler*. London: Faber Music, 1980.

Bazhanov, N. Nikolai. *Rakhmaninov*. Moscow: Raduga, 1983.

Beaumont, Antony, Editor. *Ferruccio Busoni: Selected letters*. London: Faber and Faber, 1987.

Beaumont, Antony, Editor. *Gustav Mahler, letters to his wife*. London: Faber and Faber, 2004.

Beecham, Thomas. *A mingled chime: an autobiography*. New York: Da Capo Press, 1976.

Bekker, Paul. *Beethoven*. London: J. M. Dent & Sons, 1925.

Bellasis, Edward. *Cherubini: memorials illustrative of his life*. London: Burns and Oates, 1874.

Bennett, James R. Sterndale. *The life of William Sterndale Bennett*. Cambridge: University Press, 1907.

Benser, Caroline Cepin. *Egon Wellesz (1885–1974): chronicle of twentieth-century musician*. New York: P. Lang, 1985.

Berlioz, Hector. *Evenings in the orchestra*. Harmondsworth: Penguin Books, 1963.

Berlioz, Hector. *The musical madhouse (Les grotesques de la musique)*. Rochester, New York: University of Rochester Press, 2003.

Bernard, Jonathan W., Editor. *Elliott Carter: collected essays and lectures, 1937-1995*. Rochester, New York; Woodbridge: University of Rochester Press, 1998.

Bernstein, Leonard. *The joy of music*. New York: Simon and Schuster, 1959.

Bertensson, Sergei. *Sergei Rachmaninoff: a lifetime in music*. London: G. Allen & Unwin, 1965.

Biancolli, Louis. *The Flagstad manuscript*. New York: Putnam, 1952.

Bickley, Nora, Editor. *Letters from and to Joseph Joachim*. London: Macmillan, 1914.

Bie, Oskar. *A history of the pianoforte and pianoforte players*. New York: Da Capo Press, 1966.

Blaukopf, Herta. *Mahler's unknown letters*. London: Gollancz, 1986.

Blaukopf, Kurt and Herta. *Mahler: his life, work and world*. London: Thames and Hudson, 1991.

Bliss, Arthur. *As I remember*. London: Thames Publishing, 1989.

Block, Adrienne Fried. *Amy Beach, passionate Victorian: the life and work of an American composer, 1867–1944*. New York: Oxford University Press, 1998.

Bloch, Ernst. *Essays on the philoso-

phy of music. Cambridge: Cambridge University Press, 1985.

Blocker, Robert. *The Robert Shaw reader*. New Haven; London: Yale University Press, 2004.

Blom, Eric. *A musical postbag*. London: J. M. Dent, 1945.

Blom, Eric. *Beethoven's pianoforte sonatas discussed*. London: J. M. Dent, 1938.

Blom, Eric. *Classics major and minor: with some other musical ruminations*. London: J. M. Dent, 1958.

Blum, David. *The art of quartet playing: the Guarneri Quartet in conversation with David Blum*. London: Gollancz, 1986.

Blume, Friedrich. *Classic and Romantic music: a comprehensive survey*. London: Faber and Faber, 1972.

Boden, Anthony. *The Parrys of the Golden Vale: background to genius*. London: Thames Publishing, 1998.

Bonavia, Ferruccio. *Musicians on music*. London: Routledge & Kegan Paul, 1956.

Bonds, Mark Evan *After Beethoven: imperatives of originality in the symphony*. Cambridge, Massachusetts; London: Harvard University Press, 1996.

Bonis, Ferenc, Editor. *The selected writings of Zoltán Kodály*. London; New York: Boosey & Hawkes, 1974.

Bookspan, Martin. *André Previn: a biography*. London: Hamilton, 1981.

Boros, James and Richard Toop, Editors. *Brian Ferneyhough: Collected writings*. Amsterdam: Harwood Academic, 1995.

Boulez, Pierre. *Stocktakings from an apprenticeship*. Oxford: Clarendon Press, 1991.

Boult, Adrian. *Boult on music: words from a lifetime's communication*. London: Toccata Press, 1983.

Boult, Adrian. *My own trumpet*. London, Hamish Hamilton, 1973.

Boult, Adrian with Jerrold Northrop Moore. *Music and friends: seven decades of letters to Adrian Boult from Elgar, Vaughan Williams, Holst, Bruno Walter, Yehudi Menuhin and other friends*. London: Hamish Hamilton, 1979.

Bovet, Marie Anne de. *Charles Gounod: his life and his works*. London: S. Low, Marston, Searle & Rivington, Ltd., 1891.

Bowen, Catherine Drinker. *Beloved friend: the story of Tchaikowsky and Nadejda von Meck*. London: Hutchinson & Co., 1937.

Bowen, Meiron, Editor. *Gerhard on music: selected writings*. Brookfield, Vermont: Ashgate, 2000.

Bowen, Meirion. *Michael Tippett*. London: Robson Books, 1982.

Bowen, Meiron, Editor. *Music of the angels: essays and sketchbooks of Michael Tippett*. London: Eulenburg, 1980.

Bowen, Meiron, Editor. *Tippett on music*. Oxford: Clarendon Press, 1995.

Bowers, Faubion. *Scriabin: a biography*. Mineola: Dover; London: Constable, 1996.

Boyden, Matthew. *Richard Strauss*. London: Weidenfeld & Nicolson, 1999.

Bozarth, George S., Editor. *Brahms studies: analytical and historical perspectives; papers delivered at the International Brahms Conference, Washington, DC, 5-8 May 1983*. Oxford: Clarendon Press, 1990.

Brand, Juliane, Christopher Hailey and Donald Harris, Editors. *The Berg-Schoenberg correspondence: selected letters*. Basingstoke: Macmillan, 1987.

Brandenbugh, Sieghard, Editor. *Haydn, Mozart, & Beethoven: studies in the music of the classical period: essays in honor of Alan Tyson*. Oxford: Clarendon Press, 1998.

Braunstein, Joseph. *Musica Æterna, program notes for 1961-1971*. New York: Musica Æterna, 1972.

Braunstein, Joseph. *Musica Æterna, program notes for 1971-1976*. New York: Musica Æterna, 1978.

Brendel, Alfred. *Alfred Brendel on music: collected essays*. Chicago, Iliinois: A Cappella Books, 2001.

Brendel, Alfred. *The veil of order: Alfred Brendel in conversation with Martin Meyer*. London: Faber and Faber, 2002.

Breuning, Gerhard von. *Memories of Beethoven: from the house of the black-robed Spaniards*. Cambridge: Cambridge University Press, 1992.

Briscoe, James R., Editor. (Brief Description): *Debussy in performance*. New Haven: Yale University Press, 1999.

Brott, Alexander Betty Nygaard King. *Alexander Brott: my lives in music*. Oakville, Ontario; Niagara Falls, New York: Mosaic Press, 2005.

Brown, Alfred Peter. *The symphonic repertoire. Vol. 2, The first golden age of the Viennese symphony: Haydn, Mozart, Beethoven, and Schubert*. Bloomington, Indiana: Indiana University Press, 2002.

Brown, Maurice John Edwin. *Schubert: a critical biography*. London: Macmillan; New York: St. Martin's Press, 1958.

Broyles, Michael. *Beethoven: the emergence and evolution of Beethoven's heroic style*. New York: Excelsior Music Publishing Co., 1987.

Brubaker, Bruce and Jane Gottlieb, Editors. *Pianist, scholar, connoisseur: essays in honor of Jacob Lateiner*. Stuyvesant, N.Y., Pendragon Press, 2000.

Buch, Esteban. *Beethoven's Ninth: a political history*. Chicago; London: University of Chicago Press, 2003.

Burk, John N., Editor. *Letters of Richard Wagner: the Burrell collection*. London: Gollancz, 1951.

Burnham, Scott G. *Beethoven hero*. Princeton, New Jersey: Princeton University Press, 1995.

Burnham, Scott G and Michael P. Steinberg, Editors. *Beethoven and his world*. Princeton, New Jersey; Oxford: Princeton University Press, 2000.

Burton, William Westbrook, Editor. *Conversations about Bernstein*. New York; Oxford: Oxford University Press, 1995.

Busch, Fritz. *Pages from a musician's life*. London: Hogarth Press, 1953.

Busch, Hans, Editor. *Verdi's Aida: the history of an opera in letters and documents*. Minneapolis:

University of Minnesota Press, 1978.

Busch, Hans, Editor. *Verdi's Falstaff in letters and contemporary reviews*. Bloomington: Indiana University Press, 1997.

Busch, Marie, Translator. *Memoirs of Eugenie Schumann*. London: W. Heinemann, 1927.

Bush, Alan Dudley. *In my eighth decade and other essays*. London: Kahn & Averill, 1980.

Busoni, Ferruccio. *Letters to his wife*. Translated by Rosamond Ley. New York: Da Capo Press, 1975.

Byron, Reginald. *Music, culture, & experience: selected papers of John Blacking*. Chicago: University of Chicago Press, 1995.

Cairns, David. *Responses: musical essays and reviews*. New York: Da Capo Press, 1980.

Cardus, Neville. *Talking of music*. London: Collins, 1957.

Carley, Lionel. *Delius: a life in letters*. London: Scolar Press in association with the Delius Trust, 1988.

Carley, Lionel. *Grieg and Delius: a chronicle of their friendship in letters*. London: Marion Boyars, 1993.

Carner, Mosco. *Major and minor*. London: Duckworth, 1980

Carner, Mosco. *Puccini: a critical biography*. London: Duckworth, 1958.

Carroll, Brendan G. *The last prodigy: a biography of Erich Wolfgang Korngold*. Portland, Oregon: Amadeus Press, 1997.

Carse, Adam von Ahn. *The life of Jullien: adventurer, showman-conductor and establisher of the Promenade Concerts in England, together with a history of those concerts up to 1895*. Cambridge England: Heffer, 1951.

Carse, Adam von Ahn. *The orchestra from Beethoven to Berlioz: a history of the orchestra in the first half of the 19th century, and of the development of orchestral baton-conducting*. Cambridge: W. Heffer, 1948.

Casals, Pablo. *Joys and sorrows: reflections by Pablo Casals as told to Albert E. Kahn*. London: Macdonald, 1970.

Casals, Pablo. *The memoirs of Pablo Casals as told to Thomas Dozier*. London: Life en Español, 1959.

Chappell, Paul. *Dr. S. S. Wesley, 1810–1876: portrait of a Victorian musician*. Great Wakering: Mayhew-McCrimmon, 1977.

Chasins, Abram. *Leopold Stokowski, a profile*. New York: Hawthorn Books, 1979.

Charlton, Davi, Editor and Martyn Clarke Translator. *E.T.A. Hoffmann's musical writings: Kreisleriana, The Poet and the Composer*. Cambridge: Cambridge University Press, 1989.

Chávez, Carlos. *Musical thought*. Cambridge: Harvard University Press, 1961.

Chesterman, Robert, Editor. *Conversations with conductors: Bruno Walter, Sir Adrian Boult, Leonard Bernstein, Ernest Ansermet, Otto Klemperer, Leopold Stokowski*. Totowa, New Jersey: Rowman and Littlefield, 1976.

Chissell, Joan. *Clara Schumann: a dedicated spirit; a study of her life and work*. London: Hamilton, 1983.

Chua, Daniel K. L. *The "Galitzin" quartets of Beethoven: Opp.127, 132, 130*. Princeton: Princeton

University Press, 1995.

Citron, Marcia, Editor. *The letters of Fanny Hensel to Felix Mendelssohn*. Stuyvesant, New York: Pendragon Press, 1987.

Clark, Walter Aaron. *Enrique Granados: poet of the piano*. Oxford, England; New York, N.Y.: Oxford University Press, 2006.

Clark, Walter Aaron. *Isaac Albéniz: portrait of a romantic*. Oxford; New York: Oxford University Press, 1999.

Clive, Peter. *Beethoven and his world*. Oxford University Press, 2001.

Closson, Ernest. *History of the piano*. Translated by Delano Ames and edited by Robin Golding. London: Paul Elek, 1947.

Cockshoot, John V. *The fugue in Beethoven's piano music*. London: Routledge & Kegan Paul, 1959.

Coe, Richard N, Translator. *Life of Rossini by Stendhal*. London: Calder & Boyars, 1970.

Coleman, Alexander, Editor. *Diversions & animadversions: essays from The new criterion*. New Brunswick, New Jersey; London: Transaction Publishers, 2005.

Colerick, George. *From the Italian girl to Cabaret: musical humour, parody and burlesque*. London: Juventus, 1998.

Coleridge, A. D. *Life of Moscheles, with selections from his diaries and correspondence by his wife*. London: Hurst & Blackett, 1873.

Colles, Henry Cope. *Essays and lectures*. London: Humphrey Milford, Oxford University Press, 1945.

Cone, Edward T., Editor. *Roger Sessions on music: collected essays*. Princeton, New Jersey: Princeton University Press, 1979.

Cone, Edward T. *The composer's voice*. Berkeley; London: University of California Press, 1974.

Cook, Susan and Judy S. Tsou, Editors. *Cecilia reclaimed: feminist perspectives on gender and music*. Urbana: University of Illinois Press, 1994.

Cooper, Barry. *Beethoven*. The master musicians series. Oxford: Oxford University Press, 2000.

Cooper, Barry. *Beethoven and the creative process*. Oxford: Clarendon Press, 1990.

Cooper, Barry. *Beethoven's folksong settings: chronology, sources, style*. Cambridge: Cambridge University Press, 1991.

Cooper, Barry. *The Beethoven compendium: a guide to Beethoven's life and music*. London: Thames and Hudson, 1991.

Cooper, Martin. *Beethoven: the last decade, 1817–1827*. London: Oxford University Press, 1970.

Cooper, Martin. *Judgements of value: selected writings on music*. Oxford; New York: Oxford University Press, 1988.

Cooper, Martin. *Ideas and music*. London: Barrie and Rockliff, 1965.

Cooper, Victoria L. *The house of Novello: the practice and policy of a Victorian music publisher, 1829–1866*. Aldershot, Hants: Ashgate, 2003.

Coover, James. *Music at auction: Puttick and Simpson (of London), 1794–1971: being an annotated, chronological list of sales of musical materials*. Warren, Michigan: Harmonie Park Press, 1988.

Copland, Aaron. *Copland on music.* London: Deutsch, 1961.

Corredor, J. Ma. *Conversations with Casals.* London: Hutchinson, 1956.

Cott, Jonathan. *Stockhausen: conversations with the composer.* London: Picador, 1974.

Cottrell, Stephen. *Professional music making in London: ethnography and experience.* Aldershot: Ashgate, 2004.

Cowell, Henry. *Charles Ives and his music.* New York: Oxford University Press, 1955.

Cowling, Elizabeth. *The cello.* London: Batsford, 1983.

Crabbe, John. *Beethoven's empire of the mind.* Newbury: Lovell Baines, 1982.

Craft, Robert. *An improbable life: memoirs.* Nashville: Vanderbilt University Press, 2002.

Craft, Robert, Editor. *Stravinsky: selected correspondence.* London: Faber and Faber, 3 Vols. 1982–1985.

Craw, Howard Allen. *A biography and thematic catalog of the works of J. L. Dussek: 1760–1812.* Ann Arbor: Michigan, 1965.

Crawford, Richard, R. Allen Lott and Carol J. Oja, Editors. *A Celebration of American music: words and music in honor of H. Wiley Hitchcock.* Ann Arbor: University of Michigan Press, 1990.

Craxton, Harold and Tovey, Donald Francis. *Beethoven: Sonatas for Pianoforte.* London: The Associated Board, [1931].

Crichton, Ronald: Editor. *The memoirs of Ethel Smyth.* New York: Viking, 1987.

Crist, Stephen A. and Roberta M. Marvin, Editors. *Historical musicology: sources, methods, interpretations.* Rochester, New York: University of Rochester Press, 2004.

Crofton, Ian and Donald Fraser, Editors. *A dictionary of musical quotations.* London: Croom Helm, 1985.

Crompton, Louis, Editor. *Shaw, Bernard: The great composers: reviews and bombardments.* Berkeley; London: University of California Press, 1978.

Csicserry-Ronay, Elizabeth, Translator and Editor. *Hector Berlioz: The art of music and other essays: (A travers chants).* Bloomington: Indiana University Press, 1994.

Curtiss, Mina Kirstein. *Bizet and his world.* London: Secker & Warburg, 1959.

Cuyler, Louise Elvira. *The symphony.* New York: Harcourt Brace Jovanovich, 1973.

Dahlhaus, Carl. *Ludwig van Beethoven: approaches to his music.* Oxford: Clarendon Press, 1991.

Dahlhaus, Carl. *Nineteenth-century music.* Translated by J. Bradford Robinson. Berkeley; London: University of California Press, 1989.

Daniels, Robin. *Conversations with Cardus.* London: Gollancz, 1976.

Daniels, Robin. Conversations with Menuhin. London: Macdonald General Books, 1979.

Day, James. *Vaughan Williams.* London: Dent, 1961.

Davies, Peter Maxwell. *Studies from two decades.* Selected and introduced by Stephen Pruslin.

London: Boosey & Hawkes, 1979.

Dean, Winton. *Georges Bizet: his life and work*. London: J.M. Dent, 1965.

Deas, Stewart. *In defence of Hanslick*. London: Williams and Norgate, 1940.

Debussy, Claude. *Debussy on music*. London: Secker & Warburg, 1977.

Delbanco, Nicholas. *The Beaux Arts Trio*. London: Gollancz, 1985.

Demény, Janos, Editor. *Béla Bartók: letters*. London: Faber and Faber, 1971.

Dent, Edward Joseph. *Selected essays*. Edited by Hugh Taylor. Cambridge; New York: Cambridge University Press, 1979.

Deutsch, Otto Erich. *Mozart: a documentary biography*. London: Adam & Charles Black, 1965.

Deutsch, Otto Erich. *Schubert: a documentary biography*. London: J.M. Dent, 1946

Deutsch, Otto Erich. *Schubert: memoirs by his friends*. London: Adam & Charles Black, 1958.

Dibble, Jeremy. *C. Hubert H. Parry: his life and music*. Oxford: Clarendon Press, 1992.

Dibble, Jeremy. *Charles Villiers Stanford: man and musician*. Oxford: Oxford University Press, 2002.

Donakowski, Conrad L. *A muse for the masses: ritual and music in an age of democratic revolution, 1770–1870*. Chicago: University of Chicago Press, 1977.

Dower, Catherine. *Alfred Einstein on music: selected music criticisms*. New York: Greenwood Press, 1991.

Downs, Philip G. *Classical music: the era of Haydn, Mozart, and Beethoven*. New York: W.W. Norton, 1992.

Drabkin, William. *Beethoven: Missa Solemnis*. Cambridge: Cambridge University Press, 1991.

Dreyfus, Kay. *The farthest north of humanness: letters of Percy Grainger, 1901–1914*. South Melbourne; Basingstoke: Macmillan, 1985.

Dubal, David, Editor. *Remembering Horowitz: 125 pianists recall a legend*. New York: Schirmer Books, 1993.

Dubal, David. *The world of the concert pianist*. London: Victor Gollancz, 1985.

Dvořák, Otakar. *Antonín Dvořák, my father*. Spillville, Iowa: Czech Historical Research Center, 1993.

Dyson, George. *The progress of music*. London: Oxford University Press, Humphrey Milford, 1932.

Eastaugh, Kenneth. *Havergal Brian: the making of a composer*. London: Harrap, 1976.

Edwards, Allen. *Flawed words and stubborn sounds: a conversation with Elliott Carter*. New York: Norton & Company, 1971.

Edwards, Frederick George. *Musical haunts in London*. London: J. Curwen & Sons, 1895.

Ehrlich, Cyril. *First philharmonic: a history of the Royal Philharmonic Society*. Oxford: Clarendon Press, 1995.

Einstein, Alfred. *A short history of music*. London: Cassell and Company Ltd., 1948.

Einstein, Alfred. *Essays on music*. London: Faber and Faber, 1958.

Einstein, Alfred. *Mozart: his character, his work*. London: Cassell

and Company Ltd., 1946.
Einstein, Alfred. *Music in the Romantic era*. London: J.M. Dent Ltd., 1947.
Ekman, Karl. *Jean Sibelius, his life and personality*. New York: Tudor Publishing. Co., 1945.
Elgar, Edward. *A future for English music: and other lectures*, Edited by Percy M. Young. London: Dobson, 1968.
Elkin, Robert. *Queen's Hall, 1893–1941*. London: Rider, 1944.
Ella, John. *Musical sketches, abroad and at home: with original music by Mozart, Czerny, Graun, etc., vocal cadenzas and other musical illustrations*. London: Ridgway, Vol. 1., 1869.
Ellis, William Ashton. *The family letters of Richard Wagner*. Edited and translated by William Ashton Ellis and enlarged with introduction and notes by John Deathridge. Basingstoke: Macmillan, 1991.
Ellis, William Ashton. *Richard Wagner's prose works: Vol. 1, The art-work of the future*. Edited and translated by William Ashton Ellis. London: Kegan Paul, Trench, Trübner, 1895.
Ellis, William Ashton. *Richard Wagner's prose works: Vol. 2, Opera and drama*. Edited and translated by William Ashton Ellis. London: Kegan Paul, Trench, Trübner, 1900.
Ellis, William Ashton. *Richard Wagner's prose works: Vol. 3, The theatre*. Edited and translated by William Ashton Ellis. London: Kegan Paul, Trench, Trübner, 1907.
Ellis, William Ashton. *Richard Wagner's prose works: Vol. 4, Art and politics*. Edited and translated by William Ashton Ellis. London: Kegan Paul, Trench, Trübner, 1895.
Ellis, William Ashton. *Richard Wagner's prose works: Vol. 5, Actors and singers*. Edited and translated by William Ashton Ellis. London: Kegan Paul, Trench, Trübner, 1896.
Ellis, William Ashton. *Richard Wagner's prose works: Vol. 6, Religion and art*. Edited and translated by William Ashton Ellis. London: Kegan Paul, Trench, Trübner, 1897.
Ellis, William Ashton. *Richard Wagner's prose works: Vol. 7, In Paris and Dresden*. Edited and translated by William Ashton Ellis. London: Kegan Paul, Trench, Trübner, 1898.
Ellis, William Ashton. *Richard Wagner's prose works: Vol. 8, Posthumous*. Edited and translated by William Ashton Ellis. London: Kegan Paul, Trench, Trübner, 1899.
Elterlein, Ernst von. *Beethoven's pianoforte sonatas: explained for the lovers of the musical art*. London: W. Reeves, 1898.
Engel, Carl. *Musical myths and facts*. London: Novello, Ewer & Co.; New York: J.L. Peters, 1876.
Eosze, László. *Zoltán Kodály: his life and work*. London: Collet's, 1962.
Etter, Brian K. *From classicism to modernism: Western musical culture and the metaphysics of order*. Aldershot: Ashgate, 2001.
Ewen, David. *From Bach to Stravinsky: the history of music by its foremost critics*. New York, Greenwood Press, 1968.

Ewen, David. *Romain Rolland's Essays on music.* New York: Dover Publications, 1959.

Fay, Amy. *Music-study in Germany: from the home correspondence of Amy Fay.* New York: Dover Publications, 1965.

Fenby, Eric. *Delius as I knew him.* London: Quality Press, 1936.

Ferguson, Donald Nivison. *Masterworks of the orchestral repertoire: a guide for listeners.* Minneapolis: University of Minnesota Press, 1954.

Fétis, François-Joseph. *Curiosités historiques de la musique: complément nécessaire de la Musique mise à la portée de tout le monde.* Paris: Janet et Cotelle, 1830.

Fifield, Christopher. *Max Bruch: his life and works.* London: Gollancz, 1988.

Fifield, Christopher. *True artist and true friend: a biography of Hans Richter.* Oxford: Clarendon Press, 1993.

Finson, Jon and R. Larry Todd, Editors. *Mendelssohn and Schumann: essays on their music and its context.* Durham, N.C.: Duke University Press, 1984.

Fischer, Edwin. *Beethoven's pianoforte sonatas: a guide for students & amateurs.* London: Faber and Faber, 1959.

Fischer, Edwin. *Reflections on music.* London: Williams and Norgate, 1951.

Fischer, Hans Conrad and Erich Kock. *Ludwig van Beethoven: a study in text and pictures.* London: Macmillan; New York, St. Martin's Press, 1972.

Fischmann, Zdenka E. *Janáček-Newmarch correspondence. 1st limited and numbered edition.* Rockville, MD: Kabel Publishers, 1986.

Fitzlyon, April. *Maria Malibran: diva of the romantic age.* London: Souvenir Press, 1987.

FitzLyon, April. *The price of genius: a life of Pauline Viardot.* London: John Calder, 1964.

Forbes, Elliot, Editor. *Thayer's life of Beethoven.* Princeton, New Jersey: Princeton University Press, 1967.

Foreman, Lewis. *Bax: a composer and his times.* London: Scolar Press, 1983.

Foreman, Lewis, Editor. *Farewell, my youth, and other writings by Arnold Bax.* Aldershot: Scolar Press, 1992.

Foster, Myles Birket. *History of the Philharmonic Society of London, 1813–1912: a record of a hundred years' work in the cause of music.* London: Bodley Head, 1912.

Foulds, John. *Music today: its heritage from the past, and legacy to the future.* London: I. Nicholson and Watson, limited, 1934.

Frank, Mortimer H. *Arturo Toscanini: the NBC years.* Portland, Oregon: Amadeus Press, 2002.

Fraser, Andrew Alastair. *Essays on music.* London: Oxford University Press, H. Milford, 1930.

Frohlich, Martha. *Beethoven's Appassionata' sonata.* Oxford: Clarendon Press, 1991.

Gal, Hans. *The golden age of Vienna.* London: Max Parrish & Co. Limited, 1948.

Gal, Hans. *The musician's world: great composers in their letters.* London: Thames and Hudson,

1965.

Galatopoulos, Stelios. *Bellini: life, times, music.* London: Sanctuary, 2002.

Garden, Edward and Nigel Gottrei, Editors. *'To my best friend': correspondence between Tchaikovsky and Nadezhda von Meck, 1876–1878.* Oxford: Clarendon Press, 1993.

Geck, Martin. Beethoven. London: Haus, 2003.

Gerig, Reginald. *Famous pianists & their technique.* Washington: R. B. Luce, 1974.

Gilliam, Bryan. *The life of Richard Strauss.* Cambridge: Cambridge University Press, 1999.

Gilliam, Bryan, Editor. *Richard Strauss and his world.* Princeton, New Jersey: Princeton University Press, 1992.

Gillies, Malcolm and Bruce Clunies Ross, Editors. *Grainger on music.* Oxford; New York: Oxford University Press, 1999.

Gillies, Malcolm and David Pear, Editors. *The all-round man: selected letters of Percy Grainger, 1914–1961.* Oxford: Clarendon Press, 1994.

Gillies, Malcolm, Editor. *The Bartók companion.* London: Faber and Faber, 1993.

Gillmor, Alan M. *Erik Satie.* Basingstoke: Macmillan Press, 1988.

Glehn, M. E. *Goethe and Mendelssohn : (1821–1831).* London: Macmillan, 1874.

Glowacki, John, Editor. *Paul A. Pisk: Essays in his honor.* Austin, Texas: University of Texas, 1966

Gollancz, Victor. *Journey towards music: a memoir.* London: Victor Gollancz Ltd., 1964.

Good, Edwin Marshall. *Giraffes, black dragons, and other pianos: a technological history from Cristofori to the modern concert grand.* Stanford, California: Stanford University Press, 1982.

Gordon, David. *Musical visitors to Britain.* London: Routledge, 2005.

Gordon, Stewart. *A history of keyboard literature: music for the piano and its forerunners.* Schirmer Books: New York: London : Prentice Hall International, 1996.

Gorrell, Lorraine. *The nineteenth-century German lied.* Portland, Oregon: Amadeus Press, 1993.

Goss, Glenda D. *Jean Sibelius: the Hämeenlinna letters: scenes from a musical life, 1875–1895.* Esbo, Finland: Schildts, 1997.

Goss, Madeleine. *Bolero: the life of Maurice Ravel.* New York: Tudor, 1945.

Gotch, Rosamund Brunel, Editor. *Mendelssohn and his friends in Kensington: letters from Fanny and Sophy Horsley, written 1833–36.* London: Oxford University Press, 1938.

Gounod, Charles. *Charles Gounod; autobiographical reminiscences: with family letters and notes on music; from the French.* London: William Heinemann, 1896.

Grabs, Manfred, Editor. *Hanns Eisler: a rebel in music; selected writings.* Berlin: Seven Seas Publishers, 1978.

Grace, Harvey. *A musician at large.* London: Oxford University Press, H. Milford, 1928.

(La) Grange, Henry-Louis de. *Gustav Mahler.* Oxford: Oxford University Press, 1995.

Graves, Charles L. *Hubert Parry: his life and works.* London: Macmillan, 1926.

Graves, Charles L. *Post-Victorian music: with other studies and sketches.* London: Macmillan and Co., limited, 1911.

Graves, Charles L. *The life & letters of Sir George Grove, Hon. D.C.L. (Durham), Hon. LL.D. (Glasgow), formerly director of the Royal college of music.* London: Macmillan and Co., Ltd.; New York: The Macmillan Co., 1903.

Gray, Cecil. *Musical chairs, or, between two stools: being the life and memoirs of Cecil Gray.* London: Home & Van Thal, 1948.

Gregor-Dellin and Dietrich Mack, Editors. *Cosima Wagner's diaries.: Vol. 1, 1869 - 1877.* London: Collins, 1978-1980.

Griffiths, Paul. *Modern music: the avant-garde since 1945.* London: J. M. Dent & Sons Ltd., 1981.

Griffiths, Paul. *Olivier Messiaen and the music of time.* London: Faber and Faber, 1985.

Griffiths, Paul. *Peter Maxwell Davies.* London: Robson Books, 1988.

Griffiths, Paul. *The sea on fire: Jean Barraqué.* Rochester, New York: Woodbridge: University of Rochester Press, 2003.

Griffiths, Paul. *The string quartet.* London: Thames and Hudson, 1983.

Grout, Donald Jay and Claude V. Palisca, Editors. *A history of Western music.* London: J. M. Dent, 1988.

Grove, George. *Beethoven and his nine symphonies.* London: Novello, Ewer, 1896.

Grover, Ralph Scott. *Ernest Chausson: the man and his music.* London: The Athlone Press, 1980.

Grover, Ralph Scott. *The music of Edmund Rubbra.* Aldershot: Scolar Press, 1993.

Grun, Bernard. *Alban Berg: letters to his wife.* Edited and translated by Bernard Grun. London: Faber and Faber, 1971.

Gutman, David. *Prokofiev.* London: Omnibus Press, 1990.

Hadow, William Henry. *Collected essays.* London: H. Milford at the Oxford University Press, 1928.

Hadow, William Henry. *Beethoven's Op. 18 Quartets.* London: H. Milford at the Oxford University Press, 1926.

Haggin, Bernard H. *Music observed.* New York: Oxford University Press, 1964.

Hailey, Christopher. *Franz Schreker, 1878–1934: a cultural biography.* Cambridge: Cambridge University Press, 1993.

Hall, Michael. *Leaving home: a conducted tour of twentieth-century music with Simon Rattle.* London: Faber and Faber, 1996.

Hall, Patricia and Friedemann Sallis, Editors. (Brief Description): *A handbook to twentieth-century musical sketches.* Cambridge: Cambridge University Press, 2004.

Hallé, C. E. *Life and letters of Sir Charles Hallé: being an autobiography (1819–1860) with correspondence and diaries.* London: Smith, Elder & Co., 1896.

Halstead, Jill. *The woman composer: creativity and the gendered politics of musical composition. Aldershot: Ashgate, 1997.

Hamburger, Michael, Editor and Translator. *Beethoven letters, journals, and conversations*. New York: Thames and Hudson, 1951.

Hammelmann, Hanns A. and Ewald Osers. *The correspondence between Richard Strauss and Hugo von Hofmannsthal.* London: Collins, 1961.

Hanson, Lawrence and Elisabeth Hanson. *Tchaikovsky: the man behind the music.* New York: Dodd, Mead & Co, 1967.

Harding, James. *Massenet.* London: J. M. Dent & Sons Ltd., 1970.

Harding, James. *Saint-Saëns and his circle.* London: Chapman & Hall, 1965.

Harding, Rosamond E. M. *Origins of musical time and expression.* London: Oxford University Press, 1938.

Harman, Alec with Anthony Milner and Wilfrid Mellers. *Man and his music: the story of musical experience in the West.* London: Barrie & Jenkins, 1988.

Harper, Nancy Lee. *Manuel de Falla: his life and music.* Lanham, Maryland; London: The Scarecrow Press, 2005.

Hartmann, Arthur. *'Claude Debussy as I knew him' and other writings of Arthur Hartmann.* Edited by Samuel Hsu, Sidney Grolnic, and Mark Peters. Rochester, New York; Woodbridge: University of Rochester Press, 2003.

Haugen, Einar and Camilla Cai. *Ole Bull: Norway's romantic musician and cosmopolitan patriot.* Madison: The University of Wisconsin Press, 1993.

Headington, Christopher. *The Bodley Head history of Western music.* London: The Bodley Head, 1974.

Heartz, Daniel. *Music in European capitals: the galant style, 1720–1780.* New York; London: W. W. Norton, 2003.

Hedley, Arthur, Editor. *Selected correspondence of Fryderyk Chopin: abridged from Fryderyk Chopin's correspondence.* London: Heinemann, 1962.

Heiles, Anne Mischakoff. *Mischa Mischakoff: journeys of a concertmaster.* Sterling Heights, Michigan: Harmonie Park Press, 2006.

Henderson, Sanya Shoilevska. *Alex North, film composer: a biography, with musical analyses of a Streetcar named desire, Spartacus, The misfits, Under the volcano, and Prizzi's honor.* Jefferson, N.C.; London: McFarland, 2003.

Henschel, George. *Personal recollections of Johannes Brahms: some of his letters to and pages from a journal kept by George Henschel.* Boston: R G. Badger, 1907.

Henze, Hans Werner. *Bohemian fifths: an autobiography.* London: Faber and Faber, 1998.

Henze, Hans Werner. *Music and politics: collected writings 1953–81.* London: Faber and Faber, 1982.

Herbert, May, Translator. *Early letters of Robert Schumann.* London: George Bell and Sons, 1888.

Heyman, Barbara B. *Samuel Barber: the composer and his music.* New York: Oxford University

Press, 1992.

Heyworth, Peter. *Otto Klemperer, his life and times*. Cambridge: Cambridge University Press, 2 Vols. 1983–1996.

Hildebrandt, Dieter. *Pianoforte: a social history of the piano*. London: Hutchinson, 1988.

Hill, Peter. *The Messiaen companion*. London: Faber and Faber, 1995.

Hill, Peter and Nigel Simeone. *Messiaen*. New Haven Connecticut; London: Yale University Press, 2005.

Hiller, Ferdinand. *Mendelssohn: Letters and recollections*. New York: Vienna House, 1972.

Hines, Robert Stephan. *The orchestral composer's point of view: essays on twentieth-century music by those who wrote it*. Norman: University of Oklahoma Press, 1970.

Ho, Allan B. *Shostakovich reconsidered*. London: Toccata Press, 1998.

Hodeir, André. *Since Debussy: a view of contemporary music*. New York: Da Capo Press, 1975.

Holmes, Edward. *The life of Mozart: including his correspondence*. London: Chapman and Hall, 1845.

Holmes, John L. *Composers on composers*. New York: Greenwood Press, 1990.

Hopkins, Antony. *The concertgoer's companion*. London: J.M. Dent & Sons Ltd., 1984.

Hopkins, Antony. *The seven concertos of Beethoven*. Aldershot: Scolar Press, 1996.

Holt, Richard. *Nicolas Medtner (1879–1951): a tribute to his art and personality*. London: D. Dobson, 1955.

Honegger, Arthur. *I am a composer*. London: Faber and Faber, 1966.

Hoover, Kathleen and John Cage. *Virgil Thomson: his life and music*. New York; London: T. Yoseloff, 1959.

Horgan, Paul. *Encounters with Stravinsky: a personal record*. London: The Bodley Head, 1972.

Horowitz, Joseph. *Conversations with Arrau*. London: Collins, 1982.

Horowitz, Joseph. *Understanding Toscanini*. London: Faber and Faber, 1987.

Horwood, Wally. *Adolphe Sax, 1814–1894: his life and legacy*. Bramley: Bramley Books, 1980.

Howie, Crawford. *Anton Bruckner: a documentary biography*. Lewiston, N.Y.; Lampeter: Edwin Mellen Press, 2002.

Hueffer, Francis. *Correspondence of Wagner and Liszt*. New York: Greenwood Press, 2 Vols.1969.

Hughes, Spike. *The Toscanini legacy: a critical study of Arturo Toscanini's performances of Beethoven, Verdi, and other composers*. London: Putnam, 1959.

Hullah, Annette. *Theodor Leschetizky*. London and New York: J. Land & Co., 1906.

Le Huray, Peter and James Day, Editors. *Music and aesthetics in the eighteenth and early-nineteenth centuries*. Cambridge: Cambridge University Press, 1988.

D'Indy, Vincent. *César Franck*. New York: Dover Publications, 1965.

Jacobs, Arthur. *Arthur Sullivan: A Victorian musician*. Aldershot: Scolar Press, 1992.

Jahn, Otto. *Life of Mozart.* London: Novello, Ewer & Co., 1882.

Jefferson, Alan. *Sir Thomas Beecham: a centenary tribute.* London: World Records Ltd., 1979.

Jezic, Diane. *The musical migration and Ernst Toch.* Ames: Iowa State University Press, 1989.

Johnson, Douglas Porter, Editor. *The Beethoven sketchbooks: history, reconstruction, inventory.* Oxford: Clarendon, 1985.

Johnson, Stephen. *Bruckner remembered.* London: Faber and Faber, 1998.

Jones, David, Wyn. *Beethoven: Pastoral symphony.* Cambridge: Cambridge University Press, 1995.

Jones, David Wyn. *The life of Beethoven.* Cambridge: Cambridge University Press, 1998.

Jones, David Wyn. *The symphony in Beethoven's Vienna.* Cambridge: Cambridge University Press, 2006.

Jones, J. Barrie, Editor. *Gabriel Fauré: a life in letters.* London: Batsford, 1989.

Jones, Peter Ward, Editor and Translator. *The Mendelssohns on honeymoon: the 1837 diary of Felix and Cécile Mendelssohn Bartholdy, together with letters to their families.* Oxford: Clarendon Press, 1997.

Jones, Timothy. *Beethoven, the Moonlight and other sonatas, Op. 27 and Op. 31.* Cambridge; New York, N.Y.: Cambridge University Press, 1999.

Kalischer, A. C., Editor. *Beethoven's letters: a critical edition.* London: J. M. Dent, 1909.

Kárpáti, János. *Bartók's chamber music.* Stuyvesant, New York: Pendragon Press, 1994.

Keefe, Simon P. *The Cambridge companion to the concerto.* Cambridge, New York, N.Y.: Cambridge University Press, 2005.

Keller, Hans. *The great Haydn quartets: their interpretation.* London: J. M. Dent, 1986.

Keller, Hans, Editor. *The memoirs of Carl Flesch.* New York: Macmillan, 1958.

Keller, Hans, and Christopher Wintle. *Beethoven's string quartets in F minor, Op. 95 and C minor, Op. 131: two studies.* Nottingham: Department of Music, University of Nottingham, 1995.

Kelly, Thomas Forrest. *First nights at the opera: five musical premiers.* New Haven: Yale University Press, 2004.

Kennedy, Michael. *Adrian Boult.* London: Hamish Hamilton, 1987.

Kennedy, Michael. *Barbirolli, conductor laureate: the authorised biography.* London: Hart-Davis, MacGibbon, 1973.

Kennedy, Michael, Editor. *The autobiography of Charles Hallé; with correspondence and diaries.* London: Paul Elek, 1972.

Kennedy, Michael. *Hallé tradition: a century of music.* Manchester: Manchester University Press, 1960.

Kennedy, Michael. *The works of Ralph Vaughan Williams.* London: Oxford University Press, 1964.

Kemp, Ian. *Tippett: the composer and his music.* London; New York: Eulenburg Books, 1984.

Kerman, Joseph. *The Beethoven quartets*. London: Oxford University Press, 1967, c1966.

Kerman, Joseph. *Write all these down: essays on music*. Berkeley, California; London: University of California Press, 1994.

Kildea, Paul, Editor. *Britten on music*. Oxford: Oxford University Press, 2003.

Kinderman, William. *Beethoven*. Oxford: Oxford University Press, 1997.

Kinderman, William. *Beethoven's Diabelli variations*. Oxford: Clarendon Press; New York: Oxford University Press, 1987.

Kinderman, William, Editor. *The string quartets of Beethoven*. Urbana, Ilinois: University of Illinois Press, 2005.

King, Alec Hyatt. *Musical pursuits: selected essays*. London: British Library, 1987.

Kirby, F. E. *Music for piano: a short history*. Amadeus Press: Portland, 1995.

Kirkpatrick, John, Editor. *Charles E. Ives: Memos*. New York: W.W. Norton, 1972.

Knapp, Raymond. *Brahms and the challenge of the symphony*. Stuyvesant, N.Y.: Pendragon Press, c.1997.

Knight, Frida. *Cambridge music: from the Middle Ages to modern times*. Cambridge, England.: New York: Oleander Press, 1980.

Knight, Max, Translator. *A confidential matter: the letters of Richard Strauss and Stefan Zweig, 1931–1935*. Berkeley; London: University of California Press, 1977.

Kok, Alexander. *A voice in the dark: the philharmonia years*. Ampleforth: Emerson Edition, 2002.

Kopelson, Kevin. *Beethoven's kiss: pianism, perversion, and the mastery of desire*. Stanford, California: Stanford University Press, 1996.

Kostelanetz, Richard, Editor. *Aaron Copland: a reader; selected writings 1923–1972*. New York; London: Routledge, 2003.

Kostelanetz, Richard. *Conversing with Cage*. New York; London: Routledge, 2003.

Kostelanetz, Richard. *On innovative musicians*. New York: Limelight Editions, 1989.

Kostelanetz, Richard, Editor. *Virgil Thomson: a reader ; selected writings, 1924–1984*. New York; London: Routledge, 2002.

Kowalke, Kim H. *Kurt Weill in Europe*. Ann Arbor, Michigan: UMI Research Press, 1979.

Krehbiel, Henry Edward. *The pianoforte and its music*. New York: Cooper Square Publishers, 1971.

Kruseman, Philip, Editor. *Beethoven's own words*. London: Hinrichsen Edition, 1948.

Kurtz, Michael. *Stockhausen: a biography*. London: Faber and Faber, 1992.

Lam, Basil. *Beethoven string quartets*. Seattle: University of Washington Press, 1975.

Lambert, Constant. *Music ho!: a study of music in decline*. London: Faber and Faber, Ltd. 1934.

Landon, H. C. Robbins. *Beethoven: a documentary study*. London: Thames and Hudson, 1970.

Landon, H. C. Robbins. *Beethoven: his life, work and world*. London: Thames and Hudson,

1992.

Landon, H. C. Robbins. *Essays on the Viennese classical style: Gluck, Haydn, Mozart, Beethoven.* London: Barrie & Rockliff The Cresset Press, 1970.

Landon, H. C. Robbins. *Haydn: chronicle and works/Haydn, the late years, 1801–1809.* Bloomington: Indiana University Press, 1977.

Landon, H. C. Robbins. *Haydn: his life and music.* London: Thames and Hudson, 1988.

Landon, H. C. Robbins. *Haydn in England, 1791–1795.* London: Thames and Hudson, 1976.

Landon, H. C. Robbins. *Haydn: the years of 'The creation', 1796–800.* London: Thames and Hudson, 1977.

Landon, H. C. Robbins. *Mozart: the golden years, 1781–1791.* New York: Schirmer Books, 1989.

Landon, H. C. Robbins. *1791, Mozart's last year.* London: Thames and Hudson, 1988.

Landon, H. C. Robbins *The collected correspondence and London notebooks of Joseph Haydn.* London: Barrie and Rockliff, 1959.

Landon, H. C. Robbins: Editor. *The Mozart companion.* London: Faber, 1956.

Landowska, Wanda. *Music of the past.* London: Geoffrey Bles, 1926.

Lang, Paul Henry. *Musicology and performance.* New Haven: Yale University Press, 1997.

Lang, Paul Henry. *The creative world of Beethoven.* New York: W. W. Norton 1971.

Laurence, Dan H., Editor. *Shaw's music: the complete musical criticism in three volumes.* London: Max Reinhardt, the Bodley Head, 1981.

Lawford-Hinrichsen, Irene. *Music publishing and patronage: C. F. Peters, 1800 to the Holocaust.* Kenton: Edition Press, 2000.

Layton, Robert, Editor. *A guide to the concerto.* Oxford: Oxford University Press, 1996.

Layton, Robert, Editor. *A guide to the symphony.* Oxford: Oxford University Press, 1995.

Lebrecht, Norman. *The maestro myth: great conductors in pursuit of power.* London: Simon & Schuster, 1991.

Lee, Ernest Markham. *The story of the symphony.* London: Scott Publishing Co., 1916.

Leibowitz, Herbert A., Editor. *Musical impressions: selections from Paul Rosenfeld's criticism.* London: G. Allen & Unwin, 1970.

Lenrow, Elbert, Editor and Translator. *The letters of Richard Wagner to Anton Pusinelli.* New York: Vienna House, 1972.

Leonard, Maurice. *Kathleen: the life of Kathleen Ferrier: 1912–1953.* London: Hutchinson, 1988.

Lesure, François and Roger Nichols, Editors. *Debussy, letters.* London: Faber and Faber, 1987.

Letellier, Robert Ignatius, Editor and Translator. *The diaries of Giacomo Meyerbeer.* Madison: Fairleigh Dickinson University Press; London: Associated University Presses, 4 Vols., 1999–2004.

Levas, Santeri. *Sibelius: a personal portrait.* London: J. M. Dent, 1972.

Levy, Alan Howard. *Edward Mac-*

Dowell, an American master. Lanham, Md. & London: Scarecrow Press, 1998.

Levy, David Benjamin. *Beethoven: the Ninth Symphony.* New Haven, Connecticut; London: Yale University Press, 2003.

Leyda, Jay and Sergi Bertensson. *The Musorgsky reader: a life of Modeste Petrovich Musorgsky in letters and documents.* New York: W.W. Norton, 1947.

Lewis, Thomas P., Editor. *Raymond Leppard on music: an anthology of critical and personal writings.* White Plains, N.Y.: Pro/Am Music Resources, 1993.

Liébert, Georges. *Nietzsche and music.* Chicago: University of Chicago Press, 2004.

Liszt, Franz. *An artist's journey: lettres d'un bachelier ès musique, 1835–1841.* Chicago: University of Chicago Press, 1989.

Litzmann, Berthold, Editor. *Clara Schumann: an artist's life, based on material found in diaries and letters.* London: Macmillan; Leipzig: Breitkopf & Härtel, 2 Vols. 1913.

Litzmann, Berthold, Editor. *Letters of Clara Schumann and Johannes Brahms, 1853–1896.* New York, Vienna House. 2 Vols. 1971.

Lloyd, Stephen. *William Walton: muse of fire.* Woodbridge, Suffolk: The Boydell Press, 2001.

Locke, Ralph P. and Cyrilla Barr, Editors. *Cultivating music in America: women patrons and activists since 1860.* Berkeley: University of California Press, 1997.

Lockspeiser, Edward. *Debussy: his life and mind.* London: Cassell. 2 Vols. 1962–1965.

Lockspeiser, Edward. *The literary clef: an anthology of letters and writings by French composers.* London: J. Calder. 1958.

Lockwood, Lewis, Editor. *Beethoven essays: studies in honor of Elliot Forbes.* Cambridge, Massachusetts: Harvard University Department of Music: Distributed by Harvard University Press, 1984.

Lockwood, Lewis and Mark Kroll, Editors. *The Beethoven violin sonatas: history, criticism, performance.* Urbana: University of Illinois Press, 2004.

Loft, Abram. *Violin and keyboard: the duo repertoire.* New York: Grossman Publishers. 2 Vols. 1973.

Longyear, Rey Morgan. *Nineteenth-century romanticism in music.* Englewood Cliffs: Prentice-Hall, 1969.

Lowe, C. Egerton. *Beethoven's pianoforte sonatas: hints on their rendering, form, etc., with appendices on definition of sonata, music forms, ornaments, pianoforte pedals, and how to discover keys.* London: Novello, 1929.

Macdonald, Hugh, Editor. *Berlioz: Selected letters.* London: Faber and Faber, 1995.

Macdonald, Malcolm, Editor. *Havergal Brian on music: selections from his journalism: Volume One, British music.* London: Toccata Press, 1986.

MacDonald, Malcolm. *Varèse: astronomer in sound.* London: Kahn & Averill, 2003.

MacDowell, Edward. *Critical and historical essays: lectures deliv-*

ered at Columbia University. Edited by W. J. Baltzell. London: Elkin; Boston: A.P. Schmidt, 1912.

MacFarren, Walter. Memories: an autobiography. London: Walter Scott Publishing Co.,1905.

Mackenzie, Alexander Campbell. *A musician's narrative.* London: Cassell and company, Ltd, 1927.

McCarthy, Margaret William, Editor. *More letters of Amy Fay: the American years, 1879–1916.* Detroit: Information Coordinators, 1986.

McClary, Susan. *Feminine endings: music, gender, and sexuality.* Minneapolis: University of Minnesota Press, 1991.

McClatchie, Stephen, Editor and Translator. *The Mahler family letters.* Oxford: Oxford University Press, 2006.

McVeigh, Simon. *Concert life in London from Mozart to Haydn.* Cambridge: Cambridge University Press, 1993.

Mahler, Alma. *Gustav Mahler: memories and letters.* Enlarged edition revised and edited and with and introduction by Donald Mitchell. London: John Murray, 1968.

Mai, François Martin. *Diagnosing genius: the life and death of Beethoven.* Montreal; London: McGill-Queen's University Press, 2007.

Del Mar, Norman. *Orchestral variations: confusion and error in the orchestral repertoire.* London: Eulenburg, 1981.

Del Mar, Norman. *Richard Strauss: a critical commentary on his life and works.* London: Barrie & Jenkins. 3 Vols. 1978.

(La) Mara [pseudonym]. *Letters of Franz Liszt.* London: H. Grevel & Co., 2 Vols. 1894.

Marek, George Richard. *Puccini.* London: Cassell & Co., 1952.

Marek, George Richard. *Toscanini.* London: Vision, 1976.

(De) Marliave, Joseph. *Beethoven's quartets.* New York: Dover Publications (reprint), 1961.

Martin, George Whitney. *Verdi: his music, life and times.* London: Macmillan, 1965.

Martner, Knud, Editor. *Selected letters of Gustav Mahler.* London; Boston: Faber and Faber, 1979.

Martyn, Barrie. *Nicolas Medtner: his life and music.* Aldershot: Scolar Press, 1995.

Martyn, Barrie. *Rachmaninoff: composer, pianist, conductor.* Aldershot: Scolar, 1990.

Massenet, Jules. *My recollections.* Westport, Connecticut: Greenwood Press.1970.

Matheopoulos, Helena. *Maestro: encounters with conductors of today.* London: Hutchinson, 1982.

Matthews, Denis. *Beethoven.* London: J. M. Dent, 1985.

Matthews, Denis. *Beethoven piano sonatas.* London: British Broadcasting Corporation, 1967.

Matthews, Dennis. *In pursuit of music.* London: Victor Gollancz Ltd., 1968.

Matthews, Denis. *Keyboard music.* Newton Abbot: London David & Charles, 1972.

Mellers, Wilfrid Howard. *Caliban reborn: renewal in twentieth-century music.* London: Victor Gollancz, 1967.

Mellers, Wilfrid Howard. *The sonata*

principle (from c. 1750). London: Rockliff, 1957.

Mendelssohn Bartholdy. *Letters from Italy and Switzerland*. London: Longman, Green, Longman, and Roberts, 1862.

Mendelssohn Bartholdy, Paul. *Letters of Felix Mendelssohn Bartholdy, from 1833 to 1847*. London: Longman, Green, Longman, Roberts, & Green, 1864.

Menuhin, Yehudi and Curtis W. Davis. *The music of man*. London: Macdonald and Jane's, 1979.

Menuhin, Yehudi. *Theme and variations*. London: Heinemann Educational Books Ltd., 1972.

Menuhin, Yehudi. *Unfinished journey*. London: Macdonald and Jane's, 1977.

Messian, Olivier. *Music and color: conversations with Claude Samuel*. Portland, Oregon: Amadeus, 1994.

Miall, Antony. *Musical bumps*. London: J.M. Dent & Sons Ltd, 1981.

Michotte, Edmond. *Richard Wagner's visit to Rossini (Paris 1860): and, An evening at Rossini's in Beau-Sejour (Passy), 1858*. Chicago; London: University of Chicago Press, 1982.

Mies, Paul. *Beethoven's sketches: an analysis of his style based on a study of his sketchbooks*. New York: Johnson Reprint, 1969.

Milhaud, Darius. *My happy life*. London: Boyars, 1995.

Miller, Mina. *The Nielsen companion*. London: Faber and Faber, 1994.

Milsom, David. *Theory and practice in late nineteenth-century violin performance: an examination of style in performance, 1850–1900*. Aldershot: Ashgate, 2003.

Mitchell, Donald, Editor. *Letters from a life: the selected letters and diaries of Benjamin Britten 1913–1976*. London: Faber and Faber. 3 Vols., 1991.

Mitchell, Donald and Hans Keller, Editors. *Music survey: new series 1949–1952*. London: Faber Music in association with Faber & Faber, 1981.

Mitchell, Jon C. *A comprehensive biography of composer Gustav Holst, with correspondence and diary excerpts: including his American years*. Lewiston, New York: Edwin Mellen Press, 2001.

Moldenhauer, Hans. *Anton von Webern: a chronicle of his life and work*. London: Victor Gollancz, 1978.

Monrad-Johansen. *Edvard Grieg*. New York: Tudor Publishing Co., 1945.

Moore, Gerald. *Am I too loud?: memoirs of an accompanist*. London: Hamish Hamilton, 1962.

Moore, Gerald. *Farewell recital: further memoirs*. Harmondsworth: Penguin Books, 1979.

Moore, Gerald. *Furthermoore: interludes in an accompanist's life*. London: Hamish Hamilton, 1983.

Moore, Jerrold Northrop. *Edward Elgar: a creative life*. Oxford: Oxford University Press, 1984.

Moore, Jerrold Northrop. *Elgar, Edward. The windflower letters: correspondence with Alice Caroline Stuart Wortley and her family*. Oxford: Clarendon Press; New York: Oxford University Press, 1989.

Moore, Jerrold Northrop. *Elgar, Edward. Edward Elgar: letters of a lifetime.* Oxford: Clarendon Press; New York: Oxford University Press, 1990.

Moore, Jerrold Northrop. *Elgar, Edward. Elgar and his publishers: letters of a creative life.* Oxford: Clarendon, 1987.

Moreux, Serge. *Béla Bartók.* London: Harvill Press, 1953.

Morgan, Kenneth. *Fritz Reiner, maestro and martinet.* Urbana: University of Illinois Press, 2005.

Cone, Edward T., Editor. *Music, a view from Delft: selected essays.* Chicago: University of Chicago Press, 1989.

Morgan, Robert P. *Twentieth-century music: a history of musical style in modern Europe and America.* New York: Norton, 1991.

Morgenstern, Sam., Editor. *Composers on music: an anthology of composers' writings.* London: Faber & Faber, 1956.

Morrow, Mary Sue. *Concert life in Haydn's Vienna: aspects of a developing musical and social institution.* Stuyvesant, New York: Pendragon Press, 1989.

Moscheles, Felix, Editor and Translator. *Letters from Felix Mendelssohn-Bartholdy to Ignaz and Charlotte Moscheles.* London: Trübner and Co., 1888.

Mudge, Richard B., Translator. *Glinka, Mikhail Ivanovich: Memoirs.* Norman: University of Oklahoma Press, 1963.

Munch, Charles. *I am a conductor.* New York: Oxford University Press, 1955.

Mundy, Simon. *Bernard Haitink: a working life.* London: Robson Books, 1987.

Musgrave, Michael. *The musical life of the Crystal Palace.* Cambridge: Cambridge University Press, 1995.

Music & Letters. *Beethoven: special number.* London: Music & Letters, 1927.

Musical Times. *Special Issue.* John A. Fuller-Maitland London: Vol. VIII, No. 2, 1927.

Myers, Rollo H., Editor. *Twentieth-century music.* London: Calder and Boyars, 1960.

National Gallery (Great Britain). *Music performed at the National Gallery concerts, 10th October 1939 to 10th April 1946.* London: Privately printed, 1948.

Nattiez, Jean-Jacques, Editor. *Orientations: collected writings — Pierre Boulez.* London: Faber and Faber, 1986.

Nauhaus, Gerd, Editor. *The marriage diaries of Robert & Clara Schumann.* London: Robson Books, 1994.

Nectoux, Jean Michel. *Gabriel Fauré: a musical life.* Translated by Roger Nichols. Cambridge: Cambridge University Press, 1991.

Nettl, Paul. *Beethoven handbook.* Westport, Connecticut: Greenwood Press, 1975.

Neumayr, Anton. *Music and medicine.* Bloomington, Illinois: Medi-Ed Press, 1994–1997

Newbould, Brian. *Schubert and the symphony: a new perspective.* Surbiton: Toccata Press, 1992.

Newlin, Dika. *Schoenberg remembered: diaries and recollections (1938–76).* New York: Pendragon Press, 1980.

Newman, Ernest. *From the world of*

music: essays from 'The Sunday Times'. London: J. Calder, 1956.
Newman, Ernest. *Hugo Wolf*. New York: Dover Publications, 1966.
Newman, Ernest, Annotated and Translated. *Memoirs of Hector Berlioz from 1803 to 1865, comprising his travels in Germany, Italy, Russia, and England*. New York: Knopf, 1932.
Newman, Ernest. *More essays from the world of music: essays from the 'Sunday Times'*. London: John Calder, 1958.
Newman, Ernest. *Musical studies*. London; New York: John Lane, 1910.
Newman, Ernest. *Testament of music: essays and papers*. London: Putnam, 1962.
Newman, Richard. *Alma Rosé: Vienna to Auschwitz*. Portland, Oregon: Amadeus Press, 2000.
Newman, William S. *The sonata in the classic era*. Chapel Hill: University of North Carolina Press 1963.
Newman, William S. *The sonata in the Classic era*. New York; London: W.W. Norton, 1983.
Newmarch, Rosa Harriet. *Henry J. Wood*. London & New York: John Lane, 1904.
Nicholas, Jeremy. *Godowsky: the pianists' pianist; a biography of Leopold Godowsky*. Hexham: Appian Publications & Recordings, 1989.
Nichols, Roger. *Debussy remembered*. London: Faber and Faber, 1992.
Nichols, Roger. *Mendelssohn remembered*. London: Faber and Faber, 1997.
Nichols, Roger. *Ravel remembered*. London: Faber and Faber, 1987.

Niecks, Frederick. *Robert Schumann*. London: J. M. Dent, 1925.
Nielsen, Carl. *Living music*. Copenhagen, Wilhelm Hansen, 1968.
Nielsen, Carl. *My childhood*. Copenhagen, Wilhelm Hansen, 1972.
Nikolska, Irina. *Conversations with Witold Lutoslawski, (1987–92)*. Stockholm: Melos, 1994.
Nohl, Ludwig. *Beethoven depicted by his contemporaries*. London: Reeves, 1880.
De Nora, Tia. *Beethoven and the construction of genius: musical politics in Vienna, 1792–1803*. Berkeley: University of California Press, 1997.
Norton, Spencer, Editor and Translator. *Music in my time: the memoirs of Alfredo Casella*. Norman: University of Oklahoma Press, 1955.
Nottebohm, Gustav. *Two Beethoven sketchbooks: a description with musical extracts*. London: Gollancz, 1979.
Oakeley, Edward Murray. *The life of Sir Herbert Stanley Oakeley*. London: George Allen, 1904.
Lucas, Brenda and Michael Kerr. *Virtuoso: the story of John Ogdon*. London: H. Hamilton, 1981.
Oliver, Michael, Editor. *Settling the score: a journey through the music of the twentieth century*. London: Faber and Faber, 1999.
Olleson, Philip. *Samuel Wesley: the man and his music*. Woodbridge: Boydell Press, 2003.
Olleson, Philip, Editor. *The letters of Samuel Wesley: professional and social correspondence, 1797–1837*. Oxford; New York: Oxford University Press, 2001.

Olmstead, Andrea. *Conversations with Roger Sessions.* Boston: Northeastern University Press, 1987.

Orenstein, Arbie, Editor. *A Ravel reader: correspondence, articles, interviews.* New York: Columbia University Press, 1990.

Orenstein, Arbie. *Ravel: man and musician.* New York: Columbia University Press, 1975.

Orledge, Robert. *Charles Koechlin (1867–1950): his life and works.* New York: Harwood Academic Publishers, 1989.

Orledge, Robert. *Gabriel Fauré.* London: Eulenburg Books, 1979.

Orledge, Robert. *Satie remembered.* London: Faber and Faber, 1995.

Orledge, Robert. *Satie the composer.* Cambridge: Cambridge University Press, 1990.

Orlova, Alexandra. *Glinka's life in music: a chronicle.* Ann Arbor: UMI Research Press, 1988.

Orlova, Alexandra. *Musorgsky's days and works: a biography in documents.* Ann Arbor: UMI Research Press, 1983.

Orlova, Alexandra. *Tchaikovsky: a self-portrait.* Oxford: Oxford University Press, 1990.

Osborne, Charles, Editor and Translator. *Letters of Giuseppe Verdi.* London: Victor Gollancz, 1971.

Osmond-Smith David, Editor and Translator. *Luciano Berio: Two interviews with Rossana Dalmonte and Bálint András Varga.* New York; London: Boyars, 1985.

Ouellette, Fernand. *Edgard Varèse.* London: Calder & Boyars, 1973.

Paderewski, Ignacy Jan and Mary Lawton. *The Paderewski memoirs.* London: Collins, 1939.

Page, Tim: Editor. *The Glenn Gould reader.* London: Faber and Faber, 1987.

Page, Tim. *Music from the road: views and reviews, 1978–1992.* New York; Oxford: Oxford University Press, 1992.

Page, Tim and Vanessa Weeks, Editors. *Selected letters of Virgil Thomson.* New York: Summit Books, 1988.

Page, Tim. *Tim Page on music: views and reviews.* Portland, Oregon: Amadeus Press, 2002.

Palmer, Christopher. *Herbert Howells, (1892–1983): a celebration.* London: Thames, 1996.

Palmer, Christopher, Editor. *Sergei Prokofiev: Soviet diary 1927 and other writings.* London: Faber and Faber, 1991.

Palmer, Fiona M. *Domenico Dragonetti in England (1794–1846): the career of a double bass virtuoso.* Oxford: Clarendon, 1997.

Palmieri, Robert, Editor. *Encyclopedia of the piano.* New York: Garland, 1996.

Panufnik, Andrzej. *Composing myself.* London: Methuen, 1987.

Parsons, James, Editor. *The Cambridge companion to the Lied.* Cambridge: Cambridge University Press, 2004.

Paynter, John, Editor. *Between old worlds and new: occasional writings on music by Wilfrid Mellers.* London: Cygnus Arts, 1997.

Pestelli, Giorgio. *The age of Mozart and Beethoven.* Cambridge: Cambridge University Press, 1984.

Peyser, Joan. *Bernstein: a biography: revised & updated.* New York: Billboard Books, 1998.

Phillips-Matz, Mary Jane. *Verdi: a biography*. Oxford: Oxford University Press, 1993.

Piggott, Patrick. *The life and music of John Field, 1782–1837: creator of the nocturne*. London: Faber and Faber, 1973.

Plantinga, Leon. *Beethoven's concertos: history, style, performance*. New York: Norton, 1999.

Plantinga, Leon. *Clementi: his life and music*. London: Oxford University Press, 1977.

Plantinga, Leon. *Romantic music: a history of musical style in nineteenth-century Europe*. New York; London: Norton, 1984.

Plaskin, Glenn. *Horowitz: a biography of Vladimir Horowitz*. London: Macdonald, 1983.

Pleasants, Henry, Editor and Translator. *Hanslick, Eduard: Music criticisms, 1846–99*. Baltimore: Penguin Books, 1963.

Pleasants, Henry, Editor and Translator. *Hanslick's music criticisms*. New York: Dover Publications, 1988.

Pleasants, Henry, Editor and Translator. *The music criticism of Hugo Wolf*. New York: Holmes & Meier Publishers, 1978.

Pleasants, Henry, Editor and Translator. *The musical journeys of Louis Spohr*. Norman: University of Oklahoma Press, 1961.

Pollack, Howard. *Aaron Copland: the life and work of an uncommon man*. New York: Henry Holt, 1999.

Poulenc, Francis. *My friends and myself*. London: Dennis Dobson, 1978.

Powell, Richard, Mrs. *Edward Elgar: memories of a variation*. Aldershot, Hants, England: Scolar Press; Brookfield, Vermont, USA: Ashgate Publishing. Co., 1994.

Poznansky, Alexander, Editor. *Tchaikovsky through others' eyes*. Bloomington: Indiana University Press, 1999.

Praeger, Ferdinand. *Wagner as I knew him*. London; New York: Longmans, Green, 1892.

Previn, Andre. *Antony Hopkins. Music face to face*. London, Hamish Hamilton, 1971.

Prieberg, Fred K. *Trial of strength: Wilhelm Furtwängler and the Third Reich*. London: Quartet, 1991.

Procter-Gregg, Humphrey. *Beecham remembered*. London: Duckworth, 1976.

Prokofiev, Sergey. *Prokofiev by Prokofiev: a composer's memoir*. London: Macdonald and Jane's, 1979.

Rachmaninoff, Sergei. *Rachmaninoff's recollections told to Oskar von Riesemann*. London: George Allen & Unwin, 1934.

Radcliffe, Philip. *Beethoven's string quartets*. Cambridge: Cambridge University Press, 1978.

Radcliffe, Philip. *Piano Music in: The Age of Beethoven, The New Oxford History of Music, Vol. VIII*. Gerald Abraham, (Editor), 1988, p. 340.

Ratner, Leonard G. *Romantic music: sound and syntax*. New York: Schirmer Books, 1992.

Raynor, Henry. *A social history of music: from the middle ages to Beethoven*. London: Barrie & Jenkins, 1972.

Rees, Brian. *Camille Saint-Saëns: a life*. London: Chatto & Windus, 1999.

Reich, Willi, Editor. *Anton Webern: The path to the new music.* London; Bryn Mawr: Theodore Presser in association with Universal Edition, 1963.

Reid, Charles. *John Barbirolli: a biography.* London, Hamish Hamilton, 1971.

Reid, Charles. *Malcolm Sargent: a biography.* London: Hamilton, 1968.

Rennert, Jonathan. *William Crotch (1775–1847): composer, artist, teacher.* Lavenham: Terence Dalton, 1975.

Rice, John A. *Antonio Salieri and Viennese Opera.* Chicago, Illinois: University of Chicago Press, 1998.

Rice, John A. *Empress Marie Therese and music at the Viennese court, 1792–1807.* Cambridge: Cambridge University Press, 2003.

Richards, Fiona. *The Music of John Ireland.* Aldershot: Ashgate, 2000.

Rigby, Charles. *Sir Charles Hallé: a portrait for today.* Manchester: Dolphin Press, 1952.

Ringer, Alexander, Editor. *The early Romantic era: between Revolutions; 1789 and 1848.* Basingstoke: Macmillan, 1990.

Roberts, John P.L. and Ghyslaine Guertin, Editors. *Glenn Gould: Selected letters.* Toronto; Oxford: Oxford University Press, 1992.

Robertson, Alec. *More than music.* London: Collins, 1961.

Robinson, Harlow, Editor and Translator. *Selected letters of Sergei Prokofiev.* Boston: Northeastern University Press, 1998.

Robinson, Harlow. *Sergei Prokofiev: a biography.* London: Hale, 1987.

Robinson, Paul A. *Ludwig van Beethoven, Fidelio.* Cambridge: Cambridge University Press, 1996.

Robinson, Suzanne, Editor. *Michael Tippett: music and literature.* Aldershot: Ashgate, 2002.

Rochberg, George. *The aesthetics of survival: a composer's view of twentieth-century music.* Ann Arbor, Michigan: University of Michigan Press, 2004.

Rodmell, Paul. *Charles Villiers Stanford.* Aldershot: Ashgate, 2002.

Roeder, Michael Thomas. *A history of the concerto.* Portland, Oregon: Amadeus Press, 1994.

Rohr, Deborah Adams. *The careers of British musicians, 1750–1850: a profession of artisans.* Cambridge: Cambridge University Press, 2001.

Rolland, Romain. *Goethe and Beethoven.* New York; London: Blom, 1968.

Rolland, Romain. *Beethoven and Handel.* London: Waverley Book Co., 1917.

Rolland, Romain. *Beethoven the creator.* Garden City, New York: Garden City Pub., 1937.

Roscow, Gregory, Editor. *Bliss on music: selected writings of Arthur Bliss, 1920–1975.* Oxford: Oxford University Press, 1991.

Rosen, Charles. *Beethoven's piano sonatas: a short companion.* New Haven, Connecticut: London: Yale University Press, 2002.

Rosen, Charles. *Critical entertainments: music old and new.* Cambridge, Massachusetts; London: Harvard University Press, 2000.

Rosen, Charles. *The classical style: Haydn, Mozart, Beethoven.* London: Faber and Faber, 1976.

Rosen, Charles. *The romantic generation.* Cambridge, Massachusetts: Harvard University Press, 1995.

Rosenthal, Albi. *Obiter scripta: essays, lectures, articles, interviews and reviews on music, and other subjects.* Oxford: Offox Press; Lanham: Scarecrow Press, 2000.

Rostal, Max. *Beethoven: the sonatas for piano and violin; thoughts on their interpretation.* London: Toccata Press, 1985.

Rostropovich, Mstislav and Galina Vishnevskaya. *Russia, music, and liberty.* Portland, Oregan: Amadeus Press, 1995.

Rubinstein, Arthur. *My many years.* London: Jonathan Cape, 1980.

Rubinstein, Arthur. *My young years.* London: Jonathan Cape, 1973.

Rumph, Stephen C. *Beethoven after Napoleon: political romanticism in the late works.* Berkeley; London: University of California Press, 2004.

Rye, Matthew Rye. *Notes to the BBC Radio Three Beethoven Experience, Friday 10 June 2005,* www.bbc.co.uk/radio3/Beethoven.

Sachs, Harvey. *Toscanini.* London: Weidenfeld and Nicholson, 1978.

Sachs, Joel. *Kapellmeister Hummel in England and France.* Detroit: Information Coordinators, 1977.

Saffle, Michael, Editor. *Liszt and his world: proceedings of the International Liszt Conference held at Virginia Polytechnic Institute and State University, 20—23 May 1993.* Stuyvesant, New York: Pendragon Press, 1998.

Safránek, Milos. *Bohuslav Martinu, his life and works.* London: Allan Wingate, 1962.

Saint-Saëns, Camille. *Outspoken essays on music.* Westport, Connecticut: Greenwood Press, 1970.

Saussine, Renée de. *Paganini.* Westport, Connecticut: Greenwood Press, 1976.

Sayers, W. C. Berwick. *Samuel Coleridge-Taylor, musician: his life and letters.* London; New York: Cassell and Co., 1915.

Schaarwächter, Jürgen. *HB: aspects of Havergal Brian.* Aldershot: Ashgate, 1997.

Schafer, R. Murray. *E.T.A. Hoffmann and music.* Toronto: University of Toronto Press, 1975.

Schafer, R. Murray, Editor. *Ezra Pound and music: the complete criticism.* London: Faber and Faber, 1978.

Schat, Peter. *The tone clock.* Chur, Switzerland; Langhorne, Pa.: Harwood Academic Publishers, 1993.

Schenk, Erich. *Mozart and his times.* Edited and Translated by Richard and Clara Winstin. London: Secker & Warburg, 1960.

Schindler, Anton Felix. *Beethoven as I knew him.* Edited by Donald W. MacArdle and Translated by Constance S. Jolly from the German edition of 1860 London: Faber and Faber, 1966.

Schlosser, Johann. *Beethoven: the first biography, 1827.* Edited by Barry Cooper. Portland, Oregon: Amadeus Press, 1996.

Schnabel, Artur. *My life and music.*

London: Longmans, 1961.

Schnittke, Alfred. *A Schnittke reader.* Bloomington: Indiana University Press, 2002.

Scholes, Percy Alfred. *Crotchets: a few short musical notes.* London: John Lane, 1924.

Schonberg, Harold C. *The great pianists.* London: Victor Gollancz, 1964.

Schrade, Leo. *Beethoven in France: the growth of an idea.* New Haven; London: Yale University Press, H. Milford, Oxford University Press, 1942.

Schrade, Leo. *Tragedy in the art of music.* Cambridge, Massachusetts: Harvard University Press, 1964.

Schuh, Willi. *Richard Strauss: a chronicle of the early years 1864–1898.* Cambridge: Cambridge University Press, 1982.

Schuh, Willi, Editor. *Richard Strauss: Recollections and reflections.* London; New York: Boosey & Hawkes, 1953.

Schuller, Gunther. *Musings: the musical worlds of Gunther Schuller.* New York: Oxford University Press, 1986.

Schumann, Robert. *Music and musicians: essays and criticisms.* London: William Reeves, 1877.

Schuttenhelm, Editor. *Selected letters of Michael Tippett.* London: Faber and Faber, 2005.

Schwartz, Elliott. *Music since 1945: issues, materials, and literature.* New York: Schirmer Books, 1993.

Scott, Marion M. *Beethoven: (The master musicians).* London: Dent, 1940.

Scott-Sutherland, Colin. *Arnold Bax.* London: J. M. Dent, 1973.

Searle, Muriel V. *John Ireland: the man and his music.* Tunbridge Wells: Midas Books, 1979.

Secrest, Meryle. *Leonard Bernstein: a life.* London: Bloomsbury, 1995.

Seeger, Charles. *Studies in musicology II, 1929–1979.* Edited by Anne M. Pescatello. Berkeley; London: University of California Press, 1994.

Selden-Goth, Gisela, Editor. *Felix Mendelssohn: letters.* London: Paul Elek Publishers Ltd, 1946.

Senner, Wayne M., Robin Wallace and William Meredith, Editors. *The critical reception of Beethoven's compositions by his German contemporaries.* Lincoln: University of Nebraska Press, in association with the American Beethoven Society and the Ira F. Brilliant Center for Beethoven Studies, San José State University, 1999.

Seroff, Victor I. *Rachmaninoff.* London: Cassell & Company, 1951.

Sessions, Roger. *Questions about music.* Cambridge, Massachusetts: Harvard University Press, 1970.

Sessions, Roger. *The musical experience of composer, performer, listener.* New York: Atheneum, 1966, 1950.

Seyfried, Ignaz von. *Louis van Beethoven's Studies in thoroughbass, counterpoint and the art of scientific composition.* Leipzig; New-York: Schuberth and Company, 1853.

Sharma, Bhesham R. *Music and culture in the age of mechanical reproduction.* New York: Peter Lang, 2000.

Shaw, Bernard. *How to become a musical critic.* London: R. Hart Davis, 1960.

Shaw, Bernard. *London music in 1888–89 as heard by Corno di Bassetto (later known as Bernard Shaw): with some further autobiographical particulars.* London: Constable and Company, 1937.

Shaw, Bernard. *Music in London, 1890–1894.* London: Constable and Company Limited, 3 Vols., 1932.

Shedlock, John South. *Beethoven's pianoforte sonatas: the origin and respective values of various readings.* London: Augener Ltd., 1918.

Shedlock, John South. *The pianoforte sonata: its origin and development.* London: Methuen, 1895.

Shepherd, Arthur. *The string quartets of Ludwig van Beethoven.* Cleveland: H. Carr, The Printing Press, 1935.

Sheppard, Leslie and Herbert R. Axelrod. *Paganini: containing a portfolio of drawings by Vido Polikarpus.* Neptune City, New Jersey: Paganiniana Publications, 1979.

Short, Michael. *Gustav Holst: the man and his music.* Oxford: Oxford University Press, 1990.

Shostakovich, Dmitry. *Dmitry Shostakovich: about himself and his times.* Moscow: Progress Publishers, 1981.

Simpson, John Palgrave. *Carl Maria von Weber: the life of an artist, from the German of his son Baron, Max Maria von Weber.* London: Chapman and Hall, 1865.

Simpson, Robert. *Beethoven symphonies.* London: British Broadcasting Corporation, 1970.

Sipe, Thomas. *Beethoven: Eroica symphony.* Cambridge: Cambridge University Press, 1998.

Sitwell, Sacheverell. *Mozart.* Edinburgh: Peter Davies Limited, 1932.

Skelton, Geoffrey. *Paul Hindemith: the man behind the music; a biography.* London: Victor Gollancz, 1975.

Smallman, Basil. *The piano trio: its history, technique, and repertoire.* Oxford: Clarendon Press; Oxford; New York: Oxford University Press, 1990.

Smidak, Emil. *Isaak-Ignaz Moscheles: the life of the composer and his encounters with Beethoven, Liszt, Chopin, and Mendelssohn.* Aldershot, Hampshire, England: Scolar Press; Brookfield, Vermont, USA: Gower Publishing Co., 1989.

Smith, Barry. *Peter Warlock: the life of Philip Heseltine.* Oxford: Oxford University Press, 1994.

Smith, Joan Allen. *Schoenberg and his circle: a Viennese portrait.* New York: Schirmer Books, London: Collier Macmillan, 1986.

Smith, Richard Langham, Editor. *Debussy on music: the critical writings of the great French composer Claude Debussy.* London: Secker & Warburg, 1977.

Smith, Ronald. *Alkan.* London: Kahn and Averill, 1976.

Snowman, Daniel. *The Amadeus Quartet: the men and the music.* London: Robson Books, 1981.

Solomon, Maynard. *Beethoven.* New York: Schirmer, 1977.

Solomon, Maynard. *Beethoven*

Solomon, Maynard. *Late Beethoven: music, thought, imagination.* Berkeley; London: University of California Press, 2003.

Solomon, Maynard. *Mozart: a life.* London: Hutchinson, 1995.

Sonneck, Oscar George Theodore. *Beethoven: impressions of contemporaries.* London: Oxford University Press, 1927.

Spalding, Albert. *Rise to follow: an autobiography.* London: Frederick Muller Ltd., 1946.

Spohr, Louis. *Louis Spohr's autobiography.* London: Longman, Green, Longman, Roberts, & Green, 1865.

Stafford, William. *Mozart myths: a critical reassessment.* Stanford, California: Stanford University Press, 1991.

Stanford, Charles Villiers. *Interludes: records and reflections.* London: John Murray, 1922.

Stanley, Glenn, Editor. *The Cambridge companion to Beethoven.* Cambridge; New York: Cambridge University Press, 2000

Stedman, Preston. *The symphony.* Englewood Cliffs, New Jersey; London: Prentice-Hall, 1979.

Stedron, Bohumír, Editor and Translator. *Leos Janácek: letters and reminiscences.* Prague: Artia, 1955.

Stein, Erwin, Editor. *Arnold Schoenberg: letters.* London: Faber and Faber, 1964.

Stein, Erwin. *Orpheus in new guises.* London: Rockliff, 1953.

Stein, Jack Madison. *Poem and music in the German lied from Gluck to Hugo Wolf.* Cambridge, Massachusetts: Harvard University Press, 1971.

Stein, Leonard, Editor. *Style and idea: selected writings of Arnold Schoenberg.* London: Faber and Faber, 1975.

Steinberg, Michael P. *Listening to reason: culture, subjectivity, and nineteenth-century music.* Princeton, New Jersey: Princeton University Press, 2004.

Steinberg, Michael. *The concerto: a listener's guide.* New York: Oxford University Press, 1998.

Steinberg, Michael. *The symphony: a listener's guide.* Oxford; New York: Oxford University Press, 1995.

Sternfeld, Frederick William. *Goethe and music: a list of parodies and Goethe's relationship to music; a list of references.* New York: Da Capo Press, 1979.

Stivender, David. *Mascagni: an autobiography compiled, edited and translated from original sources.* New York: Pro/Am Music Resources; London: Kahn & Averill, 1988.

Stone, Else and Kurt Stone, Editors. *The writings of Elliott Carter: an American composer looks at modern music.* Bloomington: Indiana University Press, 1977.

Stowell, Robin. *Beethoven: violin concerto.* Cambridge: Cambridge University Press, 1998.

Stowell, Robin: Editor. *The Cambridge companion to the cello.* Cambridge: Cambridge University Press, 1999.

Stowell, Robin: Editor. *The Cambridge companion to the string quartet.* Cambridge: Cambridge University Press, 2003.

Stratton, Stephen Samuel. *Mendelssohn. London: J.M. Dent & Co.; New York: E.P. Dutton & Co., 1901.

Straus, Joseph N. *Remaking the past: musical modernism and the influence of the tonal tradition.* Cambridge, Massachusetts: Harvard University Press, 1990.

Stravinsky, Igor. *An autobiography.* London: Calder and Boyars, 1975.

Stravinsky, Igor. *Themes and conclusions.* London: Faber and Faber, 1972.

Stravinsky, Igor and Robert Craft. *Conversations with Igor Stravinsky.* London: Faber and Faber, 1959.

Stravinsky, Igor and Robert Craft. *Dialogues and a diary.* London: Faber and Faber 1968.

Stravinsky, Igor and Robert Craft. *Memories and commentaries.* London: Faber and Faber, 2002.

Strunk, Oliver. *Source readings in music history, 4: The Classic era.* London: Faber and Faber 1981.

Sullivan, Blair, Editor. *The echo of music: essays in honor of Marie Louise Göllner.* Warren, Michigan: Harmonie Park Press, 2004.

Sullivan, Jack, Editor. *Words on music: from Addison to Barzun.* Athens: Ohio University Press, 1990.

Symonette, Lys and Kim H. Kowalke, Editors and Translators. *Speak low (when you speak love): the letters of Kurt Weill and Lotte Lenya.* London: Hamish Hamilton, 1996.

Swalin, Benjamin F. *The violin concerto: a study in German romanticism.* New York, Da Capo Press, 1973.

Szigeti, Joseph. *With strings attached: reminiscences and reflections.* London: Cassell & Co. Ltd, 1949.

Tanner, Michael, Editor. *Notebooks, 1924–1954: Wilhelm Furtwängler.* London: Quartet Books, 1989.

Taylor, Robert, Editor. *Furtwängler on music: essays and addresses.* Aldershot: Scolar, 1991.

Taylor, Ronald. *Kurt Weill: composer in a divided world.* London: Simon & Schuster, 1991.

Tchaikovsky, Peter Ilich. *Letters to his family: an autobiography.* Translated by Galina von Meck. London: Dennis Dobson, 1981.

Tertis, Lionel. *My viola and I: a complete autobiography; with, 'Beauty of tone in string playing', and other essays.* London: Paul Elek, 1974.

Thayer, Alexander Wheelock. *Salieri: rival of Mozart.* Edited by Theodore Albrecht. Kansas City, Missouri: Philharmonia of Greater Kansas City, 1989.

Thomas, Michael Tilson. *Viva voce: conversations with Edward Seckerson.* London: Faber and Faber 1994.

Thomson, Andrew. *Vincent d'Indy and his world.* Oxford: Clarendon Press, 1996.

Thomson, Virgil. *The musical scene.* New York: Greenwood Press, 1968.

Thomson, Virgil. *Virgil Thomson.* London: Weidenfeld & Nicolson, 1967.

Tillard, Françoise. *Fanny Mendelssohn.* Amadeus Press: Portland, 1996.

Tilmouth, Michael, Editor. *Donald Francis Tovey: The classics of music: talks, essays, and other writings previously uncollected.* Oxford: Oxford University Press, 2001

Tippett, Michael. *Moving into Aquarius.* London: Routledge and Kegan Paul, 1959.

Tippett, Michael. *Those twentieth century blues: an autobiography.* London: Hutchinson, 1991.

Todd, R. Larry, Editor. *Nineteenth-century piano music.* New York; London: Routledge, 2004.

Todd, R. Larry, Editor. *Schumann and his world.* Princeton: Princeton University Press, 1994.

Tommasini, Anthony. *Virgil Thomson: composer on the aisle.* New York: W.W. Norton, 1997.

Tortelier, Paul. *A self-portrait: in conversation with David Blum.* London: Heinemann, 1984.

Tovey, Donald Francis. *A Companion to Beethoven's Pianoforte Sonatas.* Revised by Barry Cooper. London: The Associated Board, [1931], 1998.

Tovey, Donald Francis. *Beethoven.* London: Oxford University Press, 1944.

Tovey, Donald Francis. *Essays and lectures on music.* London: Oxford University Press, 1949.

Tovey, Donald Francis. *Essays in musical analysis.* London: Oxford University Press, H. Milford, 7 Vols., 1935–41.

Tovey, Donald Francis. *The forms of music: musical articles from The Encyclopaedia Britannica.* London: Oxford University Press, 1944.

Toye, Francis. *Giuseppe Verdi: his life and works.* London: William Heinemann Ltd., 1931.

Truscott, Harold. *Beethoven's late string quartets.* London: Dobson, 1968.

Tyler, William R. *The letters of Franz Liszt to Olga von Meyendorff, 1871–1886, in the Mildred Bliss Collection at Dumbarton Oaks.* Translated by William R. Tyler. Washington: Dumbarton Oaks, Trustees for Harvard University; Cambridge, Massachusetts: distributed by Harvard University Press, 1979.

Tyrrell, John. *Janácek: years of a life. Vol. 1, (1854–1914) The lonely blackbird.* London: Faber and Faber, 2006.

Tyrrell, John, Editor and Translator. *My life with Janácek: the memoirs of Zdenka Janácková.* London: Faber and Faber, 1998.

Tyson, Alan, Editor. *Beethoven studies 2.* Cambridge: Cambridge University Press, 1977.

Tyson, Alan, Editor. *Beethoven studies 3.* Cambridge: Cambridge University Press, 1982.

Tyson, Alan. *Mozart: studies of the autograph scores.* Cambridge, Massachusetts; London: Harvard University Press, 1987.

Tyson, Alan. *The authentic English editions of Beethoven.* London: Faber and Faber, 1963.

Underwood, J. A., Editor. *Gabriel Fauré: his life through his letters.* London: Marion Boyars, 1984.

Vechten, Carl van, Editor. *Nikolay, Rimsky-Korsakov: My musical life.* London: Martin Secker & Warburg Ltd., 1942.

Vinton, John. *Essays after a dictionary: music and culture at the close of Western civilization.* Lewisburg: Bucknell University Press, 1977.

Volkov, Solomon, Editor. *Testimony: the memoirs of Dmitri Shostakovich. London: Faber and Faber, 1981.

Volta, Ornella, Editor. *A mammal's notebook: collected writings of Erik Satie.* London: Atlas Press, 1996.

Wagner, Richard. Beethoven: *With [a] supplement from the philosophical works of A. Schopenhauer.* Translated by E. Dannreuther. London: Reeves, 1893.

Wagner, Richard. *My life.* London: Constable and Company Ltd., 1911.

Walden, Valerie. *One hundred years of violoncello: a history of technique and performance practice, 1740–1840.* Cambridge: Cambridge University Press, 1998.

Walker, Alan. *Franz Liszt. Volume 1, The virtuoso years: 1811–1847.* New York: Alfred A. Knopf, 1983.

Walker, Alan. *Franz Liszt. Volume 2, The Weimar years: 1848–1861.* London: Faber and Faber, 1989.

Walker, Alan. *Franz Liszt. Volume 3, The final years, 1861–1886.* London: Faber and Faber, 1997.

Walker, Bettina. *My musical experiences.* London: Richard Bentley and Son, 1890.

Walker, Ernest. *Free thought and the musician, and other essays.* London; New York: Oxford University Press, 1946.

Walker, Frank. *Hugo Wolf: a biography.* London: J. M. Dent, 1951.

Walker, Frank. *The man Verdi.* London: Dent, 1962.

Wallace, Grace, [Lady Wallace]. *Beethoven's letters (1790–1826): from the collection of Dr. Ludwig Nohl. Also his letters to the Archduke Rudolph, Cardinal-Archbishop of Olmutz, K.W., from the collection of Dr. Ludwig Ritter Von Koĺchel.* London: Longmans, Green, 2 Vols., 1866.

Wallace, Robin. *Beethoven's critics: aesthetic dilemmas and resolutions during the composer's lifetime.* Cambridge; New York: Cambridge University Press, 1986.

Walter, Bruno. *Theme and variations: an autobiography.* London: H. Hamilton, 1948.

Warrack, John Hamilton. *Writings on music.* Cambridge: Cambridge University Press, 1981.

Wasielewski, Wilhelm Joseph von. *Life of Robert Schumann: with letters, 1833–1852.* London: William Reeves, 1878.

Watkins, Glenn. *Proof through the night: music and the Great War.* Berkeley: University of California Press, 2003.

Watkins, Glenn. *Pyramids at the Louvre: music, culture, and collage from Stravinsky to the postmodernists.* Cambridge, Massachusetts; London: Belknap Press of Harvard University Press, 1994.

Watkins, Glenn. *Soundings: music in the twentieth century.* New York: Schirmer Books London: Collier Macmillan, 1988.

Watson, Derek. *Liszt.* London: J. M. Dent, 1989.

Weaver, William, Editor. *The Verdi-Boito correspondence.* Chicago; London: University of Chicago Press, 1994.

Wegeler, Franz. *Remembering Beethoven: the biographical*

notes of Franz Wegeler and Ferdinand Ries. London: Andre Deutsch, 1988.

Weingartner, Felix. *Buffets and rewards: a musician's reminiscences.* London: Hutchinson & Co., 1937.

Weinstock, Herbert. *Rossini: a biography.* New York: Limelight, 1987.

Weiss, Piero and Richard Taruskin. *Music in the Western World: a history in documents.* New York: Schirmer; London: Collier Macmillan, 1984.

Weissweiler, Eva *The complete correspondence of Clara and Robert Schumann.* New York: Peter Lang, 2 Vols., 1994.

Whittaker, William Gillies. *Collected essays.* London: Oxford University Press, 1940.

Whittall, Arnold. *Exploring twentieth-century music: tradition and innovation.* Cambridge; New York: Cambridge University Press, 2003.

Whittall, Arnold. *Music since the First World War.* London: J. M. Dent, 1977.

Whitton, Kenneth S. *Lieder: an introduction to German song.* London: Julia MacRae, 1984.

Wightman, Alistair, Editor. *Szymanowski on music: selected writings of Karol Szymanowski.* London: Toccata Press, 1999.

Wilhelm, Kurt. *Richard Strauss: an intimate portrait.* London: Thames and Hudson, 1999.

Will, Richard James. *The characteristic symphony in the age of Haydn and Beethoven.* Cambridge: Cambridge University Press, 2002.

Willetts, Pamela J. *Beethoven and England: an account of sources in the British Museum.* London: British Museum, 1970.

Williams, Adrian, Editor and Translator. *Liszt, Franz: Selected letters.* Oxford: Clarendon Press, 1998.

Williams, Adrian. *Portrait of Liszt: by himself and his contemporaries.* Oxford: Clarendon Press, 1990.

Williams, Ralph Vaughan. *Heirs and rebels: letters written to each other and occasional writings on music.* London; New York: Oxford University Press, 1959.

Williams, Ralph Vaughan. *Some thoughts on Beethoven's Choral symphony: with writings on other musical subjects.* London; Oxford University Press, 1953.

Williams, Ralph Vaughan. *The making of music.* Ithaca, New York: Cornell University Press, 1955.

Williams, Ursula Vaughan. *R.V.W.: a biography of Ralph Vaughan Williams.* London: Oxford University Press, 1964.

Wilson, Conrad. *Notes on Beethoven: 20 crucial works.* Edinburgh: Saint Andrew Press, 2003.

Wilson, Elizabeth. *Shostakovich: a life remembered.* Princeton, New Jersey: Princeton University Press, 1994.

Winter, Robert, Editor. *Beethoven, performers, and critics: the International Beethoven Congress, Detroit, 1977.* Detroit: Wayne State University Press, 1980.

Winter, Robert. *Compositional origins of Beethoven's opus 131.* Ann Arbor, Michigan: UMI Research Press, 1982.

Winter, Robert and Robert Martin,

Editors. *The Beethoven quartet companion*. Berkeley: University of California Press, 1994.

Wolf, Eugene K. and Edward H. Roesner, Editors. *Studies in musical sources and style: essays in honor of Jan LaRue*. Madison, Wisconsin: A-R Editions, 1990.

Wolff, Christoph and Robert Riggs. *The string quartets of Haydn, Mozart and Beethoven: studies of the autograph manuscripts: a conference at Isham Memorial Library, March 15-17, 1979*. Cambridge, Massachusetts: Department of Music, Harvard University, 1980.

Wolff, Konrad. *Masters of the keyboard: individual style elements in the piano music of Bach, Haydn, Mozart, Beethoven, Schubert, Chopin, and Brahms*. Bloomington: Indiana University Press, 1990.

Wörner, Karl Heinrich. *Stockhausen: life and work*. London: Faber, 1973.

Wright, Donald, Editor. *Cardus on music: a centenary collection*. London: Hamish Hamilton, 1988.

Wyndham, Henry Saxe. *August Manns and the Saturday concerts: a memoir and a retrospect*. London and Felling-on-Tyne, New York, The Walter Scott Publishing Co., Ltd., 1909.

Yastrebtsev, V.V. Edited and Translated by Florence Jonas. *Reminiscences of Rimsky-Korsakov*. New York: Columbia University Press, 1985.

Yates, Peter. *Twentieth century music: its evolution from the end of the harmonic era into the present era of sound*. London: Allen & Unwin Ltd., 1968.

Young, Percy M. *Beethoven: a Victorian tribute based on the papers of Sir George Smart*. London: D. Dobson, 1976.

Young, Percy M. *George Grove, 1820-1900: a biography*. London: Macmillan, 1980.

Young, Percy M. *Letters of Edward Elgar and other writings*. London: Geoffrey Bles, 1956.

Young, Percy M., Editor. *Letters to Nimrod: Edward Elgar to August Jaeger, 1897-1908*. London: Dennis Dobson, 1965.

Young, Percy M. *The concert tradition: from the middle ages to the twentieth century*. London: Routledge and Kegan Paul, 1965.

Young, Rob, Editor. *(Brief Description): Undercurrents: the hidden wiring of modern music*. London; New York, N.Y.: Continuum, 2002.

Yourke, Electra Slonimsky, Editor. *Nicolas Slonimsky: writings on music*. New York, N.Y.; London: Routledge, 4 Vols. 2003-2005.

Slonimsky, Nicolas. *The great composers and their works*. Edited by Electra Slonimsky Yourke. New York: Schirmer Books, 2 Vols. 2000.

Ysaÿe, Antoine. *Ysaÿe: his life, work and influence*. London: W. Heinemann, 1947.

Zamoyski, Adam. *Paderewski*. London: Collins, 1982.

Zegers, Mirjam, Editor. *Louis Andriessen: The art of stealing time*. Todmorden: Arc Music, 2002.

Zemanova, Mirka, Editor. *Janácek's uncollected essays on music*. London: Marion Boyars, 1989.

INDEX

The order adopted for the listing of the entries in this index, for each of the string quartets under consideration, is chronological – according to the sequential unfolding of events under discussion. Thereby, the reader is provided with both a guide to the contents discussed in the main text and a timeline of the principal events bearing on Beethoven's life and work.

The Beethoven Quartet Society 2, 6, 89, 99, 127, 257-258
Paul Bekker 3-4, 54, 94, 98, 106, 111, 117, 119, 121, 125, 134, 137, 138, 160, 162, 165, 166, 177, 185, 193-194, 196, 218, 221, 224, 257, 259
Hector Berlioz 3-7, 224, 227, 229, 240, 244, 257
Bernstein, Leonard 7-8, 224, 226, 227, 245, 249, 257
Botstein, Leon 8-9, 56, 110-112, 116, 257

Chopin, Fryderyk 9-10, 119, 139, 223, 235, 250, 256, 257
Clarke, Rebecca XII, 10, 12, 102, 118, 130, 138, 143, 149, 159, 161, 191, 193, 195, 206, 213, 227, 257
Dahlhaus, Carl 12-14, 192, 195, 229, 257
Debussy, Claude 13-14, 226, 230, 235, 236, 239, 240, 244, 250, 257
Fauré, Gabriel 14-16, 237, 243, 245, 253, 257

Guarneri Quartet 16, 19, 84, 116, 207, 213, 225, 257, 259
Hadow, William Henry 19-20, 38, 66, 78, 81, 83, 105, 112-113, 115-116, 118, 132, 137, 138, 140, 144, 158, 161, 163, 177, 179, 184, 186, 188, 192, 194-195, 201-203, 212-213, 234, 257
Hensel (Mendelsohn), Fanny 20, 257
Holst, Gustav 22, 225, 242, 250, 257
Keller, Hans 22-25, 237, 242, 257
Kerman, Joseph 25-26, 38, 51, 65, 68, 81, 92, 94, 95, 97, 102, 106, 110, 112-114, 116-119, 122, 124, 129, 134, 137-139, 141, 142, 146, 149-150, 152, 156, 160-161, 166, 172, 176-179, 188, 191-195, 200-201, 208, 212-213, 238, 257
Kinderman, William 26-27, 42, 80-82, 114-119, 136-139, 147-150, 160, 172, 177-179, 191, 193-195, 208, 212-213, 238, 257
Paganini, Niccolò 27-28, 148, 248, 250, 257
Prokofiev, Sergei, 28-29, 234, 245-247, 257
Radcliffe, Philip 29-30, 39, 79, 92-93, 96, 103, 115, 117-120, 123, 130, 136, 138-139, 141, 143, 148-150, 154, 157, 160-161, 164, 177-178, 181, 184, 186, 188, 189, 192, 194-195, 197, 204, 210-214, 220, 221, 246, 257, 259
Rosé, Alma 30-31, 244, 257
Shepherd, Arthur XV, 32-33, 91, 101, 117-119, 128, 137-139, 144, 145, 149-150, 152, 160-161, 168, 172, 177-179, 184, 185, 192, 194-195, 200, 204, 207, 212-213, 250, 257
Stravinsky, Igor 34-35, 110, 229, 231, 236, 252, 254, 257
Walter, Bruno II

STRING QUARTETS OP. 18, NOS. 1–6 PP. 37-109
Beethoven's residence in Vienna
Elector Maximilian Franz
Count Ferdinand von Waldstein
Christian Gottlob Neefe
Beethoven's relationship with Haydn
Johann Baptist Schenk
Ferdinand Ries
Christian Schubart
Giuseppe Cambini
Haydn's estimation of Mozart
Beethoven as virtuoso pianist
Beethoven's early string trios
Role of music patron in Vienna
Prince Karl Lichnowsky
Ignaz Schuppanzigh
Lichnowsky's annuity to Beethoven
Allgemeine musikalische Zeitung
Beethoven and publishing houses
Anton Hoffmeister
Johann Baptist Schenk
Joseph Gelineck
Eleonore von Breuning
Franz Wegeler
Count Anton Apponyi
Emanuel Aloys Förster
Gestation of String Quartets Op. 18
Ignaz Schuppanzigh's String Quartet
Nikolaus Zmeskall von Domanovez
Karl Holz
Joseph Mayseder
Ignaz von Seyfried
Lichnowsky's gift to Beethoven of a quartet of Italian instruments
Prince Joseph Franz Lobkowitz and origins of Op. 18 Quartets
Gestation of Op. 18 Quartets
Kafka Sketchbook
Grasnick 1 Sketchbook
Grasnick 2 Sketchbook
Autograph 19 E
Landsberg 7 Sketchbook
Countess Josephine von Deym
Tranquillo Mollo
Beethoven's debt to Haydn and Mozart

Friedrich Rochlitz
Contemporary estimation of Op. 18
Ferdinand Ries String Trio arrangement of Op. 18
Louis Spohr
Prince Antoni Radziwill
Karl Möser
The Beethoven Quartet Society
Modern-day estimations of Op.18

OP. 18, NO. 1 PP. 121-136
Ignaz Schuppanzigh
Karl Amenda
Sketch origins of Op. 18, No.1
Ferdinand Ries, piano arrangement
Allgemeine musikalische Zeitung
Berliner Allgemeine musikalische Zeitung
Théophile Tilmant
Société de musique classique
The Beethoven Quartet Society
Poetic-Shakespearian association
Contemporary estimation
Haydn influence
Mozart influence

OP. 18, NO. 2 PP. 140-148
Compliment Quartet
Haydnesque spirit
Transitional work
Komplimentierungs-Quartet
Sketchbook origins
Haydn's comedy of manners
Amenda version
Scherzo as cleverest yet
Spirit of Haydn

OP. 18, NO. 3 PP. 151-159
Sketchbook origins
Conventional construction
Boldness of conception'
Haydnesque precedents
Anticipation of later *cavatina*
Influence of Mozart
Anticipation of late quartets

OP. 18, NO. 4 PP. 162-177
Use of minor key
Influence of suites and partitas
Debt to Haydn and Mozart
Sketchbook origins
Fux's *Gradus ad Parnassum*
Ferdinand Ries, arrangement
Beethoven compared with Haydn and Mozart
Arnold Schoenberg, reminiscence
Emanuel Aloys Förster
Theodor Otto Helm
Sturm und Drang
Mannheim school of composers
Comparison with *Pathétique* Sonata
Professor Giovanni Biamonti
Debt to Haydn and Albrechtsberger
Menuetto, atmosphere of courtly grace
Haydn's *Gypsy Rondo*, influence of
Theodor Otto Helm

OP. 18, NO. 5 PP. 180-193
Period of composition
Sketchbook origins
Mozart's String Quartet in G major K. 387, Carl Czerny anecdote
Contemporary estimation
Andreas Romberg
Ferdinand Ries and Philharmonic Society
Mozart's model K. 464
Robert Schuman
Menuetto, spirit of Mozart
Haydn, influence of
Richard Strauss, recollections of
Variation form, Beethoven's interest in
Haydn and Mozart, variation precedents
Variations I – V
Allegro, debt to Mozart
Contemporary estimations

OP. 18, NO. 6 PP. 196-211
Maturity and originality
Contemporary estimation

Reception in France
Haydnesque humour
Don Giovanni, affinities with
Second Symphony, parallels with
Dissentient criticism
Haydn's String Quartet Op. 77, influence of
Zopf Musik, pigtail music
Scherzo, aufgeknopft — unbuttoned
La Malinconia: Adagio — Allegretto quasi Allegro
sturm und drang, character of
Der Freymüthige, contemporary estimation
Pathétique Sonata, affinities with C.P.E. Bach
Guarneri Quartet, challenge to performers
Pathos and sustained tension
Romeo and Juliet, evocations of
Beethoven's newfound flexibility
Allegretto quasi Allegro
Dissolution into dance

STRING QUARTET ARRANGEMENT: PIANO SONATA IN E MAJOR, OP. 14, NO. 1 PP. 215-220
Not one of official string-quartet canon
Other Beethoven transcriptions
Grosse Fuge, Op. 133
Count Anton Apponyi, influence of
Kunst und Industrie komptoir, publication
Technical considerations
Estimations:
Donald Tovey
Paul Bekker
Lewis Lockwood
Robert Winter and Robert Martin
Philip Radcliffe

ABOUT THE AUTHOR

Terence M. Russell graduated with first class honours in architecture and was a nominee for the coveted Silver Medal of the Royal Institute of British Architects. He is a Fellow of the Royal Incorporation of Architects in Scotland (retired), was formerly Reader in the School of Arts, Culture and Environment at the University of Edinburgh, a Fellow of the British Higher Education Academy, and Senior Assessor to the Scottish Higher Education Funding Council. Alongside his professional work in the field of architecture – embracing practice, teaching and research – he has maintained a lifetime's interest in the music and musicology of Beethoven. He has an equal admiration for the work of Franz Schubert and was for many years an active member of the Schubert Institute, UK. His book writings in the field of architecture include the following:

The Built Environment: A Subject Index, Gregg Publishing (1989):
- Vol. 1: Town planning and urbanism, architecture, gardens and landscape design
- Vol. 2: Environmental technology, constructional engineering, building and materials
- Vol. 3: Decorative art and industrial design, international exhibitions and collections, recreational and performing arts
- Vol. 4: Public health, municipal services, community welfare

Architecture in the Encyclopédie of Diderot and D'Alemebert: The Letterpress Articles and Selected Engravings, Scolar Press (1993)

The Encyclopaedic Dictionary in the Eighteenth Century: Architecture, Arts and Crafts, Scolar Press (1997):
- Vol. 1: John Harris, Lexicon Technicum
- Vol. 2: Ephraim Chambers, Cyclopaedia
- Vol. 3: The Builder's Dictionary
- Vol. 4: Samuel Johnson, A Dictionary of the English Language
- Vol. 5: A Society of Gentlemen, Encyclopaedia Britannica

Gardens and Landscapes in the Encyclopédie of Diderot and D'Alemebert: The Letterpress Articles and Selected Engravings, 2 Vols., Ashgate (1999)

The Napoleonic Survey of Egypt: The Monuments and Customs of Egypt, 2 Vols., Ashgate (2001)

The Discovery of Egypt: Vivant Denon's Travels with Napoleon's Army, History Press (2005)

www.ingramcontent.com/pod-product-compliance
Lightning Source LLC
Chambersburg PA
CBHW011956090526
44590CB00023B/3750